The Mythopoeic Reality

Mas'ud Zavarzadeh

The Mythopoeic Reality

The Postwar American Nonfiction Novel

UNIVERSITY OF ILLINOIS PRESS
Urbana Chicago London

Publication of this work was supported in part by a grant
from the Andrew W. Mellon Foundation.

LIBRARY OF CONGRESS CATALOGING IN PUBLICATION DATA

Zavarzadeh, Mas'ud, 1938–
  The mythopoeic reality.

  Bibliography: p.
  Includes index.
  1. Nonfiction novel. 2. American fiction—20th
century—History and criticism. I. Title.
PS374.N6Z3   818'.5'407   76-49509
ISBN 0-252-00523-6

Contents

Preface

A new distribution of narrative energy in post–World War II American literature has pushed the traditional novel into the background and brought to prominence new forms of narrative, especially the nonfiction novel and various modes of transfiction. My interest in this study is the nonfiction novel, its generic features as well as its epistemological and cultural matrices. Previous criticism has shown little awareness of the nonfiction novel as a literary genre, treating books like Norman Mailer's *The Armies of the Night* or Andy Warhol's *a* as literary anomalies which hover awkwardly over what have been traditionally regarded as two antithetical narrative poles: the fictional and the factual. This bipolar approach to prose narrative is no longer capable of dealing with current literary realities. Agitated by the contemporary crisis of values and energized by technological and scientific innovations, many recent works break through the conventional boundaries of the established genres. In the present study, I shall attempt to outline a theory of the nonfiction novel and to deal with the major critical problems in reading such novels.

The poetics is followed by analyses of a limited selection of books. But the power of a critical theory, I believe, is to be measured not only in terms of its empirical applications but also in light of its ability to provide new organizing perspectives for a field of study. In the theory section, the concept of the "nonfiction novel" has been developed into a generic category with a high level of generality. My purpose here has been to identify the structural principles existing within a family of books which up to now has largely been treated as a series of isolated cases and misread in terms of concepts derived from distinctly different genres of prose narrative. The codification of various narrative systems, such as the genre of the nonfiction novel, is significant not only for critical theory and literary semantics and semiotics but also for the formulation of a deep structure grammar of narrative. A universal syntax of prose narrative with the highest degree of generality can be possible only after the preparation of what might be called "partial grammars"—poetics of specific genres.

In both the poetics and the discussion of specific texts, I have had to introduce new critical concepts and to find or, more frequently, to coin new terms to articulate them. These neologisms may irritate those who would rather discuss books with the familiar though imprecise vocabulary of criticism rather than risk the charting of new literary terrain with terms which may not always sound as "civilized" as the customary ones but which may prove more precise.

Throughout this study, I have been concerned with the newness of the new and not with the obvious ties which connect the new to the old. I have attempted to point out not only the differences which exist between the nonfiction novel and the fictive novel, but also the divergences between the traditional modernist poetics of the early part of the century and what I have called the supramodern sensibility: the aesthetics which informs both the nonfiction novel and transfiction as well as other new forms of art in nonliterary media—aleatory music, minimal art, and the like.

This study has benefited from the insights of many; any shortcomings which remain are mine. Benjamin DeMott, Teresa Ebert, Terence Martin, Robert Scholes, and Alan Zoellner have read the entire manuscript and offered many valuable suggestions. I am also grateful to Malcolm Bradbury, Haideh Daragahi, Raymond Federman, James Justus, Merritt Lawlis, David Lodge, and J. Albert Robbins for their helpful views on narrative literature in general. Richard Wentworth and Carole S. Appel of the University of Illinois Press have provided helpful advice and been extremely patient throughout the preparation of the book. A Summer Faculty Research Award and other grants-in-aid from the Office of Scientific and Scholarly Research of the University of Oregon provided time for the completion of this book. Several paragraphs of Chapter 1 and the major part of a previous version of Chapter 2 originally appeared in *Journal of American Studies* (1975) and *Journal of Literary Semantics* (1974) respectively. I wish to express my gratitude to the editors of these journals for allowing the reprinting of these materials. I also wish to thank Sue Rasmussen, who typed more than one version of this book with professional care, and John Hamacher, who assisted me in the proof-reading and indexing.

Above all it is to my sister, Mahrokh, whose intellectual and emotional support has sustained me through difficult years, that I owe the existence of this book.

—M. Z.

London
September 1976

PART I

The Narratology
of the Nonfiction Novel

one
Discontinuous Facts
and the Shape of
Supramodernist Narrative

Recent American innovative narrative, in response to the fictive behavior of the emerging actualities of a technetronic society,[1] moves beyond the totalizing modernist novel—in which the fictionist interpreted the "human condition" in the light of a comprehensive private world view—toward a supramodernist [2] narrative with zero degree of interpretation. The mistrust of the epistemological authority of the interpretive novel is mainly caused by the multifarious pressures of contemporary America which render all interpretations of "reality" arbitrary and therefore at the same time both accurate and absurd.

In this post-absurd world, daily experience eludes simple meaningful/meaningless reality testing; it is, in Robbe-Grillet's words, "neither significant nor absurd. It *is*, quite

1. A technetronic society is "a society that is shaped culturally, psychologically, socially, and economically by the impact of technology and electronics—particularly in the area of computers and communications." Zbigniew Brzezinski, *Between Two Ages* (New York: Viking Press, 1971), p. 9.

2. I shall use the term "supramodernism" to refer to the nontotalizing sensibility which has emerged since the late 1950s and whose literary manifestations can be seen in such works as Barth's *Giles Goat-Boy*, Pynchon's *Gravity's Rainbow*, Mailer's *The Armies of the Night*, Barthelme's *City Life*, Warhol's *a* and Wildman's *Montezuma's Ball*. I shall use this term in conjunction with three others to describe the various aesthetic and ideational approaches to narrative literature in the present century. I retain "Modernism" for the ideas associated with Joyce, Woolf, Faulkner, and their followers. The reaction against their poetics in the 1940s and the 1950s by such writers as Jack Kerouac, Kingsley Amis, and C. P. Snow I shall call "Antimodernism." The modified continuation of the Modernist aesthetics in the works of such novelists as Beckett, Nabokov, Borges, and B. S. Johnson I shall distinguish as "paramodernism." Some critics use the term "postmodernism" to describe all of these new developments. However, I find the term not only too general to catch the nuances in different attitudes and aesthetics but also to be "temporally oriented" rather than "sensibility directed." Thus, I shall use "postmodernism" to refer to the period following the Modernist movement during which the aesthetics and consciousnesses mentioned above developed.

simply." [3] The contemporary writer's approach to the world-as-it-is, free from any imposed scheme of meaning or extracted pattern of significance, and the emergence of such noninterpretive narrative forms as "transfiction" and the "nonfiction novel"—two radical narrative reactions to the current epistemological crisis—are telling indications of the deep changes which have taken place in the postwar consciousness and which caused a new distribution of narrative energy. Although the convention of the liberal-humanist novel grounded in the author's totalization of reality continues in the writings of such novelists as Saul Bellow, Bernard Malamud, and John Updike, over the last two decades narrative energy has found more complex expression in the forms of transfiction and the nonfiction novel. In transfiction, by means of a baroque overinterpretation of the human situation, writers like John Barth, Thomas Pynchon, Donald Barthelme, and Steven Katz have repudiated the claims of the totalizing novel to an integrated view of existing realities. Moving in the opposite direction, nonfiction novelists, through a neutral registration of experiential situations, have captured the fictive nature of technetronic culture. They reject the conventional notions of art as the creation of order out of chaos and the writer as seer. In their works the mythic underside of the surrealistic facts of post-industrial society is revealed and the indeterminacy of truth in extreme situations where fact and fiction converge is enacted.

Innovation in narrative, as in the arts in general, is not merely the result of the writer's private decision or simply the outcome of purely aesthetic processes; rather, it is largely a function of the pressures created by the new configurations of forces in reality which render the previous aesthetic forms incapable of effectively approaching new experiential *données*. The necessity for radical change in narrative modes intensifies with the increasing gap between the previous literary arrangements of reality and the shape

3. Alain Robbe-Grillet, *For a New Novel*, trans. Richard Howard (New York: Grove Press, 1965), p. 19.

of the new actualities as in the postwar period in the United States. In addition to the dynamics of literary tradition itself, the innovative impulse is generally conditioned by two closely related basic factors: scientific and philosophical ideas which define the conceptual framework of the artist, and daily facts which create the texture of the immediate cultural environment in which the artist practices. The interaction among these forces is a function of a complex network of socioeconomic processes which affect the structuring of culture and consequently the form of artistic activities in it.

In the industrializing societies, the conventional totalizing novel is the most expressive and popular literary form. In such societies, widespread anomie, caused by the subversion of agrarian social structures which had conceived and ordered life according to preestablished collective norms, creates a need, even a passion, to seek total answers which can operate as integrative forces and provide a valuational cohesion for the emerging industrial mode of life. Given the rudimentary nature of mass literacy during the early stages of industrialization, these totalizing views are usually worked out in such accepted and entertaining forms as the novel which, because of its mimetic conventions and structural flexibility, is responsive to the epistemological demands of the period while also being highly accessible to a large readership. The total answers that the conventional novel gives to the new questions raised by industrial civilization function—to a considerable extent—as the secular substitutes for religious absolutes, which were the basis of social connection and cohesion in small-scale agrarian communities but failed to provide practical guidelines for living in the new industrial metropolis. The totalization of experience in the narrative literature of such periods is also encouraged by the dominance of rational and conceptual modes of thinking which are necessary tools for planning and managing an efficient factory or society. Consequently both social and individual life are approached in terms of explainable cause and effect series of teleological events—a fact which is reflected in the structure of the bourgeois novel in which experience is organized causally in a linear plot, with careful exposition, logical development, and the strong closural effects of completeness, resolution, and stability. The summative views of industrial culture in the interpretive novel, reaching their apogee in the nineteenth century, are paralleled in the grand formulations of Marx, Darwin, Freud, and William James, to mention only the most influential thinkers, which further underscore the prevailing need for new integrative visions. Through a complete interpretation of life, the classic novel orders the chaos of experience and shapes it into a comprehensible whole endowed with purpose and governed by laws that are discoverable by the rational mind. In doing so, the conventional novel imposes necessity and certainty on life and, to the comfort of its bourgeois reader, removes the anguish of the contingent. The congruent nature of the totalizing novel and industrializing society is further indicated by the fact that at the present time, while the novel is losing its grip on the complex realities emerging in technologically advanced societies and is being replaced by new narrative forms, it is enjoying a rapid growth in the Third World countries, which are undergoing an industrialization process somewhat similar to that of the West in the eighteenth and nineteenth centuries.

The interpretive impulse, of course, also informs the prebourgeois narratives of agrarian societies. However, the interpretive perspective of these narratives is generally not only teleological but also theological, aimed at justifying the ways of God to men. Unlike the bourgeois narratives of the industrial age, which are empirical, secular, humanistic, and given to an investigation of human relationships, the narratives of the agrarian era are mythical, ritualistic, otherworldly, and interested in the nature of the relationship between human and divine. The two, nonetheless, are similar in their search for absolutes and for total answers by which life can be given coherence, direction, and significance.

With the passing of industrial civilization and the advent of postindustrial culture, the totalizing novel no longer serves as the focusing narrative form. Many literary and

extraliterary forces are involved in this redistributive process which Jakobson describes as a shift in the hierarchy of
genres.[4] One of these forces which has had an immediate
and lasting effect on the refocusing of narrative energy is
the modern communications media which developed with
technetronic cultures. The new communication technologies make the formulation of any encompassing authorita-
tive visions increasingly more difficult, since they produce
an information overload which gives such diverse and disparate views of reality that no single interpretive frame can
contain them all and still present a coherent vision of experience. The information revolution also expands the range
of the probable to the extent that it blurs the boundaries of
fact and fiction with the ultimate effect, as far as the conventional novel is concerned, being that the contemporary
reader feels uneasy entering the world of the totalizing
novel rooted in the dualistic epistemology of the actual and
the imaginal. Unlike the novel of the industrial age, the
postbourgeois novel favors the technique of "collage" for
the organization of experience rather than "plot." Collage,
typographical enactments, and innovative uses of paginal
space are more in accord with contemporary man's exposure to the multilayered nature of experience in the new
age and the ambivalent attitude that experience engenders
in defiance of being compressed into an epiphanic whole.

Mistrust and even fear of totalization not only inform the
attitude of innovative American narratists today but also
serve as their immediate subject matter. Such dread is the
basic thematic motif of Thomas Pynchon's *V.*, in which the
protagonist, Herbert Stencil, ostensibly seeks a literal synthesis of the numerous confusing manifestations of V., but
actually fears any solution to "the V. jigsaw." He welcomes
V.'s mysterious metamorphoses, since the more imperson-
ations attributed to V., the better his chances for prolonging
his "quest" and thus avoiding the final totalization of the
clues and facts into an integrated concept of V. Stencil is

4. Roman Jakobson, "The Dominant," in *Readings in Russian Poetics: Formalist
and Structuralist Views,* ed. Ladislav Matejka and Krystyna Pomorska (Cambridge,
Mass.: M.I.T. Press, 1971), pp. 82–87.

presented not as the interpreter of the V. affair, but as "purely He Who *Looks* for V." (emphasis added). In fact, the very prospect of finding—totalizing—V. has become antithetical to his existence in a technological society; it is only the act of searching itself which is significant: "Finding her: what then? Only that what love there was to Stencil had become directed entirely inward, toward this acquired sense of animateness. Having found this he could hardly release it, it was too dear. To sustain it he had to hunt V.; but if he should find her, where else would there be to go but back into half-consciousness? He tried not to think, therefore, about the end to the search. Approach and avoid." [5]

This "half-consciousness" is the state of hibernation caused by the false assurance of having obtained the harmonizing principle behind the manifold reality. Stencil's fear of piecing together the hints, clues, and signs he has come across during his search—caused by his suspicion that these are all planted in his way by some conspiracy to mislead him and prove that his integration of V. is no more than "merely a scholarly quest" for a synthetic wholeness— is opposed by the equal weight of his anguish in not being able to locate V. and separate her from various V.-like appearances. His conflicting feelings and his "approach and avoid" strategy are indications that, while he has a strong yearning for a unifying belief, the "norm" in his life has so unmistakably become the fragmentation and chaos of experience that even the thought of reaching a cohesive vision of the wholeness beneath the scattered surfaces is not only suspect but also phony. This agonizing impasse is characteristic of contemporary man's compulsive attempt to identify a solid core of trustable reality distinguishable from fictitious appearances and his mistrust that the pattern he comes up with may be a mere projection based on no more than "recurrence of an initial and a few dead objects" thrown in his way by cabals. As one character in *V.* states: "In a world such as you inhabit, Mr. Stencil, any cluster of phenomena may be a conspiracy."

5. Thomas Pynchon, *V.* (Philadelphia and New York: J. B. Lippincott, 1963), p. 55.

The view of recent reality as a form of organized chaos, resisting interpretation and inherently indeterminate to such an extent that a paralogic of conspiracy is the only kind of reasoning which can account for its strangeness, is more than just a private fantasy of a few contemporary fictionists. It is a communal *donnée*. In contrast to the scattered and bafflingly contradictory reality of present-day America, the preceding eras of human history—notwithstanding disruptions, valuational crises, and upheavals occasioned by natural and social disasters—enjoyed a cohering system of beliefs rooted in their integrative conceptual frame of reference and vision of reality. The specifics of this totalizing outlook naturally changed from period to period according to the degree of scientific and philosophical knowledge as well as the sophistication of the economic base, but in all these eras there remained a central, all-encompassing view of reality from which public and private life derived their guidelines. In contemporary America, on the other hand, the formulation of any comprehensive scheme of reality has become impossible. American reality since the late 1950s has become more and more discontinuous, inconclusive, and fictionlike in its strange and original behavior. Consequently, the structure of contemporary consciousness and the forms of recent narrative literature have changed so radically that the present seems to be more a mutation than a continuation of the past.[6]

The idea of the discontinuous present has been criticized by such divergent writers as Arthur Lovejoy, who regarded it as a dangerous "presenticentricism," and the editors of *The New Yorker*, who condemned it as a decadent search for the New,[7] as well as numerous other critics who occupy different positions between these two scholarly and journalistic standpoints. These critics see the present as a logical continuation of the past, and some, like Frank Kermode, go even further and consider the "now" to be merely the dilution of "then," a form of popular Modernism which amounts to

6. On the question of "continuity" and "mutation" see Michel Foucault, *The Order of Things: An Archaeology of the Human Sciences* (New York: Pantheon, 1970).
    7. *The New Yorker*, Aug. 11, 1975, p. 19.

nothing more than jokes, put-ons and mass apocalyptic thinking.[8]

Disruption, nihilism, chaos, and violence have, of course, existed throughout human history, and to take only the more recent period, communal and private suffering as well as moral and valuational crises have extended from the Middle Ages described by Huizinga [9] to the London portrayed by Mayhew.[10] While it is not too difficult to draw parallels between the *texture* of distrupted life in these eras and that of postwar America, the *structures* of human experience in these periods are fundamentally different. The contemporary period differs from them not only in terms of the scope and universalization of disruption and discontinuity, but more important, it lacks an all-encompassing view of itself. The conditions that Huizinga and Mayhew describe were ultimately regarded by members of these cul-

8. See, for instance, Frank Kermode's *The Sense of an Ending* (New York: Oxford University Press, 1967) and his collection of essays, *Continuities* (New York: Random House, 1968). Opposing the political conservatism of Kermode but still sharing his cultural attitudes is Gerald Graff, who, in his two essays on contemporary fiction (*TriQuarterly*, Nos. 26 and 33), reminds one of Christopher Caudwell's nostalgic comparison of the coherent view of the universe offered by dialectical materialism and the "chaotic confusion" of the world revealed by the new sciences, in *Further Studies in a Dying Culture* (New York: Monthly Review Press, 1971), pp. 210–56. For a discussion of continuities in general and Kermode's position in particular, see G. Gillespie, "New Apocalypse for Old: Kermode's Theory of Modernism," *boundary* 2, 3 (1975), 307–23, and Richard Webster's "Frank Kermode's *The Sense of an Ending*" in *Critical Quarterly*, 16 (1974), 311–24. The following passage from Webster's article is particularly relevant to the present discussions: "It might be suggested that in *The Sense of an Ending* Professor Kermode created a myth of his own which answered to a need felt deeply by many who had lived through the crisis-laden sixties, and provided us in spite of all with that sense of continuity-within-tradition we so desperately needed. For if we adopted Kermode's historiography we could lift every schismatic movement out of its immediate social context and fix it in a two thousand year old tradition of formalistically conceived history. The more desperately the sense of crisis was projected the more speedily would its projector be converted, as if by magic, into another link in the chain of continuity. When in May 1968 Paris students rose against their government and Hornsey School of Art was taken over by students, when the predictions of ecological catastrophe began to appear, many literary critics must have reached down their copy of *The Sense of an Ending* in order to read the immensely consoling pronouncement that 'there is nothing at all distinguishing about eschatological anxieties' " (p. 318).

9. See Johan Huizinga, *The Waning of the Middle Ages* (1924; rpt. New York: St. Martin's Press, 1967), especially the essay on "The Violent Tenor of Life."

10. See Henry Mayhew, *London Labour and the London Poor* (1851, 1861–62; rpt. New York: A. M. Kelley, 1967).

tural communities as passing aberrations of reality, and the suspension of a dominating order was frequently seen as a manifestation of a higher order unknowable to ordinary man. Thus, in the context of a communal belief—divine or secular—a certainty existed that a reintegration of shattered values and a restoration of order would occur even if it had to take place in the coming world. Faith in the final inclusiveness of an ordering principle provided both the individual and the culture with emotional as well as intellectual moorings. But at the present time, the pressures of cultural actualities cause the very notion of order to be regarded as a superstition suitable only for consoling less-sophisticated minds. Although surface similarities between life in nineteenth-century London and urban living in modern America do exist, the two have basically different cultural meanings and experiential qualities. The violence of nineteenth-century London street life is "local" in the sense that the violence is seen as a temporary and limited violation of still-existent regulative forces in nature and society. But, in contemporary America, the loss of conviction is "global," pervading all levels of sociocultural and emotional-familial life. The local-global distinction, in other words, marks the difference between the passing convulsive seizure and spastic paralysis.

The first wave of this metaphysical crisis, which reached its climax after World War 2, hit the consciousness of Modernist writers in the late nineteenth and early twentieth centuries. The invading chaos, arising from the disappearance of the image of an orderly universe, broken up by the discoveries of modern physics and further fragmented by the sociopolitical turbulences which led to World War 1, however, was largely contained by Modernist writers through their private mythographies. The Yeatsian vision, the Joycean adoption of Vico's philosophy of history, Poundian economics, the Lawrentian deification of flesh and religion of blood, and Eliot's early probing of the myth of the Grail (which eventually provided him with the "idea of a Christian society"), all served as defenses against the engulfing confusion and entropy of the spreading urban civilization.

But since the war, such defenses have become less and less effective, and the search for valuational stability through the invention of mythic schemes has been denounced and ridiculed as "mythotherapy" by writers like John Barth.

It is not necessary to be an orthodox Hegelian to see the significance of Hegel's concept of the dialectical transformation of quantity into quality in comprehending the great break which separates the present from the absolutist cultures of the past. The changes which started with the technological advances of the sixteenth century and gathered momentum in the succeeding eras reached, in the 1950s, a critical point at which the accumulation of various quantitative changes produced a qualitative transformation, thereby creating a new cultural situation. To understand this process which radically severs the present from the past, it is necessary to examine, very briefly, the phases of previous totalistic cultures and present conditions. Without such a context, the "local" disorders of the past may be confused with the "global" chaos of the present.

Before the onset of the technological innovations of the sixteenth century and the scientific and philosophical revolutions of the seventeenth century, a shared faith in a transcendental, inclusive, and all-embracing theocentric paradigm assured medieval man that there was an orderly reality outside his head and that the "facts" of daily life, on a mundane level, served as the touchstones of his experience. The relative material simplicity and thus stability of feudal society which had shaped this totalizing view was also responsible for the conviction that even if this order was suspended, as it was from time to time at periods of natural, economic, and social disruptions, the disappearance of order in itself was only another aspect of the higher calculus of reality; it was the limitations of the human mind which prevented understanding of the sublime logic. The artistic summa of this conception of the universe as an intelligible, ordered, and trustable system of reality was Dante's *Divine Comedy*.

Post-Renaissance people, whose faith in a Dantean vision was shaken by the ideas of such scientists and thinkers as

Copernicus, Kepler, Galileo, Newton, Descartes, and Bacon, however, did not lose the possibility of synthesizing their experience; instead, one ordering principle was simply replaced by another. John Donne's lamentation that

> new Philosophy calls all in doubt,
> The Element of fire is quite put out;
> The Sun is lost, and th'earth, and no mans wit
> Can well direct him where to looke for it.
> And freely men confesse that this world's spent,
> When in the Planets, and the Firmament
> They seeke so many new; they see that this
> Is crumbled out againe to his Atomies.
> 'Tis all in peeces, all cohaerence gone;
> All just supply, and all Relation . . .[11]

is occasioned by the disappearance of one kind of order—the familiar geocentric Ptolemaic theories challenged by the Copernican hypotheses. " 'Tis all in peeces" only in terms of the established hierarchies of the medieval world picture, which had not proven complex enough for the changing configurations of reality in the succeeding era. The Newtonian physics offered a new architectonics of reality, which accommodated the growing complexity of the bourgeois conception of the external world and devised a new epistemology in which the disjointed pieces of the medieval world view were reordered and fitted together in a totalistic system. In fact, the new scientific interpretation of reality proved so effective in providing a coherent ordering principle for the cosmos that it encouraged Laplace in the eighteenth century to announce with arrogant confidence that the universe could be mapped with perfect predictability and absolute certainty.[12] The technological innovations of the sixteenth century and the scientific revolution of the seventeenth century, in short, merely changed the form and articulation of order and provided it with a scientific foundation which emphasized that the functioning of the uni-

11. *The Poems of John Donne*, ed. Herbert J. C. Grierson (Oxford: Clarendon Press, 1912), I, 237.

12. See Michael Polanyi, *Personal Knowledge: Towards a Post-Critical Philosophy* (Chicago: University of Chicago Press, 1958), pp. 140–41.

verse was as exact and precise as a clock. As Carl Becker has observed, the followers of the new philosophy had not stopped worshiping order: "They had only given another form and a new name to the object of worship: having denatured God, they deified nature." [13] Even Goethe—who in the name of the complexities of human experience rejected the geometrical systems of thinking in all Newtonian scientific and analytical approaches to reality, going so far as to argue for discarding the use of numbers in *Optics* and to propose describing colors in terms of *deeds* and *sufferings* of light—had the epistemological assurance of a cosmic order as demonstrated in *Faust*. His dissent from the totalizing mode of the sciences of his time was only an assertion of a new, albeit nonanalytical, model of absolutization in his formulation of *Naturphilosophie* which eventually provided an alternative paradigm of order for the Romantic "rebels." [14] In all these theories concerning the nature of external reality, although "facts"—theological, scientific, or experiential—were becoming more and more complex, they nevertheless were treated as epistemologically reliable units of cognition.

The secure status of "facts" as the ultimate arbiter of truth, however, began to be challenged, beginning with Einstein's "theory of relativity," which questioned the Newtonian theory of gravitation and its assumptions of the absoluteness of time and space. The "solid, massy and hard" iron ball–like atoms, the building blocks of the Newtonian world, whose movements were governed by the laws of classic mechanics, lost their "substantiality," "stability," and "irreducibility" and were replaced by the concept of the elementary particle, which was "nothing but the nexus of various relations in which it participates." [15] Furthermore, quantum physics reformulated the body of laws associated with classic mechanics, but, in doing so, the new physics

13. Carl Becker, *The Heavenly City of the Eighteenth-Century Philosophers* (New Haven: Yale University Press, 1959), p. 63.

14. See Robert Bloch, "Goethe, Idealistic Morphology, and Science," *American Scientist*, 40 (1952), 317–22.

15. Harvey Brooks, "Scientific Concepts and Cultural Change," *Daedalus*, 94, No. 1 (1965), 70.

went far beyond just updating the old laws in the light of new experiments and discoveries: not only did it completely shatter the Laplacian image of an orderly universe rooted in the predictable chain of cause and effect, but more important, it questioned the very idea of totalization and the possibility of postulating an ordered, fully mappable cosmos. The notion of a discontinuous universe came to the fore in the wake of Max Planck's demonstration that energy was emitted not in a stream of wavelike rays but in intermittent packets or *quanta*,[16] and Heisenberg's formulation of the "principle of indeterminacy," which established the impossibility of determining the position and velocity of a particle simultaneously. Heisenberg's theories replaced the condition of certainty in classical physics with a state of probability and randomness in the microscopic world of particles. However, the larger philosophical conclusions drawn from these new theories affected the entire climate of thought. As Cecil Schneer observes,

> The behavior of the particle is uncertain and therefore the behavior of the atom is an uncertainty. The behavior of the atom can be predicted to a degree of probability. The behavior of an aggregate of atoms is therefore only a probability, and not a certainty. And it is no use saying that the degree of uncertainty is too small to effect events on the ordinary scale, for the notion of determinism is similarly based on the fundamental determinism of the individual molecules, multiplied many times to become the world of nature.[17]

The revelation of the inherent uncertainty of reality was further amplified by Niels Bohr's "principle of complimentarity," which brought to science a high degree of "tolerance of ambiguity." Bohr argued that the opposing "wave" and "particle" theories concerning the nature of matter were both valid and coexisted in complimentary relationship with each other and thus provided a complex explanation of the phenomena involved. Bohr's development of such a two-set

16. Max Planck, *The New Science,* trans. James Murphy and W. H. Johnston (New York: Meridian Books, 1959), pp. 18ff.

17. Cecil Schneer, *The Evolution of Physical Science* (New York: Grove Press, 1960), p. 364.

theory in which neither term was subsumed by the other was especially significant, because it moved beyond the strict absolutization of physical phenomena.

The community of shared values dominated by a commonsensical and logically complete view of life which pervaded Western thought thus began to disintegrate under the pressures of the discoveries made by the modern sciences. The surety of perception which could allow Joseph Addison to "solemnly declare" in the pages of *The Spectator* (No. 126) that ". . . we do in our consciences believe two and two make four; and that we shall adjudge any man whatsoever to be our enemy who endeavours to persuade us to the contrary. . . . We do also firmly declare, that it is our resolution as long as we live to call black black, and white white" was undermined. Two and two, it turned out, make four *only* in mathematical systems operating on Euclidean postulates and based on decimal sets in which objects are grouped and counted in tens and powers of ten. The stability of black and white, paralogical as it may seem, is not a reliable point of reference, since colors are a function of light, and light itself is not unequivocal but seems to have an opposing wave-particle nature.[18] The uncertainty about the nature of experience has increased as current research has put science more and more "in contact with . . . the mysterious . . . that which belongs to the physical world but which . . . might never be apprehended." [19] As a result, the contradiction-free Aristotelian causal logic has been replaced by multivalued logics, and the controlling metaphor of culture has changed from "order" to "entropy."

This invasion of the unknown into the province of the actual has largely been responsible for the dissolution of the boundaries dividing stable facts from illusory fictions in all areas of contemporary life. Even such seemingly unshakable concepts as the nature of man and his selfhood are los-

18. See Daniel McDonald, "Science, Literature, and Absurdity," *South Atlantic Quarterly*, 66 (1967), 42–49.
19. Nicola Dallaporta, "The Crises of Contemporary Physics," *Diogenes*, No. 89 (Spring 1975), p. 76.

ing their solidity. Currently, life scientists are becoming more and more preoccupied with the *destiny* of the human species rather than its *origins,* and possibilities inherent in genetic engineering are setting off a chain reaction of uncontrollable force which may eventually bring about "the end of *Homo sapiens* and the creation of a new species by man's own actions." [20] Concurrent with the breakdown of the firm outlines of his physiological and genetic shape in an indeterminate world, contemporary man faces a redefinition of his own basic psychic conditions as well. Freudian psychology, with its humanistic concept of the self, its distinction between normal and abnormal, and its prescription for regaining a temporarily obscured selfhood, has now been eclipsed by theories which refuse to provide man with the certitude of a determinate and whole self. In place of a durable selfhood, with its internal continuity, contemporary man is not only splintered into "serial selves" but also must question such basic concepts as "sanity" and "madness," which had served him as a rough-and-ready rule for ordering the internal life of himself and others. R. D. Laing's proposition that schizophrenia is not only a breakdown but also a breakthrough [21] shatters many of the protective distinctions, such as rational/irrational; appearance/reality; interior/exterior; fact/fiction, by which the boundaries of the self and the non-self have been traditionally defined.

The scientific realization that there is a whole realm beyond identifiable causality which cannot be attained by existing means of information, the eclipse of deterministic views, and the emergence of a possibility-oriented attitude toward the experiential world have all turned the totalization of experience into what Pynchon calls "an adventure of the mind"—a willed imposition of an arbitrary pattern on reality. This impossibility of totalizing life on the level of phenomena as well as above and below it is further reflected in the demise of philosophy—the ultimate synthe-

20. Victor C. Ferkiss, *Technological Man* (New York: Braziller, 1969), p. 111.

21. Peter Sedgwick, "R. D. Laing: Self, Symptom and Society," in *R. D. Laing and Anti-Psychiatry,* ed. R. Boyers and Robert Orrill (New York: Harper and Row, 1971), p. 39. See also Jan B. Gordon's "The Meta-Journey of R. D. Laing" in the same volume.

sizer of all facets of reality into integrative concepts—in contemporary times and in the short lives of such intellectual movements as Existentialism and Structuralism, which also attempted, on a smaller scale, to formulate holistic systems in the postwar period.

Science influences the imagination of innovative writers both through the changes which it brings about in their modes of perception and through certain technological advances by which it affects the texture of their environment— the facts of everyday life. Modern science, unlike its predecessor, has no integrative function in the contemporary world, but nonetheless the postwar consciousness is formed largely by the synergetics of the scientific-technological order—the processes, ideas, and procedures as well as machines. No other events have so deeply influenced contemporary thinking as the launching of the first Sputnik or the first landing of a man on the moon. Recent technology, however, like modern science and contemporary thought, is radically different from the industrial technologies of the nineteenth and early twentieth centuries, which were intimately related to the old crafts and in that sense were mere extensions of the hand and thus obedient to human ideals and the logic behind them. With the growing sophistication of technologies, the human context and therefore the ordering of technology according to ideals have been lost to the extent that not only the underlying abstract logic of new technologies but even their subjects of investigation are sometimes incomprehensible in terms of concrete human experience. The concern of nuclear technology, for instance, is, in Heisenberg's words, "the exploitation of natural forces to which every approach from the world of natural experience is lacking." [22] Present-day technology has created a new milieu which envelops man and forms his new habitat. It is in this context that talking about the "influence" of technology on man and on his moral, social, and economic institutions has become rather irrelevant, since, as

22. Werner Heisenberg, "The Representation of Nature in Contemporary Physics," *Daedalus*, 87, No. 3 (Summer 1958), 101.

Jacques Ellul observes, all these are "situated in" the new milieu and therefore are defined through it.[23] The conception of reality, in other words, is in terms of the new milieu which not only is composed of "hard" and visible machines, but also consists of what D. H. Lasswell defines as "the ensemble of practices by which one uses available resources in order to achieve certain valued ends."[24] These "valued ends," however, are set not according to preestablished human goals but by the self-augmenting, self-perpetuating needs of the new technology itself which, in Aldous Huxley's words, "tends always to obey the laws of its own logic,"[25] which is, as one writer put it: "all that is possible is necessary." The increasing advancement of technology, in other words, displaces man as the core of the social process and overturns the old humanistic distinction between "ends" and "means" connected by a preconceived table of human values. The two worlds, the old organic world of man and the new world of technology, in fact run counter to each other and "obey different imperatives, different directives and different laws which have nothing in common."[26] Thus, the vision of reality as a conspiratorial staging of events by sinister cabals who are manipulating external facts according to a plot is partly rooted in the inherent unpredictability and ambiguity of technological developments. Such developments create an open-ended and indeterminable system which defies all historical and totalizing frames of reference.

It would be too lengthy an undertaking either to discuss the technological breakthroughs which have both given a unique physical form to the environment of everyday life and affected the pattern of ongoing events in contemporary America, or to analyze the changes which they have caused in the nature of relationships among people or between

23. Jacques Ellul, "The Technological Order," in *The Technological Order*, ed. C. F. Stover (Detroit: Wayne State University Press, 1963), p. 11.

24. Quoted by Ellul in his book, *The Technological Society* (New York: Knopf, 1964), p. 18.

25. Stover, ed., *Technological Order*, p. 82.

26. Ellul, *Technological Society*, p. 79.

people and the social order.[27] Nonetheless, it is necessary to point beyond the individual technological feats to the merging of man and machine, which manifests the fundamental transformation of man and his reality in a technetronic society. Scientists in the near future, for instance, will be able to develop "Cybersex"—the transmission of sexual stimuli through computers and other electronic media to desiring partners. One Japanese firm even expects to market "Cybersex" tapes, so that people can buy them in the same way they now purchase musical records or cassette tapes. The symbiosis of man and machine may reach such a degree that, as Heisenberg predicts: "Many of our technical apparatuses will . . . belong as inseparably to man as the snail's shell does to the snail or the spider's web to the spider . . . the apparatus would then be a part of our human organism." Implanted electrodes through which people will have access to inexhaustible memory-storage banks that will extend their mental powers in unpredictable dimensions are instances of such apparatuses.[28] The mutualism of man and machine is gradually changing psychosomatic conditions of human beings; the development of both artificial and human organ transplants has already raised questions about the nature and stability of the human body and the personal self and has in many ways anticipated the passing of man, in George Steiner's words, "from the closed sphere of private being into that of collectivity." Having dissolved the established physical and mental boundaries of the human situation, contemporary technol-

27. Victor Ferkiss in his *Technological Man* gives a full bibliography of books discussing various facets of technological reality, and Emmanuel G. Mesthene's *Technological Change* (Cambridge, Mass.: Harvard University Press, 1970) has a shorter, annotated bibliography of works discussing transformations of contemporary life under the pressures of technology. For an illuminating overview of the new human milieu and the forces dominating it, see Daniel Bell, *The Coming of Post-Industrial Society* (New York: Basic Books, 1973).

28. At the 1976 annual meeting of the American Association for the Advancement of Science, Adam V. Reed of the Rockefeller University spoke of the day when people will have computers implanted in their brains. "As an aid to memory," he said, "it should provide the user with an almost infinite data capacity." He added that a computer wired to a brain can help regulate such rhythmic functions as breathing and heart rate, and also take over the work of whole portions of the brain that might be damaged by accident or stroke.

ogies and sciences have created an evanescent reality which at best can only be partially described but cannot be analyzed and compressed into a total pattern of cohesion and meaning. We are confronting a radically new phase in human history which has neither a clear precedent nor a definable future.

One of the seminal features of this new situation, this "zone of total probability," [29] is the interchangeability of what is conventionally referred to as the ascertainable "fact" of the experiential world and the made-up "fiction" of the imagination. The runaway contemporary technologies are turning the sensory world into a projected fiction and transforming unreal fantasies into actualities. Even more important, the logic of contemporary sciences and the paralogic of current events prove that there is very little difference between the two in any case. The scientific discoveries of the recent past have overthrown the traditional views of facts as the understandable, tame, verifiable, and familiar sunny core of reality, which provide a touchstone for man's experience of the external world, and instead have revealed them to be as wild, indeterminate, arbitrary, dark, and elusive as the most outrageous fantasies of speculative fiction. What used to be almost universally recognized as fictional and associated with the conjured illusion of reality in novels has now become an empirical fiction surrounding us. Observing this new "patareal" reality (to use Ishmael Reed's term), with its heavy symbolic load, fictive resonance, and ironic overtone, is like entering the fantastic world of the fabulators: "Reality itself has become so extravagant in its contradictions, absurdities, violence, speed of change, science-fictional technology, weirdness and constant unfamiliarity" [30] that, as one commentator puts it, "just to match what is with accuracy takes the conscientious reporter into the realms of the Unknown—into what used to be called 'the world of the imagination.' " [31]

29. The expression is Reyner Banham's.
30. Seymour Krim, *Shake It for the World, Smartass* (New York: Dial Press, 1970), p. 349.
31. Ibid.

Under the pressures of such a deeply altered reality, the relations of the writer, his or her fictive work, and the destabilized actual world have changed—"the gift for creating the fictional illusion of reality," as Malcolm Bradbury observes, "is shifted from the writer . . . to the culture in which he practices." [32] For today's American writer, the questions of his craft cannot be answered outside the context of this ongoing empirical fiction, which reduces his privately invented fiction to trivia and even turns him into a minor cartoon character. "I like Beckett and Burroughs and Lenny Bruce," says Elia Katz, "but fiction—even their kind—does not quite make it any more next to what goes down in this country. . . . The official level of reality is so weird that what passes for realistic fiction is totally anachronistic, like an old road map." [33] "Realistic fiction" is only one form of the totalizing narrative which has been historically canceled. Calling the *New York Times* the bible of the black humorists, Bruce J. Friedman reexamines the position of the "satirist" in contemporary America and concludes that he "has had his ground usurped by the newspaper reporter." For instance, the journalist who must "cover the ecumenical debate on whether Jews, on the one hand, are still to be known as Christ-killers, or, on the other hand, are to be left off the hook," is without doubt today's unconscious satirist. [34] The most engaging description of this change in the chemistry of contemporary public reality (the meeting ground of the classic novelist and his or her audience) is found in the opening remarks of Larry L. King's review of an extended reportage of the 1968 American presidential campaign:

> The America of 1968, with its assassinations, torched ghettos, campus wars, crime waves, alienations, deposed kings and crazed pretenders, almost seems too much for a single book.

32. Malcolm Bradbury, "The Open Form: The Novel and Reality," in *Possibilities* (London: Oxford University Press, 1973), p. 19.
33. Quoted in *Cutting Edges: Young American Fiction for the 70's*, ed. Jack Hicks (New York: Holt, Rinehart and Winston, 1973), p. 537.
34. Bruce J. Friedman, ed., *Black Humor* (New York: Bantam Books, 1965), p. x.

Offered as a novel, it might be rejected even by the lowliest of publishing house readers. "This story smacks too much of fantasy," such a low-echelon reader might report to his superiors. "There is too much random violence, nameless complications, and wild improbabilities. The Southern Governor known as George Wallace is surely overdrawn: a composite of all the Dixie demagogues of the past. That his racist appeals could enjoy enough popular support to get his name on ballots in virtually all states, through the signing of petitions by millions, is incredible. That he would name a Stone Age primitive from the military ranks as his running mate caps incredibility with foolhardiness. The aging Hollywood idol who has somehow become governor of California (!) and who within two years can reach for the Presidency, is more a satirical figure than not: I cannot determine whether we are meant to take him seriously. The young prince figure, Senator Robert Kennedy, dies so senseless and near-accidental a death in his moment of triumph (he is shot by a fanatical, anti-Israeli Jordanian in a hotel kitchen corridor after having won his most meaningful primary of the year) that only the most amateurish novelist would dare present it. Nor does it seem reasonable that a power-driven and proud President could be so easily forced from office by a handful of disgruntled Eastern intellectuals, and legions of dedicated college kids rallying around a half-mystic Midwestern Senator who alternately dabbles in poetry and sarcasm. It doesn't appear remotely possible that the leaders of the Democratic Party (old pros, after all, who have long spoken in the name of Freedom, Humanity, Equality) would permit brutal and suicidal attacks in the streets of Chicago against unarmed young dissidents—not with the whole world looking on. And certainly the author must be kidding when—after all this melodrama and the wild excesses of a dozen swashbuckling, Falstaffian main characters—he offers as the ultimate nominees of the major parties two gray, old-style, burnt-out professional politicians, both of whom talk either in cliches or merely to hear their tongues rattle. This manuscript should be rejected." [35]

35. Larry L. King, "You Must Be Kidding," *New Republic,* May 31, 1969, pp. 24–25, reviewing Lewis Chester et al., *An American Melodrama* (New York: Viking Press, 1969).

What seems to be fictitious is, of course, real. But the old logic of reality no longer orders these events: the real merges with the fantastic, and the blend approaches the surrealism that Norman Mailer believes to be our new reality.[36]

The perplexing fictivity of the "real" increases as the century drags on. The "melodrama" of 1968 is indeed an anemic show in comparison with the "happenings" known as the Watergate affair, 1972–74. Millions of alarmed Americans were mesmerized by the television broadcasts of the Senate public hearings. The "facts" of the matter, as narrated by witness after witness, did not yield themselves to any familiar code of reality; they seemed more like elements of a perverse fantasy, as if "someone had been planning to write a book." [37] Facts were so immured in the fiction they generated that Nat Hentoff talked about "the sheer novelistic drama" [38] of it all, and Norman Mailer admitted that "No novelist unwinds a narrative so well." [39] One of the senators, who had difficulty believing that what he was hearing could actually take place in real life, even addressed one witness as if he was a "character" out of a novel, asking him, "Who thought you up?" [40] The senator then acknowledged that the witness had by his actions "provided . . . at least half a dozen titles for . . . novels," which he assured him he was eager to buy. The whole spectrum of "reality" had turned into what seemed to be an invented fiction: here were operatives of one political party using a James Bondian nomenclature, nicknaming their operation "Gemstone," calling one another by such emblematic names as "Ruby I," "Ruby II," and "Crystal," wearing red wigs, using speech-altering devices and photographing themselves in front of file cabinets in "enemy" offices that were broken into by sanction of

36. From remarks made by Mailer on February 11, 1966, at Wesleyan University as reported by Paul Levine in "The Intemperate Zone: The Climate of Contemporary American Fiction," *Massachusetts Review,* 8 (1967), 505–23.

37. Pearl Wiesen, Letter to the Editor, *New York Times,* June 19, 1973, p. 36.

38. Nat Hentoff, "As the Watergate Turns," *Village Voice,* June 7, 1973, p. 11.

39. Quoted in *The New Yorker,* May 20, 1974, p. 24.

40. "Comic Relief from the Brown-Bag Man," *New York Times,* July 19, 1973, p. 18.

those who came to power with the political slogan of "Law and Order." They all behaved, in fact, like Damon Runyon characters barging around in a science fiction thriller. The empirical irony, perceived not by the subtle mind of the fictionist, but emerging directly from the naked facts, could not be more dramatically incongruous.[41] Contemporary experience is becoming so extravagantly fabulous in its shape that increasingly it resembles an invented fictional patterning in its unfolding. In *Breakfast of Champions*, Kurt Vonnegut, Jr., comments on the way life is lived now in America: "They were doing their best to live like people invented in story books. This was the reason Americans shot each other so often: it was a convenient device for ending short stories and books." As if to dramatize Vonnegut's comments, Florida television broadcaster Chris Chubbuck, after having finished reading the news on her morning program on July 15, 1974, calmly announced: "And now, in keeping with Channel 40's policy of always bringing you the latest in blood and guts, in living color, you're about to see another first—an attempted suicide." She then pulled the trigger. The station, as if to provide the clincher, switched to a travel film.[42]

Philip Roth's recent attempt at caricaturing the caricaturesque reality, *Our Gang*, failed because he himself evidently had not learned the lesson that in an extreme situation mere "quotation" serves as "parody." Roth himself had observed that ". . . the American writer in the middle of the 20th century has his hands full in trying to understand, and then describe, and then make *credible* much of the American reality. It stupefies, it sickens, it infuriates, and finally it is even a kind of embarrassment to one's own meager imagination. The actuality is continually outdoing our talents, and the culture tosses up figures almost daily

41. On technology and Watergate, see Victor Cohn's incisive commentary, "Watergate Bug Infects Technology," *Technology Review,* July/Aug. 1973, pp. 5–6. The eeriness of Watergate is enacted in Hunter S. Thompson's "Fear and Loathing at the Watergate," *Rolling Stone,* Sept. 27, 1973, pp. 31–38, 73–81. The major record companies are planning to market versions of the Nixon tapes on long-playing records and tapes when the tapes are made available to the public.

42. Reported by *Newsweek,* July 29, 1974.

that are the envy of any novelist." [43] At this cultural juncture, the old fictions seem suddenly to have become new realities, and the old verities to look like new fictions. The totalizing novel, which aims at interpreting the human situation with mimetic conventions and linear causal logic rooted in the separation of fiction and fact, reduces the charged quality of experience and consequently presents to the reader an imaginary (almost escapist) world, thin and anemic in comparison with the empirical world. In the absence of a total view of reality which can endow both the private and the public life with a sense of significance and establish if not harmony at least a certain correspondence between the facts of culture and the actions and beliefs of the individual, traditional interpretive art undergoes a radical change. It becomes "pure sensual pleasure, entertainment, therapy and other valuable things, but it no longer serves, as it has in other civilizations, as a means for orientation or for integrating oneself with the social and physical environment." [44] An air of irrelevance and immateriality has surrounded the contemporary interpretive novel because of its loss of orienting power and its inability to fulfill its traditional function, namely the exploration of the actual through the fictional and the illumination of man's experience in its public contexts through authentic aesthetic patterning.

The predicament of the totalizing novel and the emergence of new kinds of postinterpretive narratives are tied to specific facets of the changing modalities of contemporary consciousness as well as the "automatization" of novelistic devices and the narrative inertia of the novel in recent times. Traditionally many critics, including such recent ones as John Bayley, Bernard Bergonzi, and W. J. Harvey, have maintained that "the novel is the distinct art form of liberalism," which celebrates the centrality of the individual in the human community and the sanctity of his or her private space, as well as their corollaries: the diversity of

43. Philip Roth, "Writing American Fiction," *Commentary*, 31 (March 1961), 224.
44. Ferkiss, *Technological Man*, p. 236.

modes of being, limited social planning and government, the "natural harmony of interests," and a free market economy. Although liberalism is not the only ideology informing the totalizing novel—and it can be easily demonstrated that many novels of the last two centuries are energized by forces other than liberalism—nevertheless, there is truth to the suggestion that liberalism more than any other single ideology has influenced the conception and shape of the type of narrative discussed here, namely, the modern bourgeois novel.[45] Liberalism has had a lasting impact not only on the themes treated in the fictive novel but also on its structure and the handling of some of its most important narrative elements, such as "character." However, the inherent contradictions of liberalism and its inability to cope with the modern situation have become more and more evident under the onslaught of rapid socioeconomic changes over the last two decades (although the disenchantment with liberalism started with its failure to deal effectively with the problems which led to World War 1). The incompatibility, for instance, of the liberal economy of a free market energized by aggressive private enterprise and the liberal commitment to the individual's right to develop his or her moral, aesthetic, and intellectual capacities has turned the cherished ideal of what Trilling calls the "variousness" of human beings into a sick joke. The free market economy in postindustrial societies has suppressed the development of individual traits by creating standardized desires, needs, and goals which are necessary more for the efficient expansion of the production process than the self-fulfillment of the individual. The complex of technological culture, which, ironically enough, is a product of liberal policies, moves toward a collectivist rather than an individualistic future in which the simple organic community envisioned by liberal thinkers is replaced by the cybernetic technopolis of synthetic interests. The disintegration of liberalism is part of the untenability of all totalistic systems of thought in technetronic civilizations. Liberalism, contrary to what its

45. However, see Robert Scholes, "The Illiberal Imagination," *New Literary History*, 4 (1973), 521–40.

believers would like us to think, *is* a totalizing ideology and its pluralistic manner and eclectic method should not be confused with its ideational thrust. Robert Scholes, who approaches the relationship between liberalism and the novel from a different standpoint, nevertheless describes the totalizing tendencies in the supposedly pluralistic and liberal novel and the world in which it flourished:

> In the heyday of the "liberal" novel [the nineteenth century] author-narrator-entrepreneurs ruled their fictional worlds as despotically as the laissez-faire capitalists ruled their factories. And beyond this, the benevolently despotic narrator was invariably committed to the most sweeping generalizations about human nature. He was always looking for the laws of behavior that governed the actions of his puppets. The realism of the nineteenth-century was characterized by the belief that the nature of reality is determinate and discoverable but has not been discovered—until now. Whereupon, the successful realist took out a patent on his discovery and delivered it to us as the latest thing in reality, stamped "Made in Balzac" or "Bottled by Dickens."[46]

It is the disappearance of totalizing perspectives, including liberalism and the social order behind it, that have deprived the conventional novel of its old assurances about the nature of man and society and therefore impoverished it.

The epistemology of the totalizing novel, which views reality as an objective and knowable entity governed in its behavior by rational laws discoverable by the reasoning individual, is closely related to the bourgeois liberal outlook. The themes of the novel, which George Steiner sums up as "the dreams and nightmares of the mercantile ethic, of middle-class privacy, and of monetary-sexual conflicts and delights of industrial society," are usually worked out in terms of this epistemology which presupposes a system of correspondences between private experience and the facts of communal reality. The aesthetics of verisimilitude is a tacit acknowledgment of the existence of such a correspondence as well as the presence of a shared perception of

46. Ibid., p. 526.

society expressed in the novel through a common language of values. The totalizing novel, in other words, operates on a certain balance of reality: an equipoise between the self and the world. With the increasing complexity of urbanized life in a technetronic culture and the individual's growing sense of helplessness in ever coming to grips with it, this equilibrium has been lost in contemporary American society. Since World War 2, American society has been undergoing, more intensely than ever before, what Gunnar Myrdal calls the process of "dissimilation"—a fragmentation of the main culture into innumerable subcultures. In place of a communal language of values, there have developed a myriad of idiolects which have in effect created a new Tower of Babel in the nascent cybernetic metropolis. The subsequent gap between the self and the world works against the conventional mimetic balance of the fictive novel and its ability to universalize experience, since the comprehensive picture of reality offered by the novelist in his or her fiction is hardly shareable with today's reader, whose private experience contradicts the communal image at every important point. This phenomenon is in sharp contrast with the informing epistemology within which the themes of the totalizing novel used to be developed. "As recently as the nineteenth century, and the beginning of the twentieth," Erich Auerbach maintains, "so much clearly formulable and recognized community of thought and feeling remained . . . that a writer engaged in representing reality had reliable criteria at hand by which to organize it." [47] In the absence of this "community of thought and feeling," the contemporary totalizing novel becomes insubstantial and experientially meaningless.

The schism between the self and society and the eclipse of liberalism have deprived the totalizing novel of its main sources of cultural energy. Internally the novel has also lost its literary vigor through the "automatization" of its basic narrative devices such as "character" and "plot" as well as its main mediative means—a transparent and communal lan-

47. Erich Auerbach, *Mimesis*, trans. W. R. Trask (Princeton, N.J.: Princeton University Press, 1953), p. 550.

guage. For many critics, including John Bayley, W. J. Harvey, and such writers as Alberto Moravia and Iris Murdoch, the ultimate moral and aesthetic worth of a novel depends on the ability of the novelist to create free characters who enjoy the opacity and complexity of real human beings. This concern with "characterization" in the novel reflects the preoccupation of liberal thought with the "variousness" of human beings as well as with the fully developed individual and his or her self-actualization in a vast private space. The "function" of this device, which, in Robbe-Grillet's words, was operative "in a universe where personality represented both the means and the end of all exploration," has become obsolete today, when a less anthropomorphic view of the world dominates our imagination. The individual has lost his centrality in a world where the very survival of the human race is at stake. Now he not only has to live with various degrees of centralized control over his economic activities but must also allow such things as birth control into his private life if the balance between natural resources and the population on earth is to be preserved. The expansion of scientific and technological knowledge has helped to create a new planetary consciousness and thus to diminish the liberal anthropomorphism on which the device of character in the totalizing novel is structured. A new collectivist mode of thought is replacing the individualism of industrial society and making the very creation of character impossible since, as Moravia puts it, "Modern man can be seen as a mere numerical entity within the most terrifying collectives that the human race has ever known. He can be seen as existing not for himself but as part of something else, of a collective feeling, idea and organism. It is very difficult to create a character out of such a man." [48] As a result of these changes in the contemporary situation, the character in the totalizing novel today cannot fulfill its traditional narrative functions, which were to portray a fully individuated person so rooted in a "community of thought

48. Alberto Moravia, *Man as an End: A Defense of Humanism,* trans. Bernard Wall (New York: Farrar, Straus and Giroux, 1966), pp. 70–71.

and feeling" shared by his fellow human beings that he could also typify a particular group of people. The "disautomatization" of this narrative device in postwar writing is one of the literary factors responsible for the emergence of such nontotalizing genres of narratives as transfiction and the nonfiction novel. In these kinds of narratives, instead of a nostalgic projection of a vision of wholeness and an intelligibility of life as in the person of Mr. Artur Sammler, we encounter either countercharacters such as Giles or actual human persons like Ken Kesey.

The "retreat from character" is only one literary symptom of the passing of the liberal humanism which informed the novel. Other major narrative constituents of the fictive novel which have become dysfunctional and worn out are "plot" and "language." The epistemology of the fictive novel regards reality as a series of causally connected and chronologically ordered events; thus, the formalization of these events takes the shape of a linear and logically constructed plot in the novel. Such a stylization of experience is in sharp contrast with the multifaceted, kaleidoscopic view that contemporary man has of life because of the new communications technologies. The veracity and authenticity of this chronological-causal ordering of experience is also undermined by the post-Newtonian physics of randomness and uncertainty. The novel's view of progress, inherited from the liberal humanist outlook, is embodied in the movement of its plot as well as its particular conception of time, which forms the matrix of the plot; however, both are at odds with contemporary perspectives of them. The plot of the totalizing novel, therefore, seems to the contemporary reader to be a falsification of historical consciousness and daily experience. It has, in other words, become another "automatized" narative device through which the novelist willfully imposes a desired order, contradicted by the facts of culture, on unruly contemporary experience. "As the world spins in ever-crazier orbit with its moonshots and mass murders," not only does the causal plot forfeit its epistemological validity, but, as one critic of recent literature comments, "language itself loses its power to encompass or define life." [49] The novel has, of course, suffered more than other literary genres from this ever-widening gap between reality and words, since it is committed to a transparent language which can depict reality without interposing itself between the reader and the image of reality conveyed. In the postwar period, a significant portion of the reality which informs the culture is generated outside the verbal medium either in the metacodes of logics and mathematics or in visual and audial codes. Also, the criticism of language by Marxists and psychoanalysts for its failure to be faithful to the complexities of social and psychic actualities, and the reexamination of the relationship between language and reality in general by such philosophers as Wittgenstein have contributed to the devaluation of language in contemporary thought, and thus undermined the mimetic preoccupation of the novel with language. [50]

The untenability of the novel's epistemology and the disappearance of the social order which gave rise to its informing ideology as well as the erosion of its internal literary power have turned the totalizing novel into an anemic genre no longer capable of achieving its aesthetic and catalytic goal, which "has always been and is now to observe and to order the social facts about us and to dramatize them in a new imaginative interpretation of human experience." [51] In our "age of suspicion," these attempts of the totalizing novel seem inauthentic. [52] They were valid only when it was still possible for the literary artist to create in his work an epistemological correlative—a *summa mundi*—for his culture, but such grand views belong as much to the history of ideas as the comprehensivist approach of that magnificent monu-

49. "Theatre without Adventure," *Times Literary Supplement,* Dec. 29, 1972, p. 1569.

50. See also George Steiner's essay, "Retreat from the Word," in his *Language and Silence* (New York: Atheneum, 1970), pp. 12–35, and for a different approach to the issues, David Lodge, *Language of Fiction* (New York: Columbia University Press, 1966).

51. James W. Tuttleton, *The Novel of Manners in America* (Chapel Hill: University of North Carolina Press, 1972), p. 7.

52. See also Lionel Trilling, *Sincerity and Authenticity* (Cambridge, Mass.: Harvard University Press, 1972), pp. 134–39.

ment of the liberal humanist tradition, the eleventh edition
of the *Encyclopaedia Britannica* (1910–11). The information
explosion and new communications technologies which
have literally fragmented the *Encyclopaedia* into the *Propae-
dia, Micropaedia* and *Macropaedia* have also questioned the
ontological status of the fictive novel in the contemporary
world—the necessity of its very mode of being. If the task of
the novelist is, as Conrad put it, to make the reader hear,
feel, and "before all," to make him "see," then surely film
and television can accomplish such a goal more effectively
and are far more capable of narrating and capturing the
texture of daily reality. The supplanting function of the
electronic media, however, is not just limited to the reflection of the quotidian fabric of life; more significant, it has
brought about a profound change in the perception of reality by its ability to present a multidimensional view of experience and thus make the unilinear novel seem simplifying
and reductional. In addition to the challenge of the mass
media, the behavioral sciences have similarly diminished the
informing power of the novel: since the psychic wounds of
recent wars and the traumata of contemporary life have
proven too deep for the novelist to interpret, professional
psychoanalysts have had to intervene, replacing the novelists' amateur and inadequate analyses with actual case studies. The problems which have been turning the lives of the
lonely crowd into a constant nightmare are no longer mappable by the sociologizings of novelists but require the professional skills of trained social scientists. The novel, as an
interpretive genre, in short, has been backgrounded by the
historical forces which brought about a new technological
order as well as by the exhaustion of its internal literary
energies.[53]

    53. It might also be appropriate here to refer to the "publishing" problems
which such commentators as Ronald Sukenick (*New York Times Book Review*, Sept.
15, 1974, p. 55) and John Leonard (*Village Voice*, June 27, 1974, p. 30) think to be
the real cause of the current crisis of the fictive novel. The position is most suc-
cinctly put by Charles Newman: ". . . we are determined not by a genre, but by a
hopelessly anachronistic [publishing and marketing] technology. In other words,
the cost of producing and marketing what we *make* has simply exceeded the industry's profit margin, and this particular disease has been masked long enough by
theories of dying forms and metaphors of terminal illness" (*TriQuarterly*, No. 26,

However, this is not to say that the novel is "dead." The twin critical clichés of "the death of the novel" and "the death of 'the death of the novel'" have been around for quite some time now. As early as 1790 a commentator on fiction announced in the *Monthly Review* that "the manufacture of novels has been so long established, that in general they have arrived at mediocrity. . . . We are indeed so sickened with this worn-out species of composition, that we have lost all relish for it." [54] And, of course, the lines of counterstatements, denials, assurances, and predictions for a new life for the novel, and also mere emotional outbursts are familiar:

> "There was talk some years ago" said James Bellingham, "about novels going out."
> "They're just coming!" cried Miss Kingsbury.[55]

In the present century, the debate has been carried on by critics from Ortega y Gassett, through T. S. Eliot and Lionel Trilling, to John Barth and Ronald Sukenick, with the issue becoming an emotional one on which nearly every critic of the novel feels obliged to take sides.

Such analyses, however, are based on an organological theory of literary evolutionism operating on the analogy of an animal growth postulate that each literary genre is born, achieves maturity, and finally dies. Such a notion (revitalized in the nineteenth century by the theories of Darwin

1973, p. 7). Publishing economics have certainly changed, and there has been a statistical drop in the number of new novels published over the last two decades: in 1950, 14 percent of all new titles were "fiction," but by 1974 they had decreased to 8 percent. (For details see the yearly reports of *Publishers Weekly*.) However, it would be rather naïve to disregard the literary and cultural dimensions of the crisis and explain such a complex phenomenon merely in terms of publishing circumstances. A more fruitful discussion of the role of the publishing industry would be one within the larger context of the status of the novel in postindustrial cultures. In *The Situation of the Novel* (London: Macmillan, 1970), Bernard Bergonzi comes close to such an approach when he talks about the "paradox" that ". . . the novel, which seems so open to life, and to give, as Lawrence saw, a total picture of man in all his variety and fullness, is intimately connected with a particular technology and form of commercial development, neither of which may be permanently protected from obsolescence" (p. 13).

54. Aug. 1790, p. 463, quoted in J. M. S. Tompkins, *The Popular Novel in England* (London: Constable, 1932), p. 5.

55. William Dean Howells, *The Rise of Silas Lapham*, ed. Edwin H. Cady (Boston: Houghton Mifflin, 1957), p. 162.

and Spencer) sees genre as a closed and determined cycle, ignores its dialectical dynamism, and implies a continuous direct line of movement toward a predetermined end. The dynamics of genre, contrary to these views, are not entirely predictable, and, as Tynyanov demonstrates in his study *Dostoevsky and Gogol,* such an unbroken line uniting "the younger and the older representatives of a known literary branch" is nonexistent: "[The matter] is much more complicated. There is no continuing direct line; there is rather a departure, a pushing away from the known point—a struggle. . . . Any literary succession is first of all a struggle, a destruction of the old values and a reconstruction of old elements." [56] Narrative genres undergo constant changes born out of the interaction of internal generic forces and the whole literary tradition on one hand, and such extraliterary factors as new cultural necessities, the influence of the audience, and the complete reality matrix of society on the other. The genre of the totalizing novel, for example, has been subjected to the extraliterary factors previously described. As long as the changes made in the fictive novel were only an intensification of existing compositional problems and thus were merely "quantitative"—like increasing the psychological analysis of character in the Modernist novel or a more systematic use of dramatic presentation in connection with narrative point of view—they were absorbed by the existing narrative systems. Once the accumulated changes reached a critical point in the postwar period, there was a sudden transformation of these quantitative variations into "qualitative" alterations out of which the radically new constructs of nontotalizing kinds of narratives emerged. The difference between *Middlemarch* and *To the Lighthouse* is basically a matter of quantitative changes in such aspects of the novel as the psychological analysis of the character and the retardation of the plot: both are still operating within the narrative framework of the totalizing novel. However, *The Crying of Lot 49* or *La Vida,* which are widely known supramodernist narratives with overall narra-

56. *Russian Formalist Criticism: Four Essays,* trans. L. T. Lemon and M. J. Reis (Lincoln: University of Nebraska Press, 1965), p. 134.

tive concerns relatively similar to those of George Eliot's and Virginia Woolf's novels, are entirely new kinds of narratives which are not understandable in terms of the criteria used to approach traditional novels. The narrative configurations in Pynchon's and Lewis's books are the function of a technologically induced reality and a reorientation of literary tradition itself. Oedipa Maas is more a "countercharacter" than a character like Mrs. Ramsay or Dorothea, and Fernanda cannot be approached as a character at all for she is not a "literary device"; in fact, an entirely new descriptive term is needed for her. Such a change is not a gradual perfection or progress but the discontinuous and abrupt outcome of the process of "shifting dominant" discussed by Roman Jakobson. The "dominant" is that focusing element which "rules, determines and transforms the remaining components" of a given literary system.[57] In other words, it establishes a hierarchy of values, and literary change is the result of the reordering of this hierarchy under the pressures of literary and extraliterary stresses. At the genre level, the process of "shifting dominant" will bring about a situation in which "genres which were originally secondary paths, subsidary variants, now come to the fore, whereas the canonical genres are pushed toward the rear."[58] *Middlemarch* and *To the Lighthouse*, like all totalizing novels, are "dominated" by a tendency toward an "epiphanic summation of experience," a trait which does not exist in nontotalizing novels such as *The Crying of Lot 49* and *La Vida*.

The genre which is backgrounded, however, does not "die"; at any given time several kinds of narrative are in existence. The Victorian sub-genre of the totalizing novel did not expire but was backgrounded by the sub-genre of the Modernist novel, and today the two exist simultaneously with the supramodernist narrative. As John Barth observes, "a good many current novelists write turn-of-the-century-type novels, only in more or less mid-twentieth-century lan-

57. Jakobson, "The Dominant," in *Readings in Russian Poetics*, p. 83. For the origin of the concept of "dominant" see Victor Erlich, *Russian Formalism*, 3d. ed. (The Hague: Mouton, 1969), p. 199.

58. Jakobson, *Readings in Russian Poetics*, p. 85.

guage and about contemporary people and topics." Thus, according to Shklovsky, "The vanquished line is not obliterated, it does not cease to exist. It is only knocked from the throne. Moreover, in reality the matter is complicated by the fact that new hegemony is usually not a pure revival of previous forms but is made more complex by the presence of features of the younger schools and with features, now secondary, inherited from its predecessors on the throne." [59] Although the totalizing novel as a genre has become "automatized" today, it continues to be not only written but widely reviewed and read. However, because it has lost its cultural function, "the consumption of the novel," as Leslie Fiedler puts it, "has become a dull public observance like going to church. It *is* going to church, the last gesture of piety to the art on the part of the bourgeoisie who once fought so bitterly to claim this aspect of culture as their birthright." [60] The fictive quality of current realities demands radical responses which can equal their volcanic energy and accommodate their unruly behavior without imposing antiquated notions of order upon them. The emergence of new narrative forms in which the fictionist enacts contemporary actualities, rather than attempting to interpret them in terms of projected values, contrary to the thinking of some critics and writers, by no means implies the death of the imagination; rather, it means narrative energy is finding new "dominants." [61] Not surprisingly, the two most significant narrative types in which this energy is manifesting itself are acknowledgments of the impossibility of formulating an interpretive frame of reference which can decode the bizarre realities of today in aesthetic idioms without falsifying and reducing their density.

Lost in the funhouse of interpretations of the human situation, the fictionist is now trying to trace his way back out

59. *Russian Formalist Criticism*, p. 135.

60. Leslie Fiedler, "The Novel in the Post-Political World," *Partisan Review*, 23 (1956), 358. See also Fiedler, "The Death and Rebirth of the Novel," in *The Theory of the Novel*, ed. John Halperin (New York: Oxford University Press, 1974), pp. 189–209.

61. This refocusing, significantly enough, has become one of the recurring themes and controlling metaphors in recent writings. See, for example, Ronald Sukenick's *The Death of the Novel and Other Stories* (New York: Dial Press, 1969).

of the labyrinths of distorting commentaries. He is doing this either by an extravagant mimicking of interpretations of reality through a commentary on the comments or by circumventing the interpretations altogether and reaching back to the basics—the testable actualities. In either case, his narrative is nontotalizing.

Since about 1957—the year the Soviet Union's Sputnik shook America and almost overnight changed the cold war of ideological opposition between the two postwar superpowers into a planetary polarization between Man and Machine—the most radical narrative idioms for articulating the agitating content of today's extreme situation have developed in the forms of "transfiction" and the "nonfiction novel." Both of these kinds of narrative can be considered the result of what W. J. Harvey regards as the "mutation" of the novel caused by the radical experiments of novelists in a postliberal society: "the first imaginative responses to a changing world view." [62] The fictive novel, of course, contains elements of both transfiction and the nonfiction novel, and from an historical perspective one may see these two forms arising from the disintegration of the narrative, descriptive, and discursive components of the classic novel.

"Transfiction" is a type of narrative which is constructed upon the process of what might be called, in terms of the poetics of the Russian Formalists, a baring of literary devices: [63] unmasking narrative conventions and turning them into counterconventions in order to shatter the illusion of reality which is the aesthetic foundation of the totalizing novel. This use of countertechniques played off against a background of conventional devices in transfiction creates a narrative tension which varies in degree according to the different modes of transfiction ranging from "metafiction" through "surfiction" to "science fiction."

62. W. J. Harvey, *Character and the Novel* (Ithaca, N.Y.: Cornell University Press, 1965), p. 26.
63. See Shklovsky's essays in *Russian Formalist Criticism*, pp. 2–57; Eichenbaum's "O. Henry and the Theory of the Short Story," in *Readings in Russian Poetics*, pp. 227–69, as well as Robert Scholes's *Structuralism in Literature* (New Haven: Yale University Press, 1974), pp. 74–91.

"Metafiction" is ultimately a narrational metatheorem whose subject matter is fictional systems themselves and the molds through which reality is patterned by narrative conventions. In the metafictions of such writers as John Barth, Donald Barthelme, and Robert Coover, "the forms of fiction serve as the material upon which further forms can be imposed." [64] Metafiction more than other modes of transfiction is conscious of its own fictivity and, in contrast to the interpretive novel, which operates with the aesthetic assumptions of verisimilitude, exults over its own fictitiousness, which it uses as the very terms of its narrative ontology—it is a "mask which points to itself." The informing matrix of metafiction is, in Roland Barthes's words, "that asymptotic zone where literature appears to destroy itself as a language object without destroying itself as a metalanguage." [65] This intense self-reflexiveness of metafiction is caused by the fact that the only certain reality for the metafictionist is the reality of his own discourse; thus, his fiction turns in upon itself, transforming the process of writing into the subject of writing. The credibility of fiction, therefore, is reestablished not as an illuminating commentary on life but as a metacommentary on fiction itself. The main counter-techniques of metafiction are two-dimensional, flat characterization, consciously contrived plots, and paralogical, noncausal, and anti-linear sequences of events, all of which are carried out in a highly foregrounded language embedded in a counterhumor that is nondidactic, distancing, and not "concerned about what to do about life but how to take it." [66] Through an extravagant *over-totalization* and mock interpretation of the human condition, the metafictionist accentuates the arbitrariness of uniting the elements of a disjunctive universe into a significant whole. His over-totalizing approaches a parody of the ordered, causal, and realistically

64. William Gass, *Fiction and the Figures of Life* (New York: Knopf, 1970), p. 25. See also John Barth, "The Literature of Exhaustion," *Atlantic*, Aug. 1967, pp. 29–34 and Robert Scholes, "Metafiction," *Iowa Review*, 1 (1970), 100–115.

65. Roland Barthes, *Critical Essays*, trans. Richard Howard (Evanston, Ill.: Northwestern University Press, 1972), p. 98.

66. Robert Scholes, *The Fabulators* (New York: Oxford University Press, 1967), p. 43.

performed interpretation of the fictive novelist. By substituting parody of interpretation for straight interpretation, the metafictionist demonstrates the confusing multiplicity of reality and thus the naïveté involved in attempting to reach a total synthesis of life within narrative. The metafictionist's over-totalization, consequently, creates a work with low-message value at the zero degree of interpretation, thus freeing the narrative from an anthropomorphic order-hunting and insuring that, as Barthelme says, there is nothing between the lines but white spaces. Barthelme's (and the metafictionist's) attitude echoes Witold Gombrowicz's concept of the mocking of meaning and his advice to his readers (in *Ferdydurke*) to "start dancing with the book instead of asking for meaning."

"Surfiction" [67] shares many of metafiction's counter-techniques aimed at laying bare the devices and conventions of the art of narrative, but the tension between technique and countertechnique is reduced in the works of the surfic-tionists, who prefer to move out of the aesthetically incestuous world of metafiction and directly engage the reality outside (rather than inside) the fictional discourse. The surfictions of such writers as Steve Katz, Gilbert Sorrentino, Ronald Sukenick, Raymond Federman, and Ishmael Reed refuse to make any claim to interpreting reality and instead regard what Sukenick in his *98.6* calls "the law of mosaics, a way of dealing with parts in the absence of wholes" to be the only valid approach to contemporary experience.[68]

The main literary advice laid bare in "science fiction," on the other hand, is the narrative theme, which is turned into a pararealistic countertheme based on an implied "as if," thus creating an entirely subjunctive field of narration. Extrapolation is substituted in science fiction for the conventional interpretation of the totalizing novel. Even in "social science fiction," a conspicuously fictitious and hypothetical posthuman situation is projected, rather than a simulacrum

67. The term "surfiction" is Raymond Federman's; however, he is not responsible for this typology or definition. See Federman, *Surfiction* (Chicago: Swallow Press, 1975), pp. 5–15.
68. Ronald Sukenick, *98.6* (New York: Fiction Collective, 1975), p. 122.

of the experiential world. Through extrapolation, in other words, the science fiction writer creates a world discontinuous with the world in which the readers conduct their lives and thereby undermines the possibility of totalizing the present human situation.[69]

Transfiction, in all its modes, is an instance of what John Barth (with an eye on the mythic character of Modernist art) calls "mythoplastic" art: an art form aware of its own artificiality and conscious of the means it uses to "conceptualize, to grammatize, to syntactify" experience. The transfictionist renounces the conventional authority of imagination and assumes in the face of an entropic reality what Ihab Hassan calls "the ironic attitude of the wordless author binding a sheaf of blank pages." [70]

Employing a completely different set of narrative strategies, the nonfiction novel shares with transfiction this radical refusal to neutralize the contingent nature of reality by transforming it into a safe zone of unified meaning. The nonfiction novel moves toward a zero degree of interpretation of man's situation not through mock-commentary or extrapolation, but by empirically registering the experiential realities. The nonfiction novel is the most immediate narrative manifestation of the epistemological crisis of our "age of suspicion." The nonfiction novel is the narrative of the consciousness which is engulfed and overwhelmed by the enormity of the stark actualities, the consciousness in what Jaspers calls an "extreme situation." Consequently, it is no longer capable of accepting any single interpretation or reaction and can only neutrally transcribe the texture of the fictional reality whose contradictory nature and mythic dimensions resist the totalizing imagination. The direct inscription of the visible facts (as happened events, not as categories of reality) and lack of interpretive commentary confront the reader with the mind-boggling actualities of today. Jorge Luis Borges is referring to this quality of the

69. However, see Darko Suvin, "On the Poetics of the Science Fiction Genre," *College English*, 34 (1972), 372–82.

70. The theoretical model behind this brief description of transfiction is developed in my forthcoming book, "The Semiotics of Transfiction."

nonfiction novel when he says that Capote's "*In Cold Blood* is composed with an almost inhuman objectivity." [71] Facts in the nonfiction novel are used not to endorse an imposed vision or interpretation of reality but in their full literal value. By consistently refusing to go beyond the experiential *donnée* and the naked facts, the nonfiction novelist rejects the conventional aesthetic notion of art as the extraction of order out of chaos and with it the concept of the artist as *vates*. This position is best expressed in John Cage's statement: "our intention is . . . not to bring order out of chaos . . . but simply to wake up to the very life we are living."

The noninterpretive stance of the nonfiction novel is a function of changes which have taken place in contemporary reality. The fictive novel operates with the absolute of a permanent order while relativity, indeterminacy, and entropy are the shaping factors of today's reality.[72] However, this·should not be taken to mean that the nonfiction novel employs entropic elements as controlling themes or metaphors; that would be a new interpretation of reality within a different metaphysical scheme. It simply means that the presence of "entropy" has induced epistemological conditions which have made the emergence of such art forms as the nonfiction novel inevitable. The recurrence of entropic motifs in a nonfiction novel like Andy Warhol's *a*, for example, is transcriptional and not interpretational—entropy is embedded in the "unimagined existence" that the nonfiction novelist registers.

The noninterpretational approach of the nonfiction novelist does not imply either that he is a passive information-processing instrument or that he works on the assumption that there is an objective reality "out there" which can be transcribed, free from the intervention of his own consciousness. In registering objects and ongoing events, the

71. Jorge Luis Borges, *An Introduction to American Literature*, trans. L. Clark Keating and Robert O. Evans (Lexington: University Press of Kentucky, 1971), p. 73.

72. See Norbert Wiener, *The Human Use of Human Beings* (Boston: Houghton Mifflin, 1950), and Stanley Angrist and Loren G. Hepler, *Order and Chaos: Laws of Energy and Entropy* (New York: Basic Books, 1967).

nonfiction novelist enters into a transaction with them; as a human being, the post-Behaviorist psychology of perception has indicated, he cannot do otherwise. The way the external world appears to him is affected not only by his past responses and assumptions but also by his expectations about the future, as well as by such conditioning factors as his culture and language. The perceiver and the perceived do not exist independently; the perceived is part of the process of perception, and both are a function of the active participation of the perceiver in life. As Heisenberg reminds us, even "the laws of nature which we formulate mathematically in quantum theory deal no longer with the particles themselves but with our knowledge of the elementary particles. The question whether these particles exist in space and time 'in themselves' can thus no longer be posed in this form." [73]

The nonfiction novelist's transaction with the surrounding world, colored as it is with his personal history and outlook, however, remains finally a local reaction and interpretation rather than a global totalization—he does not assemble his sensory impressions into a significant form in order to formulate a particular metaphysics or convey a single vision of reality as the fictive novelist does. His observations, unlike those of the fictive novelist, are non-teleological: they are not a means for fleshing out his epiphanic vision of the ultimate structure of reality but an end in themselves. Like the contemporary scientist or painter, the nonfiction novelist

> detects that the ordinary, the commonplace, the superficial, the quotidian is the very mystery most inaccessible to reason and explanation and method. The immediate occasion is sufficient unto itself, and this recognition has led to a new humility, as well as a new frustration. If the significant is on the surface, then the need for depth explanation has gone, and the contingent, the everyday happening, is more authentic than the ultimate or absolute. . . . The old systems of meaning—the Newtonian solid geometry locating things at

73. Heisenberg, "The Representation of Nature in Contemporary Physics," pp. 99–100.

appropriate distance or the theoretic order of Alberti's perspective, which foreshortened—are suspect. . . . Plot itself
was a mode of foreshortening. To accept the accidental or
causal is to recognize the irrationality of the obvious, to dis-
pense with the need for a logic accounting for everything.[74]

The reality which is transcribed in the nonfiction novel is
inclusive and non-selective since the nonfiction novelist does
not apply axiological criteria—which is implied in a totalistic
conception of reality—to his observations and does not "select" elements of his experience in order to project a total
perspective of life. Although he does not follow the aesthetics of the closed-set novel based on the dichotomy articulated by Henry James as "Life being all inclusion and confusion, and art being all discrimination and selection," he is
nevertheless subject to the limitations imposed on him by
his medium: the book. Since durational realism is impossible, he is compelled by his medium to omit segments of his
observations. The act of omission implies selection, but a
selection which is medium-imposed, not interpretively motivated.

The transactional nature of human perception of the external world, the infeasibility of a durational realism, the
limitations of the book as a medium, and the nonfiction
novelist's use of language—which is by definition a symbolic
system charged with the communal meanings and attitudes
of a speech community [75]—have often been confused with a
metaphysical interpretation and thus have caused the nonfiction novel to be read in terms of other genres of prose
narrative. The nonfiction novelist's perspective on reality, it
should be emphasized, is a local view and not a total vista in
that it does not employ observed events as constituents of a
projected fictional world containing a private vision of real-

74. Wylie Sypher, *Literature and Technology* (New York: Random House, 1968),
p. 240.
75. Robbe-Grillet's programmatic de-metaphorization of the language of narrative—attempting to purge it of its communal values and humanizing effects—is
not only a positive metaphysical and interpretive stance, but its very limited
achievement illuminates the enormity of the epistemological problems that confront all writers of narrative. The nonfiction novelist accepts the nature of human
language. His narrative is *neutral and not neutralizing.*

ity. When Tom Wolfe, for instance, sees the Merry Pranksters' bus in their garage at the Warehouse on Harriet
Street in San Francisco, he responds to its presence with all
his accumulated experiences, sensations, and expectations.
His reaction is humanly much more complex than the Be-
haviorists' stimulus-response model implies. Nonetheless,
the fact remains that the bus, in other words, is not invented as a symbolic vehicle and thus is ontologically different, for example, from the bus in John Hawkes's *The Second Skin,* which takes the "Skipper" across the landscape of
a fictive country and his own mind, or the car in which
Jason chases Quentin in Faulkner's *The Sound and the Fury.*
The vehicle in Faulkner's novel not only is charged with
symbolic resonances about the depravity of Jason as modern man, but also serves as a metaphor for Faulkner's rejection of the invading technological culture. Wolfe's account
of the bus is, by contrast, free from such emblematic
elements, and whatever symbolic significance the bus may
have in the narrative is derived not from Wolfe's imagination but from the empirical fiction projected by the Pranksters. Similarly, Norman Mailer in *The Armies of the Night*
does not make symbolic and interpretive use of Robert
Lowell, who has an actual existence outside the narrative, in
the same sense that Bernard Malamud uses the entirely
fictive Harry Lesser in *The Tenants.* Any commentary on the
reality perspective in *The Electric Kool-Aid Acid Test* and *The
Armies of the Night* or on the subjectivity of Wolfe's and
Mailer's accounts should be made within the context of the
nature of human knowledge of the external world and with
Heisenberg's statement in mind that even "the mathematical formulas indeed no longer portray nature, but our
knowledge of nature."

The nonfiction novelist, in contrast to the fictive novelist
(who reaches for order behind the unruly and fragmentary
experience) and the transfictionist (who possesses the fabulous by inventing the metafabulous), accepts the bizarre, fictive nature of reality as the experiential *donnée* of contemporary man and transcribes it. The registered fiction of facts,
consequently, replaces the fiction of fantasy, the latter a vic-

tim of the intense pressures of this surreal reality. The generation which Bruce J. Friedman amusingly called "the surprise-proof generation" is finding it more and more difficult to suspend disbelief and relate to the make-believe world of the totalizing novel. Faced with the perplexities of surrounding actualities, one of the characters in Philip Roth's "On the Air" voices this state of mind: " 'Kill the metaphor!' the chief screamed in his delirium. 'Slaughter simile! Fuck the fable! Piss on the parable once and for all! I'm being driven literal Scully—I'm going stark raving literal at last!' " [76]

Unlike factual narratives, the nonfiction novel is written not *about* but *in* facts. This generic radical provides the epistemological foundation for a new king of literature which might be called "literal literature." Ihab Hassan sees this literalism as one of the strategies that the "literature of silence" uses to deny the time-honored totalizing function of literature. Literal literature is related to a general movement in the contemporary arts in which works aspiring to a noninterpretive stance enact the neutral but concrete surfaces of life. Manifestations of this tendency range from the *musique concrete* of Luigi Nono and Karl Stockhausen, through the "Song of the Humpback Whale" recorded with underwater microphones off the coast of Bermuda, to John Cage's works, including a four-movement piece composed by holding up a microphone to the environmental sounds of four different locations in New York; [77] from Robert Rauschenberg's all-white paintings in which the only image is the spectator's own shadow to Andy Warhol's signed Brillo box or soup can, and from *cinéma vérité* to "An American Family" (which Margaret Mead regards as a breakthrough in mapping existing actualities).

The distrust of the imagined and made-up and an almost hysterical embracing of the actual are connected to the valuational crisis of the times, when only the tangible elements of experience, clearly located in the empirical world, are

76. Philip Roth, "On the Air," *New American Review*, No. 10 (1970), p. 46.
77. Program honoring Cage's sixtieth birthday, at the New School, New York, June 30, 1972.

treated as "real." For the nonfiction novel, facts—objects of the senses—are the only available ultimate reality. This is, by the Modernist criteria, a "reduced reality" which eliminates, as far as possible, the pattern-making mind of the artist and substitutes for private mythologies the myths outflowing from contemporary facts. This fiction of fact can be mapped out only in an intermediary zone of experience, located between the "factual" and the "fictional," an area which language with its entrenched factual-fictional polarization of experience cannot currently identify. The nonfiction novel deals with this area of experience which is the matrix of reality in extreme situations.

To read the nonfiction novel on its own terms, it is necessary first to examine its narrational features: those elements constituting the deep structure of generic codes which—the uniqueness of each individual work notwithstanding—inform the nonfiction novel's singular narrative configuration. There has been, especially since Croce's attack on the concept of genre in the opening years of this century, a lingering suspicion among critics that any literary study which aspires to go beyond a given work will inevitably violate the aesthetic integrity of that work and obscure its uniqueness. Croce's aesthetic atomism (shared by the American New Critics and the British Practical Critics and "Close Readers") is based on a monistic contrasting of the universal and the particular.[78] However, the findings of the modern sciences, especially the research in modern linguistics from Saussure to Chomsky, have indicated that the universal and the particular are, contrary to the Crocean doctrine, in complimentary and not contradictory relationship. The creativity of language, its open-endedness and the speaker's ability to constantly produce unique new sentences, for in-

78. In his *Aesthetic*, Croce discusses literature in the context of its medium; an implicit comparison between a single work of literary art and the sentence, which he regards as the "linguistic unit," informs his criticism. "Language," he says, "is a perpetual creation" unrepeatable and the source of "ever-new expressions." To seek an underlying structure ("model language") of which all these expressions are individual manifestations is, according to him, "to seek the immobility of motion." In other words, to analyze the elements of linguistic and literary creation into smaller units or to relate them to larger contexts such as discourse or genre according to Crocean dogma, is to damage their irreplaceable identity.

stance, is a manifestation of the existence of an underlying system in terms of which "ever-new expressions" are formulated and decoded.[79] In the same manner generic orders, as Claudio Guillen suggests, are no more alien to the unique works of the creative literary artist than the "linguistic code is to the actual utterances in his speech." [80] The uniqueness of a work and its creator should not be considered as an expression of separateness and non-contiguity with the works of various writers. Their individuality, Mikhail Khrapchenko maintains, does not mean that no inner links exist among them, or that general principles do not manifest themselves in the writings of different writers.[81] Rather, the "general principle," the generic code, serves as a norm or expectation "to guide the reader in his encounter with the text." [82] The purpose in the following chapters of this study of the nonfiction novel's generic features is not to find a classificatory system or formulate a set of prescriptive rules, but to explore a type of narrative meaning and its generic signals. Such an examination, as Todorov has indicated, aids the reader in becoming aware of the properties that a particular text shares with the "texts belonging to one of the sub-groups of literature" (genre) and at the same time heightens the reader's understanding of the uniqueness of that text, since no text is merely "the product of a pre-existing combinatorial system (constituted by all that is literature *in posse*); it is also a transformation of that system." [83] Thus, the dialectical tension between the particular

79. See, among other sources, Noam Chomsky, *Topics in the Theory of Generative Grammar* (The Hague: Mouton, 1966); *Aspects of the Theory of Syntax* (Cambridge, Mass.: M.I.T. Press, 1965); and *Language and Mind,* enlarged ed. (New York: Harcourt, Brace, Jovanovich, 1972).

80. Claudio Guillen, *Literature as System* (Princeton, N.J.: Princeton University Press, 1971), p. 390.

81. Mikhail Khrapchenko, "The Typological Study of Literature," *Social Sciences* (*USSR Academy of Sciences*), No. 4 (10), 1972, p. 116.

82. Jonathan Culler, *Structuralist Poetics* (London: Routledge and Kegan Paul, 1975), p. 136.

83. Tzvetan Todorov, *The Fantastic,* trans. Richard Howard (Ithaca, N.Y.: Cornell University Press, 1975), pp. 6–7. See also Alastair Fowler, "The Life and Death of Literary Forms," *New Literary History,* 2 (1971), 199–216; Robert Scholes, "Towards a Poetics of Fiction: (4) An Approach through Genre," *Novel,* 2 (1969), 101–11, and Thomas G. Pavel, "Some Remarks on Narrative Grammars," *Poetics,* 8 (1973), 5–30.

features of a narrative and its universal generic order, which is an integral part of its mode of being, is grasped. In the study of the nonfiction novel, such an investigation is all the more necessary, because the newness of the genre has caused many generic misreadings of nonfiction novels in terms of established kinds of prose narrative.

two
A Typology
of Prose Narrative

The current theories of prose narrative suffer from a restrictive taxonomy which distributes works of narrative into "fictional" and "factual" categories according to the type of reality they contain. If the content of the narrative directly corresponds to the empirical realities of the world outside, then the book is considered to be "factual"; otherwise, it is labeled "fictional." Within the context of such an approach, the "nature of literature," as René Wellek states,

> emerges most clearly under the referential aspects. The center of literary art is obviously to be found in the traditional genres of the lyric, the epic, the drama. In all of them, the reference is to a world of fiction, of imagination. The statements in a novel, in a poem, or in a drama are not literally true; they are not logical propositions. There is a central and important difference between a statement, even in a historical novel or a novel by Balzac which seems to convey "information" about actual happenings, and the same information appearing in a book of history or sociology.[1]

Similarly, Northrop Frye, whose critical perspective is very different from the formalism of Wellek, suggests that "verbal structures may be classified according to whether the *final* direction of meaning is outward or inward." In "descriptive and assertive" writing, Frye considers the final direction of meaning to be outward, while "in all literary verbal structures the final direction of meaning is inward."[2] According to these theories, the inward-directed meaning which is found in fiction focuses on the coherence of the

1. René Wellek and Austin Warren, *Theory of Literature*, 3d ed. (New York: Harcourt, Brace and World, 1962), p. 25.
2. Northrop Frye, *Anatomy of Criticism* (Princeton: Princeton University Press, 1957), p. 74.

discourse, but the function of the outward-directed meaning of nonfictive discourse is to establish a correspondence
between the external phenomenon and the internal verbal
sign with such a high degree of accuracy that "truth" is
captured.

Critics by and large have squeezed all prose narratives
into these categories, which are hardly any more sophisticated than the librarian's pathetically naïve fiction and
nonfiction pigeonholes into which the entire output of the
human imagination is divided. Narratives not snugly suited
to either category have, as a result, been misread or completely ignored. Some critics are still puzzled by Defoe's *A
Journal of the Plague Year,* unable to decide whether it fits in
the "fictional" or "factual" slot. Clemens's generically ambiguous *Life on the Mississippi* still awaits the critic who can provide appropriate terms for its reading as an achieved work
of the imagination. The problems created by the haphazard
pigeonholing of narratives are more complex than these
examples suggest. The encyclopedic whaling sections of
Moby-Dick have puzzled critics who insist on approaching literary realities within the confines of the conventional fictional-factual framework. Reporting that in his college library Agee's *Let Us Now Praise Famous Men* was shelved with
the books on Alabama history, Samuel Hynes agrees this is
like classifying *Moby-Dick* as a book about whales, but sym-
pathizes with the librarian and declares Agee's book "fundamentally unclassifiable." [3]

The tension between the fictive and the real, which I
believe to be the central issue here, has never been investigated in a systematic manner. Even critics who show a
special interest in a poetics of narrative are trapped in the
bipolar, factual-fictional framework. Frye, for example,
equates fictional with creative, and then, instead of mapping
the "vague limbo of books which are not quite literature
because they are 'thought,' and not quite religion or philosophy because they are Examples of Prose Style," he rede-
fines the concept of fiction so it can absorb the generically

3. Samuel Hynes, "James Agee: Let Us Now Praise Famous Men," in *Landmarks
of American Writing,* ed. Hennig Cohen (New York: Basic Books, 1969), p. 328.

ambiguous works and give "several of our best prose works a definable place in fiction." He dethrones the "novel-centered view of prose fiction" only to substitute a fiction-centered view of prose narrative, the result of his working with a bipolar theory.[4] Given the limitations of bipolar approaches to the study of narrative, it is necessary that critics begin addressing themselves to the shared problems of all forms of narrative. They must work with a more general concept such as "prose narrative," rather than "prose fiction," or they will fail to deal with the narrative universals—those narrational features or properties of the deep structure of all modes of narrative and thus common to all narrative forms. Without an adequate study of these universals, no comprehensive theory of fiction or any other kind of narration can be formulated.

Robert Scholes and Robert Kellogg in *The Nature of Narrative* also suggest a scheme that is not novel-centered, and, as their title shows, they even replace the concept of "fiction" with that of "narrative." But they still operate with a two-term epistemological set which divides the conception of reality and its stylization in narrative works into the factual and the fictional. "The two antithetical types of narrative" which they believe emerge from the disintegration of epic are labeled "empirical" and "fictional." The allegiance of empirical narrative, with its two main components, the *historical* and the *mimetic,* is to reality while the allegiance of fictional narrative, with its two main components, the *romantic* and the *didactic,* is to the ideal.[5] For all the differences in terminology, Scholes's and Kellogg's *empirical* and *fictional* categories correspond very closely to the fictional-factual classes. Indeed, they maintain that "the distinction between fact and fiction, once it is clearly established, forces storytelling to choose the rubric under which it will function: truth or beauty. The result is a separation of narrative streams into the factual and the fictional, producing forms we have learned to call history and romance." [6] This polar-

4. Frye, *Anatomy of Criticism,* pp. 307, 304.
5. Robert Scholes and Robert Kellogg, *The Nature of Narrative* (New York: Oxford University Press, 1966), pp. 13–14.
6. Ibid., p. 58.

ity is further reflected in their analysis of meaning in narrative. The semantic identity of prose narrative, according to their theory, is understandable in terms of two basic aims: representation of the factuality of the outside world or illustration of essences and concepts.[7]

A similar critical dualism lies behind the five papers so far published in the journal *Novel* under the general series title "Towards a Poetics of Fiction." [8] The critical views of all participants in the two symposia arranged by the journal to deal with "Realism, Reality and the Novel" [9] and "Wrestling (American Style) with Proteus" [10] are shaped by factual-fictional contraries. I do not intend to review the entire spectrum of recent criticism, though I must note that narrative theories based on fictional-factual oppositions constitute only one aspect of the Modernist aesthetics which approaches (verbal) arts in terms of "artscript" and "craftscript"—a dichotomy rooted in the life-art contraries in the Modernist critical orthodoxy.[11]

Such critical approaches have led to inadequate readings of narrative works which do not lend themselves to a bipolar typology. These works have been generally regarded as some kind of aesthetic deviation from the norm and thus have been misread. Most of the critical debate about Mailer's *The Armies of the Night* or Capote's *In Cold Blood* centers on whether these books are novels (fictional) or reportage (factual), while the possibility that they may be neither has evidently not occurred to the critics or, at least, has not been articulated in any systematic way.

Changes in contemporary life have created new literary realities which cannot be dealt with in terms of orthodox Modernist aesthetics. The current typology of prose narra-

7. Ibid., pp. 82–105.

8. The contributors to the series "Towards a Poetics of Fiction" in *Novel* were: Malcolm Bradbury, "Structure," 1 (1967), 45–52; David Lodge, "Language," 1 (1968), 158–69; Barbara Hardy, "Narrative," 2 (1968), 5–14; Robert Scholes, "Genre," 2 (1969), 101–11; and E. N. Hutchens, "The Novel as Chronomorph," 5 (1972), 215–24.

9. Transcription edited by Park Honan, *Novel,* 2 (1969), 197–211.

10. Report by Roger Henkle, *Novel,* 3 (1970), 197–207.

11. Allan Rodway and Brian Lee, "Coming to Terms," *Essays in Criticism,* 14 (1964), 109–25. The works of such Modernist critics as I. A. Richards, William Empson, Cleanth Brooks, and John Crowe Ransom contain similar dichotomies.

tive is incapable of dealing with some of the most important narratives written since the war under the pressure of these new realities. To read *La Vida* as a fictive novel or as a piece of reportage is to distort the narrative and to violate its generic singularity in order to place it within the established categories. A more flexible typology of prose narrative is required to overcome the problems created by the transformation of literary genres and to provide a fresh view of past narrative works damaged by previous misreadings.

Polaristic theories are based on the assumption that all forms of prose narrative can be reduced to two essentially different modes of narration: the fictional and the factual. If the work generates its own unique "truth" and enjoys total internal believability by being self-referent and self-contained, it is fictional. On the other hand, if the "truth" embodied in the narrative has to be supported by the external evidence—documents of happened events—the mode is factual.

The most commonly known form of the fictional mode is, of course, the fictive novel. Novels may or may not draw their subject matter from the events of the author's real life or the actual, historical lives of other people. The novelist, however, according to the conventional aesthetics of fiction, should transform, with the power of his or her inventive imagination, the raw material of life into the finished product of art, and thus imbue the completed work, regardless of its sources, with an internal consistency and a credible world of its own. The truth formulated by the invented discourse, it is argued, exists within the fictional field established by the verbal construct and therefore is self-referential. This essentially religious and magical view of Modernist aesthetics is best phrased by Joyce in *A Portrait of the Artist*, notwithstanding the ambiguity of the narrative voice. The artist becomes a cleric, for Stephen Dedalus is a "priest of eternal imagination, transmuting the daily bread of experience into the radiant body of everliving life."

Biography and history, in contrast to the fictive novel, are considered specimens of the factual mode of narration in which the events (and therefore the people and things re-

lated to them) described in the discourse are true to the extent that they correspond with their originals. The truth in
a biography or history not only is generated by the discourse itself but also depends on the verifiable world outside the discourse. It is, of course, clear that the limitations
of the verbal medium, which require the biographer or the
historian to select details rather than transcribe everything
which occurred in the past, force him to adopt a viewpoint.
But behind all biographies, such as, for example, those on
D. H. Lawrence, stands the subject of the biographies—in
this case, David Herbert Lawrence (1885–1930)—to whom
the biographies owe their existence and by reference to
whose life their "truth" is tested. Lawrence's own novels,
however, according to the Modernist poetics, although very
much influenced by this life, and in many instances almost a
partial transcription of it, exist by virtue of the unified field
of fiction created from his life by the transmuting power of
his imagination. The factual mode, then, unlike its antitype,
refers not to itself but to the external world, populated not
by imaginary characters but by real people, all of whom
exist independently of the verbal construct. The points of
departure and the destination of the factual narrative lie
outside the two covers of the book—they lie in the world
comprehensible via the sensory organs.

The factual and fictional modes, considered to be diametrically different and regarded as either the generator or the
reflector of truth, have more in common than the polarist
theories of narrative would lead us to believe. The two
modes differ according to the criterion of experiential veri-
fiability, but they are quite similar from the more literary
perspective of the scope of the narrative field of reference:
both the fictional and the factual modes have only a single
field of reference. Their referents, of course, differ, but ultimately each has as its referent either an internal unified
field of fiction mapped out within the book (in-referential)
or an external configuration of facts verifiable outside the
book (out-referential). Both of these narrative modes, regardless of the nature of their field of reference, are mono-
referential.

Fictional and factual narratives as examples of the mono-referential mode are thus each static narrational systems; once the field of reference is established, the writer sticks within the set modal norm largely because the Modernist poetics of fiction does not favor oscillation between life and art, the fictional and the factual, within the same work. Such shifts in the field of reference are usually regarded as signs of a lack of artistic control, and of an inability to transform life completely into a work of art.

Not all works of narrative, however, are mono-referential. Another mode of narration, responding to a more complex reality, explores more than a single circle of reference and orchestrates, in its movement between the allegedly antithetical poles of art and life, the aesthetically justified truth of the fictional and the experientially valid truth of the factual. This manifold narrative mode exercises both the aesthetic control associated with the fictional mode and the analytical approach characteristic of the factual mode. It is, in other words, simultaneously self-referential and out-referential and is modally more complex and sophisticated than either form of the mono-referential narratives. In contrast to the mono-referential mode, this mode of narration is *bi-referential.*

The bi-referential mode is the narrative form through which the consciousness, engulfed in fabulous reality and overwhelmed by the naked actuality, articulates its experience of an extreme situation. This area of reality, however, where the factual and the fictional converge in a state of unresolved tension, needs a special term of identification. I shall call this puzzling merging of the fictional and the factual the *fictual:* a zone of experience where the factual is not secure or unequivocal but seems preternaturally strange and eerie, and where the fictional seems not all that fictitious, remote and alien, but bears an uncanny resemblance to daily experience.

This "fictuality" of current experience escapes the mono-referential narratives which require an unequivocal pledge to fact or fiction. The nonfiction novel, in contrast to these modes of narrative, is a bi-referential work which refuses an either/or approach to experiential situations and establishes, through its dual fields of reference, a double perspective on contemporary fictuality. It is a narrative which is simultaneously self-referential and out-referential, factual and fictional, and thus well equipped to deal with the elusive fusion of fact and fiction which has become the matrix of today's experience. The nonfiction novel has the shapeliness of fiction and the authority of reality usually reserved for factual narrative but transcends both, becoming the concrete narrative correlative for the fictuality of the present times. Norman Mailer's *The Armies of the Night* and Tom Wolfe's *The Electric Kool-Aid Acid Test,* for example, are self-referential narratives which have the aesthetic control associated with works of art, but at the same time remain out-referential; they are externally verifiable. The ultimate meaning of these books, however, lies neither in their internal aesthetic shape nor in their correspondence to the actualities of the empirical world, but in the fictuality which emerges out of the counterpointing of fact and fiction through their bi-referential mode: an acting out of the contemporary experience which defies being labeled as fact or fiction and interpreted in terms of any single metaphysical framework.

The nonfiction novel is a distinct genre, a unique mode of apprehending and transcribing reality, requiring its own particular set of critical assumptions which can deal with such central problems in the phenomenology of reading it as the tension created by the centrifugal energy of the external reality and the centripetal force of the internal shape of the narrative. For without this tension, the fictuality of the narrative is reduced to the factuality of a document (*The Armies of the Night* becomes history) or the fictionality of a novel (*In Cold Blood* becomes a crime story).

Not all works of narrative are written entirely in either a mono-referential or a bi-referential mode. Some books have employed more than a single mode of narration and thus are not *unimodal. Moby-Dick,* for example, uses more than one mode of narration to satisfy the demands of the total narrational situation. It opens with a mono-referential mode (fictional section), changes to a bi-referential mode (sections dealing with the facts of the whaling industry), then reverts to a mono-referential mode (fiction). *Moby-Dick* thus represents a *multimodal* narrative.

Unlike the fictive narratives which operate as closed static sets, the bi-referential narratives form open dynamic systems in active tension with the experiential world outside the book. The dialectical quality of these systems is partly derived from their attitude toward facts. Reading the non-fiction novel in its full bi-referential complexity requires a reexamination of the question of the function of fact in fiction.

In a prose narrative, facts are used as either elements of composition or objects of comprehension. The ultimate meaning of experience in the fictive novel is ultra-factual; facts are employed by the novelist essentially to give veracity and density to his imaginary world in order to convey his personal vision of life and point out the significant pattern of meaning behind the chaotic sensory impressions. The totalizing novel resembles an extended epiphany objectified in terms of concrete recognizable daily facts and events. The novel, in other words, is the narrative correlative of the writer's metaphysics—his private reading of reality—and facts are a *means* for communicating this interpretation. To the fictive novel, facts give circumstantiality, internal believability, and specificity, all of which make the imaginary world of the writer lifelike. A letter of Joyce's to his aunt while he was composing *Ulysses* manifests the nature of the novelist's interest in facts: "Is it possible for an ordinary person to climb over the area railings of no. 7 Eccles street, either from the path or the steps, lower himself from the lowest part of the railings till his feet are within 2 feet or 3 of the ground and drop unhurt[?] I saw it done myself but by a man of rather athletic build. I require this information in detail in order to determine the wording of a paragraph." [12] In Mary McCarthy's words, "The presence of fact in fiction, of dates and times and distances, is a kind of reas-

---

12. *Letters of James Joyce*, ed. Stuart Gilbert (New York: Viking Press, 1957, 1966), I, 175.

surance—a guarantee of credibility." [13] Not only the fictive novelist but also other writers, such as the transfictionist, the detective novelist, and the fantasist, use facts in this manner. Their main purpose is to flesh out the shadowy world of their imagination, to endow it with dimension, and make it seem continuous with life.

The traditional critical approach to the question of the use of fact in fiction is essentially an assessment of the success of the novelist in creating, by means of factual details, "an air of reality" which James thought was the "supreme virtue of a novel." [14] The "air of reality" is, of course, not an end in itself but a necessary rhetorical environment within which the novelist is capable of patterning his interpretation of life in a believable manner. Too much attachment to facts, however, is as undesirable for the Modernist critic as too little: a mimetic balance must exist in the novel between the factuality of the events and people, and the transcendental vision of the artist. Robert E. Kuehn's comments on *In Cold Blood* are typical of this attitude. Complaining that Capote's book "remains stuck in the mire of factuality," he urges writers to use facts to support their vision of life. "The older novelists—Fielding, Dickens, Joyce, Faulkner—" Kuehn maintains, "used facts to create a new order of reality; they forced history to yield poetry." [15] Confronted with fictual reality, the nonfiction novelist refuses to impose a pattern of interpretation on events or to force them to "yield poetry"—an overly simplistic assumption in view of the ambiguity of current reality. The nonfiction novel rejects the verisimilar use of facts in favor of a neutral transcription and registration. Thus, in order to arrive at a comprehensive analysis of the diametrically different function of facts in bi-referential as opposed to mono-referential narratives, a closer examination of the various levels of facts in fictive and nonfiction narratives is needed.

13. Mary McCarthy, *On the Contrary* (New York: Farrar, Straus and Cudahy, 1961), p. 263.
14. "The Art of Fiction," in *Theory of Fiction: Henry James,* ed. James E. Miller (Lincoln: University of Nebraska Press, 1972), p. 35.
15. Robert E. Kuehn, "The Novel Now: Some Anxieties and Prescriptions," *Wisconsin Studies in Contemporary Literature,* 7 (1966), 127.

Compositionally, facts are used in fictive narratives on two distinct but closely related levels, the "figurational" and the "elemental," both of which have the ultimate rhetorical purpose of providing truthfulness to the imagined world of the narrative. The figurational use of facts is essential to all fictional constructs while the elemental use of facts, on the other hand, is optional and more common in the "realistic" and "naturalistic" narratives. It is the figurational employment of facts that shapes the totalizing vision of the novelist and gives it the tone, the texture, and the substance of felt experience. Examples of the figurational use of facts in fiction include the use of representational settings, patterns of speech, and references to actual people and places, which all help to bring the sights and sounds of the bustling world of everyday life into the fictional milieu. The word "fact," however, is not quite correct when used to describe such experiential details which endow the narrative with the "air of reality." "Facts" used figurationally are not verifiable and more often than not are patently made-up and invented. Even when such "facts" are verifiable, they are refracted as they pass through the patterning imagination of the writer in order to fit his projected view of life: the details, for example, in Conrad's *Heart of Darkness* are based on an actual physical journey which symbolizes an internal psychic journey. Facts on this level of usage should, more appropriately, be called "factoids"—factlike details of empirical reality which help to create a fictional likeness of the real world. A typical example of such use of factoids is Kafka's *The Metamorphosis*. Whether Gregor Samsa actually is transformed into a "gigantic insect" or not, the story itself, in terms of its internal rhetoric, achieves believability through Kafka's consistent use of quotidian details. Although the writers of all narrative fictions make use of facts figurationally, the writers of nonrealistic fictions such as metafiction, surfiction, and science fiction as well as such popular forms of narrative as gothic romances especially depend on factoids for developing their fictional universe.

In realistic and naturalistic narratives, facts are more commonly used as the elements of the composition. Dreiser's *An American Tragedy* is one of the many novels in which facts are used as the basic elements and substance of the narrative. Although from the Modernist point of view factual accuracy is ultimately not directly relevant to the criticism of fiction since, as W. K. Wimsatt states, "poetry [imaginative literature] is truth of 'coherence,' rather than truth of 'correspondence,' "[16] when facts are used elementally in a narrative a new dimension is added to the narrative ontology. The aesthetic purity of the narrative is reduced and its mode of being depends on the extraliterary circumstances under which the fiction was written. This may explain why naturalistic and realistic novels as well as such sub-genres as satire and the historical novel—which are all rooted in the ethos, mores, and manners of particular communities—are held in relatively low aesthetic esteem. In most of these narratives, the "truth of coherence" is at least partially eclipsed by the "truth of correspondence," and a knowledge of the facts used in the narrative and the areas of human experience to which they refer becomes necessary for a total reading of the narrative.

Narratives which employ facts elementally, and thus assume a quasi referentiality, superficially resemble the factual narrative and the nonfiction novel. In both Zola's *Nana* and Agee's *Let Us Now Praise Famous Men*, the observed facts of life are the elements of the narratives, but the two works are quite different. The former is a naturalistic fictive novel interpreting the demimonde society from a particular viewpoint, and the latter is a noninterpretive narrative registering life without imposing an ordering design on its inherent chaos. Facts and factoids in all fictive narratives are distributed in a pattern that is shaped by the lines of force created by the magnetic field of the narratist's totalizing vision of life. In Zola's book facts are used as building blocks of composition while in Agee's book they are used comprehensionally. Various types of realistic novels, or such sub-genres of fictive novels as the muckraking novel (Upton Sinclair's *The Jungle*), the fact novel (Dan Wakefield's *Island in the City:*

16. William K. Wimsatt, Jr., and Cleanth Brooks, *Literary Criticism: A Short History* (New York: Knopf, 1957), p. 748.

The World of Spanish Harlem), and the *roman à clef* (Hemingway's *The Sun Also Rises*), are all instances of the elemental use of facts in a compositional manner. The *roman à clef*, in its close adherence to the facts of experienced life, most nearly resembles factual narratives.

In the *roman à clef*, as in other forms of the fictive novel, the facts are manipulated for their rhetorical effects; the characters and events, although real and verifiable, are woven into a fictional pattern which eventually represents the vision of the writer. The characters and events of *The Sun Also Rises*, though taken from real life, are incorporated into Hemingway's interpretive fictional pattern. Philip Young comments that "Various personages known to Paris of the twenties have thought they recognized without difficulty the originals—Donald Ogden Stewart, Harold Stearns, Harold Loeb, Lady Duff-Twysden, Ford Madox Ford, and Pat Guthrie—and even Jake had his counterpart in actuality," but he adds " . . . Hemingway has changed the characters to suit his purposes, and it is clear that whatever his origins, Jake, for instance, owes most to the man who created him." [17] In other words, Hemingway has altered them to fit his metaphysics, his interpretation of reality. Thus, the distinguishing feature of all compositional uses of facts in fiction is their function of authenticating the artist's metaphysics, whether moral, political, or theological.

The difference between the fictive novelist who uses facts compositionally to give veracity to the narrative and the narratist who approaches facts comprehensionally is one of vision versus probing. The former has a vision of life (a view of mankind in relation to a larger order) which he wants to substantiate and communicate through facts. He thus subsumes the elemental to the figurational use of facts in order to establish a unified field of fiction. The narratist who approaches facts comprehensionally, however, wants to record events in order to comprehend them. Of course not all narratists who approach facts comprehensionally do so

17. Philip Young, *Ernest Hemingway: A Reconsideration* (University Park: Pennsylvania State University Press, 1966), p. 85.

with the same intention. The biographer and the historian, for example, use facts in their narratives comprehensionally, but their ultimate goal is to discover the significance behind the random facts. They want to find out about the "real" man behind the facts or the "real" social and cultural conditions of a particular period in history. In their effort to discover the "truth" behind the isolated facts, the biographer and the historian are very much like the fictive novelist. The fictive novelist starts with an interpretation of experience and then supports and communicates that interpretation by employing facts as units of composition in his book; the biographer or the historian, on the other hand, starts with little preexisting interpretation and instead probes facts in the hope of revealing their ultimate meaning. In other words, the fictive novelist starts with a vision and uses facts to support that vision; the biographer or the historian starts with facts and ends with vision. The approach of such factual narratists as the biographer, the historian, the fact novelist, and the New Journalist [18] is essentially *noumenalistic.*

The New Journalist's final commitment, like that of all reporters, is to the "truth" behind the facts. He seeks, according to Gay Talese, "a larger truth than is possible through the mere compilation of verifiable facts." [19] However, in order to penetrate the facade of the announced reality and provide an experiential context for that hidden "truth," he makes use of such narrative techniques as "scene," "point of view" and "flashback" as a means of capturing the gesture, the facial expressions, and the texture of dialogues. Through these devices, he assures the reader that he has been there, that he has tested the reality he is reporting. But, as Tom Wolfe is quick to point out, a New Journalistic

18. "New Journalist" is a term believed to have been coined in the mid-sixties by Pete Hamill to identify new trends in journalism under the pressure of new realities in that decade. (See Seymour Krim's letter to the editors of the *Village Voice,* May 25, 1972, p. 4.) Krim himself uses the term, "Journalit." See "The Writer's Situation, II," *New American Review,* No. 10 (1970), p. 232, and also *Iowa Review* 3 (1972), 59–62.

19. Gay Talese, *Fame and Obscurity* (New York: World, 1970), p. vii.

piece stands or falls on its depth of information and the veracity of the content of its report.[20] The difference between the conventional journalism and the New Journalism is less epistemological than is commonly thought. The employment of narrative techniques gives New Journalistic copy a fictional texture rather than a fictual tension. Like history, biography, or the fact novel, the piece is a mono-referential narrative and thus is diametrically different from the nonfiction novel.

The fact novel is another kind of mono-referential factual narrative which aims at a presentation of the reality behind appearances. It is novelized sociology, psychiatric case history, and anthropology. Unlike the monograph of the specialist, the fact novel is organized according to a narrative logic rather than a conceptual model. The narrative framework and devices are used to assimilate the data into a full-length narrative which is addressed to the general reader. Irving Stone's *The Passions of the Mind,* for instance, presents the ideas and life of Sigmund Freud and attempts to discover the "real man" behind the legend. Elenore Smith Bowen's *Return to Laughter* is an anthropological novel which, according to a reviewer, "provides deep insight into the indigenous culture of West Africa, the subtle web of tribal life, the power of the institution of witchcraft." Cornelius Ryan's *The Longest Day* is devoted to unveiling the "truth" of the D-Day invasion of June 6, 1944, and Theodore White's *The Making of the President* series, Gay Talese's *The Kingdom and the Power,* and William Manchester's *The Death of a President* also fall into this category. The fact novel is a mono-referential narrative which is more concerned with truth, information, and smooth, pleasurable presentation than with the inherent fictual ambiguity of extreme situations. The noumenalist approaches facts for their inner truth value, which he believes he can discover after proper investigation; the internal shape of the narrative eventually containing these facts as cognitive units is of secondary importance.

20. Tom Wolfe and E. W. Johnson, eds., *The New Journalism* (New York: Harper and Row, 1973), p. 21.

The nonfiction novelist, like most factual narratists, approaches facts comprehensionally (not merely for building up a plausible verisimilar world but in order that he may understand them). However, unlike the biographer, the historian, the fact novelist, or the New Journalist, he does not believe in the informing truth behind the facts (noumenon) which, in a sense, is a remnant of the order-oriented-universe view. The non-totalizing approach of the nonfiction novelist to the actualities of the outside world and life experiences makes his narrative radically different from those of the fictive and factual narratists. He does not totalize the chain of events and experiences (facts) in terms of either a pre-existing (*a priori*) interpretation of life, like the fictive novelist, or an emerging (*a posteriori*) "truth," similar to the factual narratist. His use of facts is post-mimetic and *phenomenalistic.*

The functions of fact in prose narrative may be formulated in rules shown below.

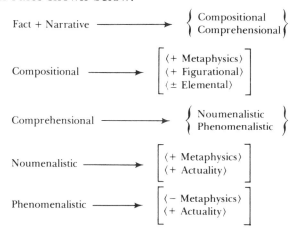

The nonfiction novelist uses facts phenomenalistically to capture the dimensions of facts as facts; for him facts become not a means but an end. The phenomenalistic use of fact in narrative is post-mimetic, non-verisimilar (the narrative is an open system), transcriptive, anti-symbolic, and purely literal. It is a mode of dealing with appearances as knowable by the senses. By using facts phenomenalistically, the nonfiction novelist merely registers facts without the accompaniment of an interpretive pattern, which makes an observed fact part of an imposed metaphysical scheme. The nonfiction novelist's arrangement of facts is not endorsive (authenticating) but mythopoeic: it reveals the disorienting fictiveness inherent in the facts. In other words, facts are not used to establish or unveil an order but are allowed to enact, in their totality and entirety, the ambiguity, unpredictability, and disorder—in short, the entropy—of the actual. The nonfiction novel is a narrative of observation which opposes the illusionistic Jamesian aesthetics. The counterpointing of an external factuality with the internal fictiveness of the facts operates in the nonfiction novel as a kind of Brechtian alienation effect which distances the reader, prevents an easy emotional identification with the characters and situations, and forces the reader to confront the charged actuality. This non-illusionistic approach to the presentation of experience agitates, revolutionizes, and liberates the consciousness of the reader from order-hunting.

To understand fully the phenomenalistic approach of the nonfiction novelist to facts in the narrative, one must surrender the notion that a fact is necessarily an embodiment of order, predictability, and what used to be known as commonsensical reality. When Mary McCarthy, in her essay "The Fact in Fiction," regards the absence of the "supernatural" as the sole criterion for distinguishing the novel from other forms of narrative, she exhibits a positivistic attitude toward the fact as a solid, identifiable unit of reality, almost an antidote for fantasy.[21] In so doing, she is only reiterating a kind of nineteenth-century Gradgrindian view which looked at facts as a category of supposedly objective reality. But what could be more fantastic than the events recorded by a tape recorder in Andy Warhol's *a,* or the incidents withnessed by Norman Mailer in *The Armies of the Night,* or the happenings reported in *The Pentagon Papers* and *The White House Transcripts?* The dark, mythical, and fabulous aspects of facts, however, are not just the discovery of our own day, as is clear from Defoe's *A Journal of the Plague Year*

21. McCarthy, *On The Contrary,* p. 251.

(1722). Nevertheless, the epistemological crisis of the twentieth century, especially the paroxysms of the last two decades, have exposed these facets of facts with more dramatic and terrifying intensity.

The nonfiction novel is the genre created by our times of continual crisis and value disorder, for through its modal duality it offers a double vision of the bizarre fictuality of contemporary reality, a vision not unlike the schizophrenic view of experience in our age.[22] The writer who approaches facts not to invoke their facade of reality but to enact through his registration their inner turbulence becomes the mythographer of contemporary consciousness.

22. R. D. Laing, *The Politics of Experience* (New York: Pantheon, 1967).

three
The Anatomy
of the Nonfiction Novel

The nonfiction novel is the "fiction" of the meta-physical void. In the absence of shared, preestablished norms, it maps the surrounding objectal world, without imposing a projected pattern of meaning on the neutral massiveness and amorphous identity of actual people and events. Its response to the confused and contradictory interpretations of reality, which are all the product of an Aristotelian compulsion to explain and label experience at all levels, is to return to noninterpretive, direct contact with actuality. Faced with the fictuality of contemporary experience, the nonfiction novelist doubts that there is more to the world than what can be apprehended through the senses and that an informing "truth" lies behind the ordinary world of appearances. He shares the attitude of postmodern writers such as Beckett, who, through his everlasting tautology in, for instance, *The Unnamable,* denounces the "stupid obsession with depth." Such a skeptical view is the result of the epistemological crisis of the times. The engulfed consciousness, unable to find its bearings with the help of traditional reality guideposts, chooses to circumvent the intervening imposed interpretations and to return to the elementals.

The nontotalizing narrative has the same relation to our times as poetic drama had to the Elizabethan period, discursive literature to the Augustan epoch, narrative verse to the Romantic era. Every cultural period has its own "dominant" genre which most perfectly articulates its concerns. Contemporary reality, whose special nature, in Elizabeth Hardwick's words, has made it difficult for "fiction to compete with the aesthetic satisfaction of the actual," [1] has found an

1. Elizabeth Hardwick, "Reflections on Fiction," *New York Review of Books,* Feb. 13, 1969, p. 16.

expressive narrative medium in the nonfiction novel—the narrative of extreme situations in which fact and fiction are fused and the conventional segmentations of reality are rendered invalid. Although man has been acquainted with crises, from the communal plight of antiquity to the predicament of working-class people in modern times, the nonfiction novel, as I have previously suggested, has moved to a more dominant generic position in contemporary literature, because continual upheavals and the ongoing crisis of norms have tensed the total contemporary environment into an extended extreme situation.

The prehistory of the nonfiction novel in English can be traced back to the periods of moral, cultural, or societal disruptions, which have forced the attention of writers away from the dominant genres of their times. Thomas Harman's *A Caveat for Common Cursitors* (1566), Robert Greene's *A Notable Discovery of Cozenage* (1591), and other Elizabethan writings on cony-lore as well as such works as Thomas Dekker's *The Wonderful Year* (1603) contain elements of the nonfiction novel. However, these writers, following the period's habit of thought, often affected a rhetorical style and lofty moral intention. These rhetorical and moral affectations are nonexistent in such later developments as Defoe's *Journal of the Plague Year* (1722), which for the most part enacts the fictuality of the visitation of the Great Plague (1665), although it is not, strictly speaking, a first-hand document— the plague having occurred when the writer was only five years old. Another manifestation of the prototypes of the genre, this one written under a more private impulse in the past century, is Clemens's *Life on the Mississippi*.

The increasing exposure to extremities, or what James Agee has called "the stature of a portion of unimagined existence," in the early part of the present century has helped to produce a number of books which might be described as proto-nonfiction novels. e. e. cummings's *the enormous room* records the brute facts of life in a French detention camp where, through some Kafkaesque bureaucratic error, he was kept during the Great War. Henry Miller's *Tropic of Cancer* is also written in the same vein, but it does not have the Bunyanesque, quasi-allegorical structure of *the enormous room*. Although the narrator in *Tropic of Cancer* is more an actual person than a fictional persona and is firmly rooted in actualities, the narrative is shaped novelistically in terms of the projected ephiphanic vision of the narratist; it is, like Thoreau's *Walden* (another book preoccupied with telling facts), ultimately a blueprint for how to live. However, in spite of all its "novelizing," *Tropic of Cancer* is energized by a noninterpretive force pushing the narrative toward becoming what Anaïs Nin calls a "naked book": by "stripping away the vestiture of art," it attempts to bring the "restorative value of experience" to a world "grown paralyzed with introspection." Thus, Miller's narrative refuses to indulge in creating full portraits of its "characters" similar to those found in conventional novels, because, according to Nin, "the individual today has no centrality" and not the "slightest illusion of wholeness." Faced with chaos, the individual must return to "fundamental realities" unclouded by intervening interpretations.[2]

In the course of a lengthy analysis of Henry Miller's writing, George Orwell, himself a keen observer of the fabulous realities of the times, comments on the disintegration of liberal-Christian culture and the death of order-seeking bourgeois literature and, praising Miller's receptivity and openness to experience, concludes, "The passive attitude will come back, and it will be more consciously passive than before. Progress and reaction have both turned out to be swindles. Seemingly there is nothing left but quietism— robbing reality of its terrors by simply submitting to it. Get inside the whale—or rather, admit that you are inside the whale (for you *are*, of course). Give yourself over to the world-process, stop fighting against it or pretending that you control it; simply accept it, endure it, record it."[3] Or-

2. Anaïs Nin, "Preface to *Tropic of Cancer*," in *Anaïs Nin Reader*, ed. Philip K. Jason (Chicago: Swallow Press, 1973), pp. 227–79. Miller's own comments on *Tropic of Cancer* are also of interest. "The theme of the book," he wrote to the *New Republic* (May 18, 1938), rebutting Edmund Wilson's review of the book, "is myself, and the narrator, or hero, as your critic puts it, is also myself. . . . I don't use 'heroes,' incidentally, nor do I write novels."

3. "Inside the Whale," in *The Collected Essays, Journalism and Letters of George Orwell*, I: *An Age Like This 1920–1940*, ed. Sonia Orwell and Ian Angus (New York: Harcourt, Brace and World, 1968), p. 526.

well's remarks not only are a penetrating commentary on Miller's approach to life; they also shed light on some of the intellectual and cultural conditions informing the nonfictive narrative of other writers, including Orwell's own *Homage to Catalonia* and Hemingway's *Green Hills of Africa.* As vulnerable to raw experience as Miller, Hemingway published his *Green Hills of Africa* a year after *Tropic of Cancer* and in his "Foreword" asserted his artistic premises and goals: "Unlike many novels, none of the characters or incidents in this book is imaginary. Anyone not finding sufficient love interest is at liberty, while reading it, to insert whatever love interest he or she may have at the time. The writer has attempted an absolutely true book to see whether the shape of a country and the pattern of a month's action can, if truly presented, compete with a work of the imagination." [4]

Like Hemingway's attempt to write a "true book," Agee's *Let Us Now Praise Famous Men,* one of the great nonfictive narratives, aspires, in Agee's own words, to a "non-'artistic' view" of the subject in an "effort to suspend or destroy imagination," so that without its mediation there may open "before consciousness and within it, a universe luminous, spacious, inculpably rich and wonderful in each detail." [5] Begun in the mid-1930s, Agee's book is an intimate prying "into the lives of an undefended and appallingly damaged group of human beings" [6]—a verbal record of the daily existence and environment of three poor white southern sharecropping families, whose lives Agee attempts to capture in his narrative not so much "by means of art" as through "open terms." *Let Us Now Praise Famous Men* is not so much a *book* as "an effort in human actuality." Indeed, Agee offers advice to the reader about the appropriate response to the narrative: "above all else: in God's name don't think of it as Art." [7] Regarding it as "Art" will diminish the immeasurable weight of the actual existence of its subject and thus will tame the force of reality in the narrative.

4. Ernest Hemingway, *Green Hills of Africa* (New York: Scribner's Sons, 1935), p. v.

5. James Agee, *Let Us Now Praise Famous Men* (1941; rpt. New York: Ballantine Books, 1972), p. 11.

6. Ibid., p. 7.

7. Ibid., p. x.

Agee's narrative, however, fails to establish the dialectical interaction with the actualities that he desires, mainly because his own overprotective tone and self-consciousness impose the totalizing view of a liberal-humanist on the book.

Various elements of the nonfiction novel can also be found in the works of such writers as Dos Passos and Steinbeck as well as in the writings of the muckrakers during the opening years of the century. But the total generic configuration of the nonfiction novel is fully achieved during the turbulent decades following World War 2, a period marked by radical changes in the literary and cultural climate and a distinct shift from the Modernist "preoccupation with values as the ground of experience" to a Postmodernist "preoccupation with experience as the ground of values." [8] The nonfiction novel thus becomes, in Tynyanov's term, one of the "dominant" narrative forms of the period.

The term "nonfiction novel," however, is of recent origin. It became publicly known and widely used only after the jacket of *In Cold Blood* announced that the book "represents the culmination of [Capote's] long-standing desire to make a contribution to the establishment of a serious new literary form: the Nonfiction Novel." But this was by no means the first use of the term. Capote promoted some confusion by claiming the invention of a new art form and a term for it —the nonfiction novel—in his interviews and statements soon after the publication of his book.[9] As a result of such public statements and the fanfare accompanying the publication of *In Cold Blood*, most critics seem to have accepted Capote's claims.[10] However, neither the term nor the genre

8. Theodore Solotaroff, *The Red Hot Vacuum* (New York: Atheneum, 1970), p. ix.

9. See the interviews with Capote in *Life*, Jan. 7, 1966, and *Playboy*, March 1968.

10. See, among others, Melvin J. Friedman, "*The Confessions of Nat Turner:* The Convergence of 'Nonfiction Novel' and 'Meditation on History,'" *Journal of Popular Culture*, 1 (1967), 168; David Lodge, "Novelist at the Crossroad," *Critical Quarterly*, 11 (1969), 110 (reprinted in his book of the same title); Louis D. Rubin, Jr., *The Curious Death of the Novel* (Baton Rouge: Louisiana State University Press, 1967), p. 15; and Robert Langbaum, "Capote's Nonfiction Novel," *American Scholar*, 35 (1966), 570. The term "nonfiction novel" is so closely associated with Capote's work in the minds of book reviewers and critics that they feel obliged to refer to *In Cold Blood* or its author after every use of the term. See, for example,

was invented by Capote, although he must be given credit for making both part of the active vocabulary of the criticism of narrative.

In the 1950s and 1960s the term was used, almost always with a disapproving tone, by such critics and commentators as Jacques Barzun, Geoffrey Wagner, and Brock Brower. In a review article published in *The Griffith,* Barzun laments what might be called the "failure of imagination" of contemporary novelists and adds:

> The novelist needs no virtues, but powers. We see this very clearly today when we follow the productions of some of our non-fiction novelists such as Mr. C. P. Snow and Mr. Arthur Koestler. Their works are "interesting," full of observation and talent and even wisdom, but as far as fictional faith goes we are left to make the effort by ourselves. On the witness stand, after reading one of their highly-charged essays on the contemporary scene, one would have to hold up one's right hand and say "I don't believe a word of it." [11]

He then concludes that, in contrast to these "non-fiction novelists," Proust is a "born fictionist." Barzun's "fictional faith" is very much an integral part of the conventional Modernist aesthetics which, operating on the basis of the dichotomy between life and art, critical and creative, rejects the concept of the work of art as an open system. For Barzun, the "non-fiction novel" is the result of the failure of the imagination of the literary artist to transubstantiate the "raw materials" of life into the finished work of art.

Some of the tonal implications of Barzun's use of the term become clearer in his essay on Stendhal: "When idea overcomes feeling and technical appreciation shackles freedom, every impulse emerges as either 'cagey' or 'corny' and is chosen accordingly. By degrees the storyteller turns into our familiar figure, the non-fiction novelist: he is full of intelligence, 'insight,' and talent but his every story is mere ex-

Alan Trachtenberg's "Mailer on the Steps of the Pentagon," *The Nation,* May 27, 1968, p. 701; Michael R. French, "The American Novel in the Sixties," *Midwest Quarterly,* 9 (1968), 366; and William Nance, *The Worlds of Truman Capote* (New York: Stein and Day, 1970), p. 176.
    11. Jacques Barzun, "Proust's Way," *The Griffin,* 5 (1956), 6.

position, a still-born child." [12] Barzun uses the term again, with the same Modernist bias, in his "Suspense Suspended," and *Science, the Glorious Entertainment*. [13] Geoffrey Wagner, in his essay "Sociology and Fiction," echoes Barzun in the disparaging use of the term: "the non-fiction novel is a further attempt to reduce art, oddly paralleled with movements of extreme abstraction in modern painting, and to reduce art—if we regard ourselves seriously at all—is simply to reduce man." [14] In an article published a year before *The New Yorker*'s serialization of *In Cold Blood*, Brock Brower used the term "nonfiction novel," with more neutral aesthetic overtones than either Barzun or Wagner, in reference to the contemporary interest in factual literature.[15] What these critics share with others who have employed the term in the framework of Modernist aesthetics is a belief that the obsession with fact in contemporary literature is a sign of the inability of the writer to control his materials and deal with them imaginatively.[16] The term "imaginative," as I mentioned in my discussion of Northrop Frye's views, stands for "fictional," and such an approach, in the last analysis, is based on the opposition of the fictional and factual, an opposition which simply does not apply to supramodernist literature including the nonfiction novel.[17]

I have used the term "nonfiction novel" as a descriptive, not a normative, concept for a genre of prose narrative whose works are characterized as bi-referential in their narrative mode and phenomenalistic in their approach to facts.

12. Jacques Barzun, "Stendhal on Love," in *The Energies of Art* (New York: Harper and Brothers, 1956), p. 125.

13. Jacques Barzun: "Suspense Suspended," *American Scholar*, 27 (1958), 500, and *Science, the Glorious Entertainment* (New York: Harper and Row, 1964), p. 242.

14. Geoffrey Wagner, "Sociology and Fiction," *Twentieth Century*, 167 (1960), 114.

15. Brock Brower, "Of Nothing but Facts," *American Scholar*, 33 (1964), 614.

16. See, for instance, Dwight Macdonald, "The Triumph of the Fact," *Against the American Grain* (New York: Random House, 1962), pp. 393–427.

17. Dietmar Haack refers to Capote's *In Cold Blood*, Mailer's *The Armies of the Night*, and Hersey's *Algiers Motel Incident* as "faction." See his "Faction: Tendenzen zu einer Kritischen Faktographie in den USA," in *Amerikanische Literatur im 20. Jahrhundert*, ed. Alfred Weber and Dietmar Haack (Göttingen: Vandenhoeck and Ruprecht, 1971), pp. 127–46.

In order to move from this rather abstract, highly technical definition of the nonfiction novel and examine the specifics of its generic identity, it is necessary to first discuss its particular formal properties and narrational constituents.

Critics are not usually hesitant to employ such concepts as "character," "setting," and "plot" in discussing nonfiction novels;[18] even the writers of the nonfiction novels themselves often discuss their books in the conventional terms originally developed for the criticism of the fictive novel.[19] Such readings of nonfiction novels can be misleading by suggesting that the nonfiction novel picks up the narrative tools of the fictive novel and applies them to "real" situations which have narrative potentiality.[20] This is the approach of such New Journalistic pieces as Terry Southern's *Red Dirt Marijuana and Other Tastes* or fact novels like those in White's *The Making of the President* series in which facts are made more palpable by the use of fictional techniques. In such fact-novels, fictional techniques are used decoratively rather than functionally; they have, in other words, only a fictional texture and not a fictual tension. For the criticism of the nonfiction novel, which has completely different epistemological premises than the fictive novel and other forms of prose narrative, we must develop a new set of critical concepts and appropriate terms. How can a critic, for example, talk about the "probability" of "plot" in a nonfiction novel where all the events narrated are "true"? Or how can one discuss the role of "suspense" in such a narrative work when all the incidents and the resolution of the themes are known beforehand? How useful is it to talk about the "characters" of a nonfiction novel in terms of their "roundness" and "flatness" while all the people whose lives are registered in the book are living, complex human beings? Other common critical terms, such as "theme" and

18. See, for example, Nancy Sullivan's review of *La Vida* in *Novel*, 1 (1967), 92–93.

19. See Truman Capote's interviews in *Playboy*, March 1969, pp. 51–62, 160–70 and in the *New York Times Book Review*, Jan. 16, 1966, pp. 2–3, 38–43. See also interview with Norman Mailer in *Playboy*, Jan. 1968, pp. 69–84.

20. See, for example, the description of the nonfiction novel in the *Micropaedia*, Vol. 7 (*Encyclopaedia Britannica*, 15th ed.).

"narrative voice," or such concepts as the "reliability of the narrator" and "implied author," add very little to the understanding of a genre of narrative which does not organize the fictional techniques developed over the last two centuries to convince the reader, through the internal rhetoric of the book, of the metaphysics of the author. Until a relevant and appropriate critical terminology is developed, any formal analysis of the genre remains partial and limited. James Agee articulates the essential problems in his introductory remarks to *Let Us Now Praise Famous Men:* "actually, the effort is to recognize the stature of a portion of unimagined existence, and to contrive techniques proper to its recording, communication, analysis." [21]

The main narrational nodes of the nonfiction novel can be shown by a binary branching of its upper-level constituents in the form of a tree diagram designating a set of phrase-structure rules of the grammar of the nonfiction novel, as shown below.

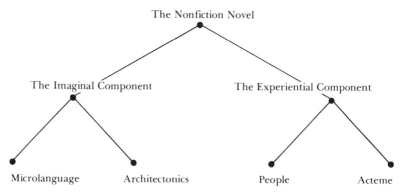

The two components—the experiential and the imaginal—formally correspond to the two referential fields I have described as the essential modal features of the nonfiction novel. The nonfiction novel enacts a model of experience as complex and ambiguous as the fictual reality of life by juxtaposing the inevitability and "persuasiveness of fact" (the external field) with what Capote calls the "poetic

21. Agee, *Let Us Now Praise Famous Men,* p. xiv.

altitude" of the internal shape of the fiction outflowing from the facts (the internal field). As I have suggested, the nonfiction novel, unlike the conventional totalizing novel or such factual narratives as biography and fact novel, has two fields of reference—the internal world of the narrative, which enjoys the aesthetic control of the verbal arts in general, and the outer world of its experiential context, which possesses the "authority of reality."

The in-referential elements of the nonfiction novel constitute the imagined frame or design through which the verbal matrix articulates the phenomenal world of the out-referential domain. The effectiveness of the writer's technique is to be judged by the way he explores, discovers, and expresses the unique inner shape of the narrative generated by the actual situation itself. This means that the nonfiction novelist, like all other practitioners of the verbal arts, exercises an artistic selectivity, which, of course, implies that he occupies a vantage point and chooses the details of his narrative according to a pattern. This pattern, as I discussed in the first chapter, unlike the organizing design of the fictive novelist, is medium-imposed rather than interpretively shaped; the nonfiction novelist is forced by his medium, which makes a total durational transcription impossible, to select details. In other words, the details are chosen and arranged not to reveal a private vision of reality (the writer's interpretation of life) but to find an exact narrative correlative for the happened events. Such a selectivity is quite different in aim from the fictional selectivity of novelists like Mann and Joyce, who choose the details that most convincingly embody their interpretation of the "human condition" in terms of the solid texture of everyday life and thus give their fictions credibility and internal believability.

The two higher-level components of the nonfiction novel, namely the experiential and the imaginal, are fused together by what I shall call the "angle of reference." The angle of reference in a nonfiction novel determines the degree of closeness of the narrative to either of its referential axes and shows whether the modal balance between the two is preserved or whether the narrative, by the loss of such balance, is moving toward the fictive novel or the factual narrative. To the degree it leans toward either axis, it loses the tension between the fictive and the factual. In losing its bi-referentiality, its fields of reference merge into one single mode; thus, it becomes a mono-referential narrative and enters another generic circle. The balanced angle of reference—the "right angle" and its variations—is shown by the three figures below.

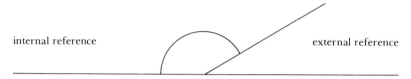

internal reference   external reference

Figure a: A narrative with an "obtuse angle of internal reference" moves toward the fictive novel (e.g., *The Confessions of Nat Turner*)

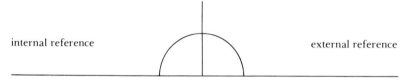

internal reference   external reference

Figure b: A narrative with a "right angle of reference" preserves its bi-referential tension (e.g., *In Cold Blood*)

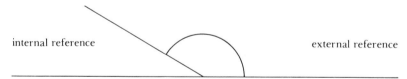

internal reference   external reference

Figure c: A narrative with an "obtuse angle of external reference" moves toward the factual account (e.g., *A Journal of the Plague Year*)

The nonfiction novel preserves the two fields of reference and presents the fictuality of experience by counterpointing the factual and the fictive when it maintains a "right angle of reference." The narrative which moves toward an "obtuse angle of internal reference" emphasizes the imaginal component and moves toward a conventional interpretive novel, while the narrative with an "obtuse angle of external reference" leans in the opposite direction and moves toward a historical novel, a fact novel, a biography, or other forms of factual narrative. The concept of the angle of reference, therefore, enables us to judge the effectiveness and success of a nonfiction novel at the genre level. This is not to say, however, that one kind of narrative is "better" than other kinds; an achieved biography is surely "better" than a clumsy nonfiction novel, but it is not a nonfiction novel. In other words, the concept of the angle of reference, although primarily a descriptive term, functions on the genre level as a means for critically distinguishing the nonfiction novel from other kinds of narrative as well as for determining the generic power of an individual narrative work as a bi-referential mode of narration. It helps us to discern a failed nonfiction novel which uses facts only to entertain or amuse (a narrative with an obtuse angle of internal reference), or the narrative which uses fictional techniques to make facts more available to the reader (a narrative with an obtuse angle of external reference). Thus the evaluation of individual nonfiction novels—those narratives which possess the right angle of reference and therefore enjoy a dual modality—is basically an assessment of their technical power to capture a portion of what Agee has called "unimagined existence."

The most significant constituents of the experiential and imaginal components which are responsible, either directly or through their subordinate components, for the working of a nonfiction novel are what I shall call "acteme," "people," "architectonics," and "microlanguage." In addition, each of these has its own lower-level nodes: actemes, for example, are made up of such elements as "suspense"; the component "people" consists of "actant" and "actee"; "architectonics" includes "narrative point of view." There are also such structural properties as "documentation" which are formed by combining two or more of the higher-level nodes.

In the fictive narrative, plot is the stylization of the writer's private vision and ultimately, as David Lodge argues, one of the "verbal complexes" which make up a novel.[22] It provides the narrative with a pattern of movement, whether causal or non-causal, which serves to distribute the dramatic intensity of the narrative, so that it objectifies and forcefully depicts the order of reality envisioned by the author while simultaneously sustaining the interest of the reader. Such a plot is a closed system of events which enables the fictive narrative to abstract "from the flux of experience something which has beginning, middle and end." [23] Although the plot of the fictive novel may be taken in greater or lesser degree from actual events, it is, in its entirety, a narrative correlative for the author's reading of the "human condition."

There is no "plot" in this sense in the nonfiction novel; rather, the "plot" of the nonfiction novel is one with the author's *donnée:* he cannot change or modify it in order to convey a private vision through it. In fact, even to talk about the "plot" in *La Vida* or *Hiroshima* is absurd. The plots in these books are shaped by the same forces that mold actuality. We can talk about "plot" in the nonfiction novel only if we choose to describe the unfolding events of our own human lives as a cosmic "plot" designed to bring out some metaphysical meaning conceived by an omnipotent being. Therefore, I shall use the term "actemes"—the result of the configuration of experiential events—instead of "plot" to describe the open pattern of situations in the nonfiction novel.[24]

The organization of plot in the fictive novel is *dramatic;* the arrangement of actemes in the nonfiction novel is *mimetic.* Situations pattern themselves in the nonfiction novel with the existential inevitability that informs actuality; thus, the actemes in a nonfiction novel are registered chronologically, and their geometry is a function of the rhythm of external events. The grouping of actemes in the nonfiction novel is also without that dominant characteristic of the fic-

22. David Lodge, *Language of Fiction* (New York: Columbia University Press, 1966), p. 47.

23. Simon O. Lesser, *Fiction and Unconscious* (Boston: Beacon Press, 1957), p. 151. See also Elizabeth Dipple, *Plot* (London: Methuen, 1970), pp. 32–53.

24. "Acteme" is analogous with "morpheme," "phoneme," "toneme" and the like—the minimal unit of unfolding acts in a nonfiction novel.

tive plot traditionally identified as "suspense"—the conventional anticipation and expectation of the reader about the development of situations in the narrative. Because occurred events and their outcome are increasingly common public knowledge, the author of the nonfiction novel cannot use them as narrative elements for sustaining reading interest by creating "an anxious uncertainty about what is going to happen." Instead, the narrational engagement one finds in reading a nonfiction novel arises out of an intense and deep scrutiny of happenings and ongoing events which are charged with an existential urgency. Using a moment-by-moment transcription of events, the nonfiction novel provides an epistemological interest in its system of actemes similar to the one aroused by looking through the eyepiece of a microscope at the molecular world. Thus, if suspense is interpreted in a broad sense to mean an "engagement with structure" [25] at all levels of narration, one can refer to the reading interest generated by the manner of registration and transcription in the nonfiction novel as a kind of suspense. This type of suspense, which is responsible for differentiating various accounts of the same events transcribed by several writers, is "inscriptional suspense" as distinguished from traditional "situational" suspense. In *The Armies of the Night,* for instance, the reader is aware of the geometry of the actemes: he knows the march on the Pentagon actually took place and is informed about what is traditionally referred to as the "what, why, when, how, where, and who" of the narrated events. Mailer's narrative thus contains very little, if indeed any, situational suspense, but it enjoys an inscriptional suspense, which is the function of such conditioning factors as the limitations of the medium, the nature of human response to events, and the employment of a conventional recording tool—language. Similarly, the system of actemes in a nonfiction novel, unlike the plot of the fictive novel, does not have the shape of Freytag's Pyramid and therefore has little conventional climactic tension; instead, the general movement of the ac-

25. Eric S. Rabkin, *Narrative Suspense* (Ann Arbor: University of Michigan Press, 1973), p. 186.

temes is in a straight line created by the chronological recording of actual events. Readers who approach such
nonfiction novels as *a* expecting a twisted, circular, or semi-
circular plot structure containing suspense and a climax are
imposing their reading habits derived from classic novels on
new narratives with radically different generic characteristics. The lack of plot in the nonfiction novel, however,
should not be confused with the "plotless" narrative design
of some totalizing novels. A plotless novel like *Ulysses* or *To
the Lighthouse* manipulates the reader's interest in and expectations about plot in narrative and by making the reader
aware of its "plotlessness" directs his or her response to the
work. Plotlessness, in other words, is as much a part of the
internal rhetoric of the fictive novel as an elaborate plot—it
represents a conscious patterning as an antiplot narrative.
The nonfiction novel, on the other hand, is neither plotic
nor even antiplotic; it is rather aplotic.

Character in the fictive novel, like plot, is a narrative device for structuring the private vision of the writer. It has
played such an important role in the development of the
totalizing novel that for many readers "character is to the
novel what the melody is to music and what the identifiable
representational subject is to painting and sculpture. It provides the element of the familiar and recognizable." [26] And
the liberal imagination has always looked to the character in
the novel for, in the words of Cleanth Brooks, "an image of
man" which can help one "in a world increasingly dehu-
manized to realize himself as a man—to act like a responsible moral being, not to drift like a mere thing." [27] The supramodernist narratist, however, cannot provide the reader
with either the assurance found in discovering recognizable
characters or a paradigm of moral order, since for him the
age of the moralized and individual self is over.

To the nonfiction novelist, "no authentic child of man," as
Norman Douglas puts it, "will fit into a novel," because fic-

26. Sharon Spencer, *Space, Time and Structure in the Modern Novel* (New York:
New York University Press, 1971), p. xv.
27. Cleanth Brooks, *The Hidden God* (New Haven, Conn.: Yale University Press,
1963), p. 4.

tive narratives are filled with characters that are invented representatives of values that are valid only within the field of fiction stylized by the verbal medium. Characters are, as William H. Gass argues, made by words, out of words.[28] In the nonfiction novel, on the other hand, as Oscar Lewis explains, those involved in the events "are not constructed types but are real people."[29] We can see and even talk to them about the books in which they appear, as Norman Cousins did with the people portrayed in John Hersey's *Hiroshima*.[30] Such people are not composite figures invented and projected by the author to substantiate an interpretive pattern of human experience. They are individuals, and their individuality (or "roundness" as E. M. Forster calls it in his discussion of the fictive novel) is not an achievement of aesthetic control but the result of their existential uniqueness.

As with the term "plot," the word "character" is not suitable for analytical discussion of the nonfiction novel, since it is overloaded with connotations that are more a hindrance than a help. Therefore, the term "people" will be used to designate those who appear in a nonfiction novel. These people in the narrative, it must be noted, do not have a fixed and assigned function; they change as the combinations and new permutations of actemes take them into various situations. Through the grammar of events, people acquire different meanings in the same way that the semantic load of words is modified according to their syntactic context. The conventional terminology of narrative criticism, however, does not recognize this dynamic nature of people and instead continues to treat them for the most part as static fictional entities. To account for this changeable quality and to distinguish between two important functions of people in a nonfiction novel, the terms "actant" and "actee" are needed: actant for the initiator of actemes (Ken

28. William Gass, *Fiction and the Figures of Life* (New York: Knopf, 1970), pp. 34–54.

29. Oscar Lewis, *Five Families* (New York: Basic Books, 1959), p. 5.

30. Norman Cousins, "John Hersey," *Saturday Review of Literature*, March 4, 1950, p. 15.

Kesey in *The Electric Kool-Aid Acid Test,* Perry Smith in *In Cold Blood*) and actee for the recipient of ideas or actions (the Pranksters in *The Electric Kool-Aid Acid Test,* the Clutters in *In Cold Blood*). These concepts will enable us to deal with such complex persons as Norman Mailer, who is both the actant and the actee in *The Armies of the Night.* Since the actant and the actee in a nonfiction novel are related to each other through actemes, a person who is an actant at one level of narration may become an actee at another point and vice versa. However, I shall use the word *people* when I am referring to those involved in a nonfiction novel regardless of their functional position in the system of actemes.

In profiling the people in his book, the nonfiction novelist tends more to record the visible surface than to analyze the imagined inner life, for the nonfiction novel, like metafiction, surfiction, and science fiction, is what Leslie Fiedler calls a "thin novel"—the novel with minimum inwardness.[31] The method of depicting persons in the nonfiction novel is essentially contextual: gathering information about other people in life through their behavioral signals, signs, and gestures. The internal psychological analysis present in the nonfiction novel is performed not by the writer himself but usually by an expert in the field (a psychiatrist in *In Cold Blood*) or the person himself (the dreams and fantasies of Ken Kesey in *The Electric Kool-Aid Acid Test*). Capote and Wolfe are not the analysts but recorders of analyses performed by someone else in order to avoid interpreting internal reality—which cannot be directly tested. The character analyses that the fictive novelist provides are projections of his own private views which, in the context of the fictual realities of our times, lead to reductive psychologism. Consequently, such narrative techniques as stream-of-consciousness, dream-sequence, and conventional interior monologue developed by the Modernist novelists have no place in the nonfiction novel and are usually replaced by psychiatric reports, clinical tests, and recorded free associations and dreams.

31. Leslie Fieldler, "Cross the Border—Close the Gap" in *Collected Essays,* II (New York: Stein and Day, 1971), p. 476.

People usually appear under their own names in nonfiction novels because, as John Hersey says in *The Algiers Motel Incident,* "when you change a man's name you change the whole man." [32] Norman Mailer presents himself under his own name in *The Armies of the Night* and preserves the names of the other persons in the book. Sometimes, however, the writer, finding it legally or ethically impossible to strictly follow this ideal, changes the names of some people in the book. In *In Cold Blood,* for example, the names of three persons (Mr. Bell, Perry's Sister, and Willie-Jay) are not real names, and in *La Vida* names of people and places are changed to "maintain the anonymity" of the persons in the book. Such changes, however, do not compromise the nature of the nonfiction novel. The question, "does nonfiction become fiction if the facts of a case are followed but the names are changed?" [33] is rather naïve. The generic identity of a nonfiction novel is determined by its phenomenalistic, non-endorsive use of fact and its double mode of reference, not merely by adherence to the real names of people and places. Empirical data alone do not change the generic nature of a literary work.

The actemes, actants, and actees in the nonfiction novel are part of the experiential component of the narrative and belong to the external field of reference which reflects the experiential world. They are real, and the book itself usually provides the reader with enough clues to check their authenticity. The evidence thus furnished inside the book amounts to a "core of documentation" which leads the reader to the outside world. This supplies the means for counterpointing the actual and the fictional and also turns the narrative work into an open system. The core of documentation is composed of such evidence as references to dates, people, places, public events, newspaper accounts, interviews, eyewitness reports, and the like. Together they form a self-verifying system within the book which enables us to see that the documents are not imagined. Forged doc-

32. John Hersey, *The Algiers Motel Incident* (New York: Knopf, 1968), p. 33.
33. Robert Tracy, "In Cold Blood," *The Southern Review,* n.s. 3 (1967), pp. 251–54.

uments are devices of the fictive novel and, within the field
of fiction, are "documents" only as inventions of the author
to give his narrative veracity and believability.

Aesthetic control of the materials in the nonfiction novel
is primarily related to the imaginal component of the narrative—the in-referential field. The two higher nodes of this
component, namely, architectonics and microlanguage, are
closely related. The architectonics of the nonfiction novel
involves such issues and techniques as point of view, the
narrative voice, and the role of montage and arrangement.

The non-subjectivism which distinguishes the nonfiction
novelist's approach to persons and actemes also marks his
treatment of the "narrator." However, the available critical
terminology, which follows the polaristic theories of narrative based on modernist aesthetics and identifies the narrator as either a *persona* [34] or *author*,[35] is incapable of ade-
quately dealing with the "registrar" in a nonfiction novel. A
persona is a fictional identity, while the *author* is a factually
locatable, controlling consciousness, which, in a biography
for example, selects the significant data, discards the trivial,
and eventually through the exercise of judgment weaves a
meaningful pattern from the data to produce a version of
the life and times of his subject. The narrator of *The Priest
of Love,* a mono-referential biography of D. H. Lawrence,
can be identified as Harry T. Moore. Behind the orches-
trated voices of *The Sound and the Fury,* the voice of all the
voices can be called the "second self" of William Faulkner.
But who is the "narrator" of *a,* the transcription of a taped
account of a twenty-four-hour period in the lives of a group
of people? Like "plot" and "character," the very term "narrator," with the connotations it has accumulated through its
frequent use in discussions of the fictive novel, is distorting
when applied to an analysis of the nonfiction novel. The
"narrator" of a nonfiction novel is non-projective, anti-sub-

34. "Persona" is usually further refined as "implied author," "second self," or
"official scribe," and similar categories. However the dual distinction between a
"historical" man—author—and a projected fictional self—narrator—is an integral
part of the Modernist aesthetics.

35. The person whose name appears on the title page.

jective, ajudgmental, and the core of his "self" seems to have been affected by the force of the actualities which constitute his experiential *données*. In some instances, out of exposure to an extreme situation, he is re-born with a new sense of self and a complex identity as ambiguous and manifold as the fictual situation itself. Norman Mailer, the "narrator" of *The Armies of the Night*, is an example of the reborn "self"—a self whose established "I" is fissioned by the pressure of actualities. As "narrator," he reflects the duality of his experiential situation and enacts the schizophrenic nature of his culture. The narrator of the nonfiction novel is more similar to the teller of an orally composed tale than to the narrators of either the totalizing novel or factual narratives. He is a medium through which the already existing events are transmitted. It would thus be more accurate to refer to him as a "narratist," since a narrator is usually the projected persona within the narrative and an integral part of its fictional apparatus. Tom Wolfe is not the narrator of the Pranksters' saga in the sense that Skipper is the narrator of *The Second Skin*. The range of creativity, selection, and composition of the nonfiction novelist also resembles that of the teller of orally composed narratives: both work within the restrictions and limitations of what might be called the existing syntax of events.

As with the other fictive devices, the concept of time is radically different in nonfiction narratives. The narratist of the nonfiction novel is concerned with what Kermode, adopting earlier uses of the term, calls "chronos"—the passing time; the narrator of the fictive novel is usually preoccupied with "kairos"—"a point in time filled with significance, charged with a meaning derived from its relation to the end." [36] In the nonfiction novel, the world is seen as a process free from the meaning of a beginning or the significance of an end. The nonfiction novelist rarely uses what Kate Hamburger calls "epic preterite"—the past mode which is used as a device for labeling the world of narrative as a fictive world and hence a world which exists exclusively

36. Frank Kermode, *The Sense of an Ending* (New York: Oxford University Press, 1967), p. 47.

in the imagination.[37] The past in the nonfiction novel has a literal value, asserting the actuality of the happened events.

Another important constituent of the nonfiction novel is the linguistic matrix. I shall use the term "microlanguage" to discuss the way the "macrolanguage" (the language in its normal use) is employed in the registration of events, persons, and atmosphere in a nonfiction novel. The aesthetic control exercised in establishing the internal field of reference and the overall inner shape of the narrative is very much the product of the register of the language used. Tom Wolfe's stylistic pyrotechnics and Norman Mailer's epic metaphors are enactments, in the very texture of the prose, of the fictuality of the reality they deal with. One of the central characteristics of the microlanguage of the nonfiction novel is that it does not contain the polarity between imaginal and discursive discourse of the fictive novel in which the presence of discursive discourse is usually regarded as a mark of artistic immaturity and lack of control. In the nonfiction novel, the two modes mix, and the texture of prose has a wider range of variety than that of the fictive novel or the strictly expository medium of the factual narrative.

The total configuration of a nonfiction novel depends on what, adopting Franz Stanzel's term, I shall call the "narrative situation." [38] Without trying to reduce the wide range of these narrative situations, we may, in order to provide a basis for a taxonomy of the nonfiction novel, classify them into three major prototypes: exegetical, testimonial, and notational. The distinguishing characteristic of these situations is the position of the narratist in relation to the event. In the exegetical nonfiction novel, the narratist is not a witness to the event, but rather subjects whatever evidence he can find to an intensive exegesis, so that he can overcome the temporal distance and repossess the density of the haunting facts (*In Cold Blood*). The nonfiction novelist who adopts a

---

37. Kate Hamburger, *The Logic of Literature*, trans. M. J. Rose (Bloomington: Indiana University Press, 1973), pp. 64–81.

38. Franz Stanzel, *Narrative Situations in the Novel*, trans. James P. Pusack (Bloomington: Indiana University Press, 1971), pp. 3–37.

testimonial narrative situation is himself a witness to the events. He usually appears under his own name in the narrative, and the narrational axis evolves around his personal voice(s) (*The Electric Kool-Aid Acid Test*). In the notational nonfiction novel, through use of sophisticated technological devices, the concept of a conventional uni-authorial work disappears, and the polyphony of voices of the "narrator-authors" is directly registered (*La Vida*). These three narrative situations, however, rarely exist in a "pure" form but instead tend to be frequently mixed with one another. Yet, regardless of the different angle of approach each of these narrative situations takes toward the empirical *données*, the narratist never projects an interpretive scheme on them nor does he suggest an informing principle behind them. The world which emerges from such narratives with a zero degree of interpretation is a naked universe presented in its unadorned ambiguity and fictional complexity.

PART II

Modes of
the Nonfiction Novel

four
The Stubborn Fact:
The Exegetical
Nonfiction Novel

The exegetical nonfiction novel is a fictual narrative
registering the public or private events which have taken
place, usually in the absence of the author, in the past. In
attempting to repossess the empirical constituents of the occurred events and to recover their original configurations
and mythic resonance, the exegetical nonfiction novelist
subjects all the available evidence to an intensive exegesis.
This kind of nonfiction novel, in its concern with past occurrences, resembles fictive novels like Proust's *A la recherche
du temps perdu*, some historical novels, and such factual narratives as *Science and Civilization in China* by Joseph Need-
ham (whom George Steiner considers "Proust's only succes-
sor").[1] But a radically different use of facts distinguishes the
exegetical nonfiction novel from fictive novels and from factual narratives.

The novelist, using a private interpretive scheme,
reorders the seemingly random incidents of the past into
what Clive Bell calls "a significant form." He dramatizes his
vision of life in a new personal patterning of events within a
narrative structure. The rhythm of his narrative follows his
chiaroscuro of experience: the distribution of light and
shade in the total picture of reality according to his metaphysics. The factual narratist is also preoccupied with the
interpretation of the past and the discovery of its underlying shape. His procedures, however, are quite different
from those of the novelist. Rather than beginning with a
totalization of experience in the light of his private vision of
life, he moves toward such a grand synthesis by examining

1. George Steiner, "A Future Literacy," *Atlantic,* Aug. 1971, p. 43.

all the documents. The tempo and rhythm of his narration are determined by the informing force behind the original movement of events which he has uncovered through his researches. The narrative attitude of the novelist is "epiphanic"; that of the factual narratist is "expositional."

In crisis situations, when "the complexities and the relative safety of a fully functioning society have been suspended and replaced by an environment at once unfamiliar and dangerous," [2] the pressures of psychic and social actualities are so intense that both the private and the communal experiences refuse to be tamed into a coherent system of meaning. Such extreme situations demand a narrative method which goes beyond the search for an anthropomorphic meaning and accommodates the *is*ness of the manifold events by capturing their charged textures. The nonfiction novel is the embodiment of such a method: it dispenses with conventional narrative expectations and, instead of neutralizing the contingency of events through an imposed aesthetic necessity, acknowledges the discontinuity of facts in a pervading freakish reality.

In his attempt to register the past events in their full existential inevitability and in their original shape, the nonfiction novelist employs a variety of research techniques. He investigates the public documents, such private records as letters, diaries, and journals, and interviews eyewitnesses and participants, if possible. In *Hiroshima,* an example of an exegetical nonfiction novel, John Hersey employs most of these methods. The main problem in dealing with the haunting facts of such events as Auschwitz, Hiroshima, Dresden, or My Lai, as Alfred Alvarez observes, is "the enormity and the truth of the events." [3] The six survivors of the first atomic explosion whose lives in a city in crisis are recorded in *Hiroshima* were six characters in search of an author. Their lives had almost instantaneously been transformed into a dark fable. To become visible to themselves

2. Louis Landa's description of the London of *A Journal of the Plague Year,* in his introduction to the Oxford edition of the book (London, 1969), p. xxxiv.

3. Alfred Alvarez, "The Literature of the Holocaust," *Commentary,* Nov. 1964, p. 65.

and others on a new plane of reality, these six lives needed to be written into a book. Their author had to be a scribe, not an interpreter who would project values into this alien world and tame it by a humanistic obsession with meaning.

Hiroshima is a literalization of Thoreau's belief that "if men would steadily observe realities only," they would realize that "reality is fabulous." [4] The tension and the ambiguity of the fictual experience endured by each of the six persons and their shared destiny is articulated through the tension of the book's narrative mode, which moves alternately to the world outside the book and to the inner fiction generated within it.

The book details the fate of about a quarter of a million people in Hiroshima on and after the day of the first atomic blast. It registers the metamorphosis of their private and communal lives through an examination of six survivors: a secretary, a doctor with a private practice, an impoverished war widow, a German Jesuit missionary, a Red Cross physician, and a Japanese Methodist minister.

The first chapter retrieves a precise moment: "exactly fifteen minutes past eight in the morning, on August 6, 1945, Japanese time." Throughout the entire chapter, Hersey subjects this frozen moment to a narrational exegesis, showing what each person was doing at this moment and the hours preceding it. The six survivors are introduced in a quasi prologue, partly narrational, partly explanatory, which serves as an annotated *dramatis personae*. Each person is then individually portrayed on this morning as he or she prepares for the daily routine. The juxtaposition of the portraits of these six persons, and those of less-exposed people, is the basic organizing device used throughout the book. The narrative interest created by contiguous portraits generates the energy of *Hiroshima*. Hersey substitutes portrait for incident or situation; the entire book uses the technique of portraiture as narration. Portrait, in other words, gives the actemes a forward thrust.

Among the six opening portraits, that of Dr. Sasaki espe-

4. *The Writings of Henry David Thoreau* (Boston: Houghton Mifflin, 1906). II, 106.

cially adds to the narrational momentum by relating the transference from one level of reality to another and by blurring the line between the private dream and public nightmare. Dr. Sasaki has had a restless night. But the nightmare which disturbed his sleep does not vanish as the morning sun comes up. It lingers. The doctor, a young graduate of Eastern Medical University in Tsingtao, China, is appalled by the inadequacy of medical facilities in the country town where his mother lives. Without a permit, he has begun visiting a few sick townspeople in the evenings, after his eight hours at the Red Cross Hospital and four hours of commuting. Recently, he has learned through a fellow doctor that the penalty for practicing without a permit is severe. In his nightmare, he was at the bedside of a country patient when the police and the fellow doctor burst into the room, dragged him outside, and beat him cruelly. On the morning train, while still preoccupied with the dream, he decides to abandon the practice. He arrives at the hospital at seven-forty, and reports to the head surgeon. In a few moments, on the first floor of the hospital, he draws blood from the arm of a man to perform a Wassermann test. With the blood specimen in his left hand and walking in a kind of distraction, perhaps because of the nightmare, he moves toward the laboratory. He is one step beyond an open window when the light of the bomb reflects "like a gigantic photographic flash" in the corridor. Ducking down on one knee, he says to himself, "Sasaki, gambare!" (Be Brave!). The building trembles, his glasses fall off, the bottle of blood crashes against one wall, his Japanese slippers are ripped from his feet. At that moment, Dr. Sasaki forgets his private dream: it has merged with a public Kafkaesque nightmare in the broad daylight.

In the frozen moment of the blast, the habitual boundaries between such concepts as real-unreal, sooner-later, here-there, and most important, the various facets of "I," blur; the person is transferred to a different sphere of actuality. The dislodging of consciousness is mapped in *Hiroshima* not by imposing a pattern of meaning or commenting on the raw experience, but through registering the actual.

The reorientation of the people to the actualities of this layer of existence is also recorded without comments about either the conceiving consciousness of the survivors or the atmosphere in which they try to regain their bearings. Any comment or search for pattern is based on the conception of values which would be alien, and therefore distorting, to this emerging actuality. The fullness is captured by exegetically retrieving the experiential *données*. In Dr. Sasaki's portrait, for example, the continuation of the personal dream into the public nightmare is not treated in any fabular manner. The dream and the nightmare are juxtaposed, and the tension between the two is enacted not by drawing attention to it, but by a noninterpretive registering of the two. When the Reverend Tanimoto, the lifelong preacher of an ethics of caring for other human beings, in a moment of confusion and dislodgment leaves a friend under the ruins and dashes into the street to save himself, no attempt is made to point out the irony. No ethical rule is applicable to this moment of patareal actuality, and interpretation of the act as "ironical" would be rather naïve. Registration and juxtaposition map the transference of the person to a new area of experience where fact and fiction converge.

The portraits in the first chapter are introduced into the narrative by the technique of "synchronic narration." In synchronic narration, the flow of time is stopped, and the contents of the moment are registered simultaneously. The only link among the contained elements is the moment itself. The technique of synchronic narration is frequently used in nonfiction novels to emphasize the solidity of measurable external time. Contrary to the practice of such Modernist writers as Joyce, Proust, Woolf, Faulkner, and others, who counterpoint clock time with interior time to show the ultimate unreality of surface time, the nonfiction novelists are suspicious of any juggling with testable clock time. To re-order time is to re-order the experience and thus to interpret it according to a private vision. Taking the chronological axis as the narrational point of reference, Hersey records the blast experiences of the six main persons in the first chapter, and then transcribes their new life in the remaining three chapters. As time passes, the people reorient themselves to the new actualities and develop an increasing awareness of the sufferings of one another. *Hiroshima* follows this movement from personal introspection to communal cooperation. The first part of the book (chapter one and the main part of chapter two) deals with the private agonies of the six persons portrayed, while the second part puts the personal anguish in the context of the public disaster. Portraits in the first part are therefore mostly of individuals examined in a given series of actemes. In the following part, the individual portraits are combined with group or composite portraits which delineate one or more of the six persons with less-exposed figures. Chapter three, for instance, opens with such a group portrait, depicting Mrs. Nakamura, Father Kleinsorge, and the Reverend Tanimoto, plus a number of friends in Asano Park. In this part, panoramic views of the city and its inhabitants are also offered, and discursive passages are interposed between the portraits. Discussions, arguments, figures, statistics, official announcements, and bulletins comprise the body of these discursive sections. They form the core of the book's documentation and help to create the self-verifying component or built-in check system, providing evidence that the events in the book are indeed authentic, not figments of the author's imagination.

Individual portraits, general scenes, and discursive passages are all put together by narrative collage, which enacts the randomness, chaos, and horror which have disrupted the life of the city and its inhabitants. (The function of collage as used by Hersey and such transfictionists as Barthelme and Federman differs radically from that of Dos Passos, Joyce, and Eliot. For the latter, collage is an interpretive and totalizing device: "fragments" which are "shored against ruins" of the "panorama of futility and anarchy" of the times. In the works of the nonfiction novelists and transfictionists, on the other hand, collage is a function of "imitative form" (the technique which Yvor Winters and other Modernist critics rejected as a "fallacy"), a means, in other words, for following the contours of the surrounding

discontinuous world.) After the blast, the city is swept by a
great fire and the streets are filled with bloodied, terrified,
half-naked people, running aimlessly in their torn un-
dergarments. On their bodies, "the burns had made patterns—of the undershirt straps and suspenders and, on the
skin of some women (since white repelled the heat from the
bomb and dark clothes absorbed it and conducted it to
the skin), the shapes of the flowers they had on their kimo-
nos." [5] The patterns bear an uncanny resemblance to the
"designs" needled on the bare skins of the condemned men
by the "harrow" of that "remarkable piece of apparatus" in
Kafka's *In the Penal Colony*. What is happening in the broad
daylight in Hiroshima preempts the imagined and fictional.
Some survivors, stunned and dazed, rush toward the fire;
some are unable to move: "a great number sat and lay on
the pavement, vomited, waited for death, and died." The
usual responses and even reflexes seem to have been suspended. The energetic Mr. Yoshida, former head of the
Nobori-cho Neighborhood Association and director of the
air-raid defenses, had boasted that fire might eat away all
Hiroshima but would never come to Nobori-cho. When the
Bomb blows down his house, a joist pins him by the legs, in
full view of people hurrying along the street. His cries for
help bring no response from the passers-by; he is merely
part of the general blur of misery. He sees the houses
around him surge into flames; heat sears his face. Then
flames reach his side of the street and lick at his house. In a
paroxysm of terrified strength, he frees himself and runs
down the alleys of Nobori-cho, hemmed in by the fire he
said would never come. He begins at once to behave like an
old man; in two months his hair will be white.

The city is in the grip of an actual collective nightmare
whose intensity and depth of horror would have been all
but distorted by any conventional novelistic form with its
preoccupation with a dramatic ordering of experience. The
events themselves are charged to the highest possible degree. They require a registrational narrative which, through

5. John Hersey, *Hiroshima* (New York: Alfred A. Knopf, 1946), pp. 19–40.
Subsequent page references to this edition will appear in the text.

exegesis of details, is capable of mapping the vibrant surface which contains the experience. The actuality itself, at this intersection of fact and fiction, is darkly reflective of the nature of the relationship between man and technology. Any aesthetic reordering or symbolic interpretation of the observed is patently redundant in bringing out the moral dimension of what, for example, Father Kleinsorge witnesses in Asano Park. While bringing water for the maimed and badly wounded, he hears a voice call to him:

> "Have you anything to drink?" He saw a uniform. Thinking there was just one soldier, he approached with the water. When he had penetrated the bushes, he saw there were about twenty men, and they were all in exactly the same nightmarish state: their faces were wholly burned, their eye-sockets were hollow, the fluid from their melted eyes had run down their cheeks. . . . Their mouths were mere swollen, pus-covered wounds, which they could not bear to stretch enough to admit the spout of the teapot. So Father Kleinsorge got a large piece of grass and drew out the stem so as to make a straw, and gave them all water to drink that way. [p. 68]

To criticize *Hiroshima* for substituting "artful detail" for "moral intelligence" is to read the book as if it were a conventional fictive novel dealing with a tamed reality.[6] The experiential event here is self-defining and need only be registered. To attempt to impose any pattern on the event is to violate its fullness and complexity. One is reminded again of Thoreau's statement in his *Journal* (November 9, 1851): "I would so state facts that they shall be significant, shall be myths or mythologic."[7]

The harrowing story of the soldiers with melted eyes is recorded in chapter three, which covers the period from the evening of August 6 to August 15. The title of the chapter, "Details Are Being Investigated," taken from a Japa-

6. See Kingsley Widmer, "American Apocalypse: Notes on the Bomb and the Failure of Imagination," in *The Forties: Fiction, Poetry, Drama,* ed. Warren French (Deland, Fla.: Everett/Edwards, 1969), p. 143.

7. *The Journal of Henry D. Thoreau,* ed. Bradford Torrey and Francis H. Allen (Boston: Houghton Mifflin, 1906), p. 99.

nese radio broadcast on August 7, indicates its general tenor. Extensive discursive passages accompany individual and group portraits. In Modernist aesthetics, the mingling of narrative with discursive discourse is regarded as impure and inartistic. Such mixing shows that the artist has been unable to control his materials and turn "life" into "art." Distinctions of this kind, however, are irrelevant to the reading of supramodern literature, which is essentially the writing of mixed levels of experience through mixed levels of discourse. The status of discursive discourse in supramodern writing is very similar to that of real objects in a contemporary painting; it opens up the closed set of the work of art and asserts the original source of experience.

Among the references to the verifiable facts, which comprise the core of documentation and help to create the out-referentiality of *Hiroshima*, are the announcements made by President Truman (p. 65) and Emperor Hirohito (p. 84), the investigations and findings of the Japanese scientists (pp. 95–97), and the inclusion of such identifiable persons as Lieutenant John D. Montgomery (p. 105) and Professor Y. Hiraiwa of Hiroshima University of Literature and Science (p. 115). The six major persons are, of course, identifiable figures of life. In his biographical note on John Hersey in *Saturday Review of Literature* for March 4, 1950, Norman Cousins describes his own visits to Dr. Fujii and Mrs. Nakamura.[8] The Reverend Mr. Tanimoto, despite his loss of energy, asked to translate *Hiroshima* into Japanese.[9]

In the final chapter, unlike the first two and the nucleus of the third, summary narration is used more freely. The time span extends from August 15 to the author's interview with the six persons in the spring of 1946. In this chapter, the depth of the bomb's violent disturbance of the balance in nature is captured by a graphic presentation of the sickness and suffering of the six survivors. Father Kleinsorge suddenly faints during a Mass; Mrs. Nakamura and

8. Norman Cousins, "John Hersey," *Saturday Review of Literature*, March 4, 1950, p. 15.

9. David Sanders, *John Hersey* (New Haven, Conn.: College and University Press, 1967), p. 50.

her daughter grow bald, and are forced to stay indoors; Mr. Tanimoto is afflicted with a general weariness and feverishness.

Discussing the illness of these four persons, the narrator's voice becomes quite audible: "These four did not realize it, but they were coming down with the strange, capricious disease which came later to be known as radiation sickness" (p. 90). This is one of the few occasions when the narrator "intrudes" into the narrative. The general narrative point of view of the book is a controlled omniscience, the most frequently adopted point of view in the exegetical nonfiction novels. I shall discuss it more fully in my analysis of Capote's *In Cold Blood*. The narrator, at all times, has a very subdued and quiet tone—the tone of the receptive and accommodating registrar—in accord with the approach of the book to the inherently ambiguous actualities.

The intermingling of the facts and the dark fiction which oozes from them in *Hiroshima* establishes the double modes of the narrative. It is possible, of course, to read any nonfiction novel as if it were a mono-referential work. In the case of *Hiroshima*, the book can be read as a factual report or a fictive novel (the sudden destruction of an alien city with a strange weapon). However, such readings fail to account for a narrative mode which counterpoints the factual and the outflowing fiction to map the responses of the overwhelmed consciousness at the borderline area of experience, an area where the various facets of perception converge and a fictual zone emerges.

Although this book focuses upon postwar American nonfiction novels, a discussion of Defoe's *A Journal of the Plague Year* (1722) will clarify some of the issues and problems involved in the study of the nonfiction novel as a literary genre, and thus aid our understanding of contemporary examples. None of the narratives discussed in this chapter has aroused more critical debate as to its generic and, eventually, its aesthetic status than Defoe's *Journal*. The argument as to the "factuality" or "fictionality" of the *Journal* persists.[10] The dilemma of scholars and critics is perhaps best expressed by Sir Walter Scott in his "Advertisement" to an edition of the book. *"The History of the Great Plague,"* he believes, "is one of that particular class of compositions which hovers between romance and history." [11]

My primary concern is with the inadequate theoretical conception of narrational mode which, it seems to me, underlies the critical debate about the generic identity of the *Journal.* The reasoning of all these critics and scholars is based on a bipolar theory of narrational mode: the fictional and the factual. They have, perhaps unwittingly, read the *Journal* as a mono-referential work (fiction or history) and thus have ignored the most important aspect of the book's narrative status. In the absence of a general theory, it is not surprising that such a well-informed scholar as F. Bastian declares the *Journal* "an incoherent jumble which defies analysis." [12] James Sutherland echoes this view in deciding that "the work is a hodge-podge." [13] Defoe's work, like Clemens's generically complex *Life on the Mississippi,* which has also been called "a hodge-podge," [14] is essentially a bi-referential narrative with two fields of meaning: the external and the internal.

10. See, among other sources, the following: "Londinesis" note in *The Gentlemen's Magazine,* 79 (1809), 1127; E. W. Brayley, *The Beauties of England and Wales* (1801–15), 10, pt. 1, pp. 374–404; Brayley's remarks in *The Gentlemen's Magazine,* 80 (1810), 215; Brayley's introduction to his famous 1835 edition of the *Journal;* Watson Nicholson, *The Historical Sources of Defoe's "Journal of the Plague Year"* (Boston: Stratford Co., 1919); A. W. Secord, *Studies in the Narrative Method of Defoe* (Urbana: University of Illinois, 1924); Secord's introduction to his 1935 edition of the *Journal* (Garden City, N.Y.: Doubleday, Doran and Co., 1935); Walter Bell, *The Great Plague in London in 1665* (New York: Dodd, Mead, 1924); E. A. Barker, *The History of the English Novel* (London: H. F. and G. Witherby, 1929), Vol. III; Anthony Burgess's "Introduction" to the Penguin edition of the *Journal* (Harmondsworth, Middlesex, 1966), pp. 6–19; and Burgess's interview in *Playboy,* Sept. 1974, p. 76. See also references elsewhere in this chapter.

11. Daniel Defoe, *The History of the Great Plague of London* (1722; rpt. New York: Derby & Jackson, 1857), p. 5.

12. F. Bastian, "Defoe's *Journal of the Plague Year* Reconsidered," *Review of English Studies,* n.s. 25, No. 62 (1965), 169.

13. James Sutherland, *Daniel Defoe: A Critical Study* (Boston: Houghton Mifflin, 1971), p. 170.

14. H. A. Pochmann and Gay Wilson Allen, *Introduction to Masters of American Literature* (Carbondale: Southern Illinois University Press, 1969), p. 128.

The *Journal,* however, is not a firsthand registration of the events in the same sense that, for instance, Capote's *In Cold Blood* or Hersey's *Hiroshima* is. This compositional factor has also added to the critical problems of reading the book and determining its generic status. Since a time gap exists between the happening of the events and Defoe's recording of them, and also because of the use of secondary sources, some critics have regarded Defoe's *Journal* as a historical novel. The *Journal,* however, yields its narrative meaning more fully if approached as an exegetical nonfiction novel rather than as a historical novel, a factual narrative, or a fictive novel. In the exegetical nonfiction novel, a time gap usually exists between the actual occurrence of events and their registration. The nonfiction novelist attempts to overcome this gap through use of various research techniques. The major factor in determining the generic identity of narratives with an external field of reference is the manner in which the narratist approaches the "facts" of the outside world rather than the time span which separates him from the incidents.[15] In the *Journal,* Defoe does not use facts as a means for endorsing a totalization of experience but employs them phenomenalistically: he transcribes the myth of the visible through registering the charged surfaces without imposing an aesthetic or epistemological pattern on them. The circumstances under which the *Journal* was composed are not, as some critics seem to think, all that unusual. Other events of the past which evoke a similar resonance have suddenly assumed new dimensions for people under the pressures of current actualities. These past events as archetypal happenings haunt the consciousness of those living in the present. The volatile climate of the 1960s in the United States, for instance, created a mood in which the facts of Nat Turner's revolt in 1831 found an immediacy of impact as forceful as the urgent events of the day—a mood partly reflected in

15. "Most novels set in the past—beyond an arbitrary number of years, say 40–60 (two generations) are liable to be considered historical." Avrom Fleishman, *The English Historical Novel: Walter Scott to Virginia Woolf* (Baltimore: Johns Hopkins University Press, 1971), p. 3.

William Styron's *The Confessions of Nat Turner.* In 1721, the spread of bubonic plague through Provence posed the threat of a new epidemic in England. Although the last time a serious outbreak of the plague had attacked England was in 1665, when Defoe was a small boy, the arrival of the contagious disease in France revived among Englishmen the horror associated with the Great Plague of half a century earlier. The past events suddenly acquired a new urgency and a powerful mental actuality. The premonition of chaos obsessed Defoe, like Styron, with the facts of the past.

In composing the *Journal*, Defoe used such sources as *Orders Conceived and Published by the Lord Mayor and Aldermen of the City of London concerning the Infection of the Plague, 1665; Bills of Mortality;* Dr. Nathaniel Hodges's *Loimologia;* and, perhaps, Thomas Vincent's *God's Terrible Voice in the City,* but, as Bastian has pointed out, "there is a great deal" in the *Journal* "which cannot be convincingly traced back to these, or any other published sources." It is this "residual material," he concludes, which must determine the character of the *Journal*." [16] The fictuality of the Great Plague transcribed in the *Journal* is mainly generated by this "residual" material. Defoe obtained these "materials" by the same means—interviewing—that Capote, Hersey, and other contemporary nonfiction novelists use to acquire theirs. He interviewed many people whom he refers to as "ancient Persons still alive"—those people who were adults at the time of the outbreak of the Great Plague of 1665. The stories told him by his own elder relatives, including his uncle, Henry Foe (the H.F. of the *Journal*), were also important in his retrieving of the texture of the past events. [17] As Virginia Woolf has commented, Defoe's assumption is " 'let the naturalists . . . explain these things, and the reason and the manner of them; all I can say to them is, to describe the facts.' " [18] Although Defoe's narrative, like Styron's, does

16. Bastian, "Defoe's *Journal*," p. 163.
17. In addition to Bastian and Sutherland, see J. H. Plumb's "Foreword" to the Signet edition of *A Journal of the Plague Year* (New York: New American Library, 1960), pp. v–x.
18. Virginia Woolf, *Collected Essays* (London: Hogarth Press, 1966), I, 74.

not have a "right angle" of reference, and the events in his book are those of the past resurrected under the pressures of the exigencies of the present, Defoe's approach to the facts nonetheless remains nontotalizing.

A Journal of the Plague Year is the recording, by a lonely observer who signs himself H.F., of a few months of continuous crisis during which "the face of London was . . . strangely altered." "H.F., the supposed author of the *Journal*, can be identified with Defoe's uncle, Henry Foe, with complete certainty," according to Bastian.[19] The verified contents of the *Journal* show that Defoe approaches H.F. not as a fictional persona but as a source of information, the same way he uses other documents available to him. Whether Henry Foe left behind an actual journal, scattered notes, or merely passed on oral accounts of the incidents that he had witnessed during the visitation of the Great Plague, Defoe's attitude toward H.F. is exegetical, not dramatic. The voice of H.F. throughout the *Journal* is similar to that of Perry Smith in his autobiographical sketch in *In Cold Blood* (chapter 71) and to the author-narrators in Studs Terkel's *Working*. The voice of H.F. in the *Journal*, however, is not conventionally juxtaposed with other narrators' voices. The counterpointing is achieved by putting the collective voice of the Londoners and what is called "speaking sights"[20] into the mainstream of narration. Contrasting the *Journal* with Tolstoy's *Sevastopol* and Hauptmann's *Weavers*, James Joyce concludes,

> But in these two works we are aware of a lyric surge, a self-conscious art, a musical theme which would appear to be the emotional revolt of modern man against human or superhuman iniquity. In Defoe there is nothing of the kind: neither lyricism nor art for art's sake nor social consciousness. The saddler walks through the deserted streets, listens to the cries of anguish, keeps his distance from the sick, reads the orders of the Lord Mayor, chats with the sextons, who chew garlic

---

19. Bastian, "Defoe's *Journal*," p. 158. See also P. D. Mundy, "The Ancestry of Daniel Defoe," *Notes and Queries*, 174 (1938), 112–14.

20. *A Journal of the Plague Year*, ed. Landa, p. 61. Subsequent page references to this edition will appear in the text.

and rue, discusses matters with a waterman at Blackwall, faithfully compiles his statistics. . . .[21]

The organization of the book, as with all nonfiction novels, is essentially mimetic rather than dramatic; it imitates life in its formlessness: narrative shape is dictated by external forces, not merely by the imagination of the author. The shaping force here is, of course, the movement of the plague which the *Journal* follows chronologically, geographically, and numerically. Chronologically it moves from "about the beginning of September 1664," actively records the happenings in London from "the latter end of November or the beginning of December 1664 when two men, said to be Frenchmen, died of the plague in Long Acre, or rather at the upper end of Drury Lane" (pp. 1–2), and concludes in December 1665, when things begin "to return to their own channel" (p. 229). Geographically, the book follows the plague from the parishes of St. Giles and St. Andrews in the western part of London to the east side, Aldgate, where the narrator lives. Numerical coverage focuses on statistical reports which convey the intensity of the plague. The structure of the book, however, is not consistent on any of these planes; because of temporal and geographical jumps and also because of some overlapping coverage, the book's registration of events is repetitious and, by the standards of dramatic impact usually applied to fictive novels, even monotonous. However, the monotony is that of the life portrayed. It focuses the minds of the reader on the single most important subject of the book.

The external field of meaning, which is responsible for the out-referentiality of the book, is established by a hard core of documents. The *Journal* opens with the support of mortality bills:

> . . . the usual number of burials in a week, in the parishes of St. Giles-in-the-Fields and St. Andrew's, Holborn, were from twelve to seventeen or nineteen each, few more or less; but from the time that the plague first began in St. Giles's parish,

21. James Joyce, "Daniel Defoe," edited from Italian manuscripts and translated by Joseph Prescott, *Buffalo Studies*, 1, No. 1 (1964), 17.

it was observed that the ordinary burials increased in number considerably. For example:-

From *Dec.*   27th   to *Jan.*   3.   St. *Giles's* ------------------------ 16
                               St. *Andrew's* -------------------- 17
      Jan.   3   to —— 10.   St. *Giles's* ------------------------ 12
                               St. *Andrew's* -------------------- 25
      Jan.   10.   to —— 17.   St. *Giles's* ------------------------ 18
                               St. *Andrew's* -------------------- 18
      Jan.   17   to —— 24.   St. *Giles's* ------------------------ 23
                               St. *Andrew's* -------------------- 16
      Jan.   24.   to —— 31.   St. *Giles's* ------------------------ 24
                               St. Andrew's -------------------- 15
      Jan.   30.   to *Feb.*   7.   St. Giles's ------------------------ 21
                               St. Andrew's -------------------- 23
      Feb.   7.   to —— 14.   St. Giles's ---------------------- 24
                               whereof one of the Plague [p. 3]

The bills are an integral part of the narration, serving as essential evidence for the statements of the book. Their numbers are supplemented by "ORDERS CONCEIVED AND PUBLISHED BY THE LORD MAYOR AND ALDERMEN OF THE CITY OF LONDON CONCERNING THE INFECTION OF THE PLAGUE, 1665" (pp. 38–46), which, like the statistics, are verifiable, and point to the world outside the covers of the book. The historical reality of persons mentioned in the *Journal* is now established, and this includes not only the famous Hodges, Brooks, Upton, Berwick, and rich men such as Sir Robert Clayton, but also people like Solomon Eagle, Dr. Heath, and the sleeping piper, all of whom, because of the bizarre situations in which they are portrayed, have long been considered fictitious characters.[22] The topography of the narrative, which establishes the solidity of the city in the *Journal*, has also been checked and found accurate.[23]

The veracity of the *Journal* is not merely a matter of abstract statistics and identification of people mentioned in it.

22. For a detailed study and further references, see Bastian, "Defoe's Journal," pp. 156–60.
23. Manuel Sconhorn, "Defoe's *Journal of the Plague Year:* Topography and Intention," *Review of English Studies*, n.s. 19 (1968), 387–402.

The urban environment is captured by recording elements of popular culture and lore. A number of advertisements, all exploiting the fears of the less-informed citizens, are reproduced in the *Journal.* They include ads for over-the-counter medicine:

INFALLIBLE preventive pills against the plague. [p. 30]

INCOMPARABLE drink against the plague, never found out before. [p. 30]

THE ROYAL-ANTIDOTE against all kinds of infection. [p. 30]

Also there are advertisements by "doctors":

An eminent High Dutch *physician, newly come over from* Holland, *where he resided during all the Time of the great plague last year in* Amsterdam, *and cured multitudes of people that actually had the plague upon them.* [p. 30]

An experienc'd Physician, who has long studied the Doctrine of Antidotes against all Sorts of Poison and Infection, has after 40 Years Practise, arrived to such, as may, with God's Blessing, direct Persons how to prevent their being touch'd by any Contagious Distemper whatsoever. He directs the Poor gratis. [p. 31]

To the poor, however, they give only their "advice" for nothing; for their "physic," they charge a very high price. The psychology of the people during the plague is revealed by the *Journal* in its detailing of their new interest in charms, philtres, exorcisms, amulets, signs of the zodiac, papers tied up with so many knots, and words or figures written on them:

```
A B R A C A D A B R A
A B R A C A D A B R
A B R A C A D A B
A B R A C A D A
A B R A C A D
A B R A C A
A B R A C
A B R A
A B R
A B
A
```

[p. 33]

Such interests resemble the contemporary preoccupation with astrology in times when the arbitrary rationale of events is sought in the paralogic of the occult. Although the elements of popular culture are not as easily verifiable as the identities of persons, the locations of buildings, or the authenticity of statistics and documents, they are "Specimen" from which one may "apprise any one of the Humour of those Times" (p. 31).

The second field of meaning, the area of internal reference, is created by the felt reality which is evoked by the documents and the fiction flowing from the fabulous facts. "Feelings," Alfred Alvarez has written about another form of the writing of consciousness in crisis, "are so fiercely present in the barest recital of the facts that any attempt to elaborate, underline or explain them seems like wild overstatement." [24]

To render the atmosphere of doom in a metropolis where people are dying by the thousands and the foundation of moral, social, and religious institutions is breaking down, Defoe uses a technique of transcribing what he calls "speaking sights"—the fictive resonance of discontinuous facts. The presence of death is felt throughout the city with the rumble of death carts, and heard in the bellman's shout: "Bring out your Dead." And the "shrieks of women and children at windows and doors of their houses, where their dearest relations were perhaps dying or just dead," are echoed in the streets where nothing is to be seen but "wagons and carts with goods, women, servants, children &c.; coaches filled with people of better sort, and horsemen attending them and all hurrying away." The enemy is invisible and attacks without warning: ". . . sometimes a man or woman dropped down dead in the very markets, for many people that had the plague upon them knew nothing of it till the inward gangrene had affected their vitals, and they died in a few moments." Chaos is so predominant that the very moral fabric of the community is coming apart; nurses put wet cloths upon the faces of dying patients or smother, starve, medically mistreat, and rob them. The plague-

24. Alvarez, "The Literature of the Holocaust," p. 66.

stricken are imprisoned in their houses, domestic animals are killed, "forty thousand dogs, and five times as many cats." The exposure of the fictivity of the "real" through the mapping of the actual is nowhere more successful than in the nocturnal visit of H.F. to the burial pit in Aldgate, where he describes the misery of a man witnessing the burial of his wife and several children:

> He mourned heartily, as it was easy to see, but with a kind of Masculine Grief, that could not give it self Vent by Tears, and calmly desiring the Buriers to let him alone, said he would only see the Bodies thrown in, and go away . . . but no sooner was the Cart turned round, and the Bodies shot into the Pit promiscuously, which was a Surprize to him, for he at least expected they would have been decently laid in . . . no sooner did he see the Sight, but he cry'd out aloud unable to contain himself . . . he went backward two or three Steps, and fell down in a Swoon. . . . He look'd into the Pit again, as he went away, but the Buriers had covered the Bodies so immediately with throwing in Earth, that tho' there was Light enough, for there were Lanterns and Candles in them, plac'd all Night round the Sides of the Pit, upon the Heaps of Earth, seven or eight, or perhaps more, yet nothing could be seen.

The nucleus of fact in this scene generates a dark fiction.

The two fields of meaning, the actual and the fictional, are not, of course, two layers of structure. The total experience of the book involves a simultaneous grasping of the internal flowing fiction of the narrative and the mapping of the raw external actualities. The two areas operate at the same time on the intellective and emotive faculties of the reader and prevent a one-dimensional response: either an escapist reaction which would read the book as a series of gothic anecdotes, or a documentarian response which would see the book as raw material for a social history. The bi-referential nature of the *Journal* will perhaps become clearer if one compares the book with two mono-referential works about the plague. Walter Bell's *The Great Plague in London in 1665* is a historical treatment, a work which examines available documents, to reach the "truth" behind the data. Camus's *The Plague,* on the other hand, is a fictive novel about a plague-stricken city which starts with the private "truth" of the artist and then, to make that private "vision" a universal, shared reality, uses *plague* as a metaphor. In its thematic and structural configuration of experience, *The Plague* becomes an allegory about the human condition. Defoe, although very much influenced by the intellectual forces of his time which were trying to discover the causes of the plague in a theological interpretation of the "visitation" or in some rationalistic explanation, seeks neither to impose an interpretation on the disaster nor to discover its ultimate causes.[25] As a nonfiction novel with modal duality, the *Journal* enacts the ambivalence in the experience. In *Due Preparations for the Plague as Well for Soul as Body,* which Defoe published about two months before the *Journal,* he used a mono-referential mode and a didactic tone to discuss the cause and cure of the plague. He came to the *Journal* knowing full well that the only way to deal with a disaster like the plague, which dislodges the established pattern of response and transfers consciousness to a fictual zone of experience, is not to impose a pattern or aim at truth, but to register the "speaking sights."

The nonfiction novel with its balance of the actual and the fictional is a very vulnerable genre. Lack of compositional equilibrium can easily turn a nonfiction novel into an unsuccessful historical novel, an unimaginative fictive narrative, a book of routine reportage, or some other form of mono-referential narrative. This balance, even when sufficiently achieved, varies among members of the genre. To formalize this modal gradation, I introduced (in Chapter 3) the concept of "angle of reference." Defoe's *Journal,* for example, leans more on the external world than Hersey's *Hiroshima,* and thus has an obtuse angle of external reference. The factual in the *Journal* is not compositionally bal-

25. See also W. Austin Flanders, "Defoe's Journal of the Plague Year and the Modern Urban Experience," *Centennial Review,* 16 (1972), 347; and Everett Zimmerman, "H.F.'s Meditations: *A Journal of the Plague Year,*" *PMLA,* 87 (1972), 417–23.

anced with the fictional, but the book keeps its dual mode of reference throughout. An example of a book unbalanced in the opposite direction is William Styron's *The Confessions of Nat Turner.*

In his "Author's Note," Styron shows his awareness of the generic aspects of his book, and, in anticipation of questions they may raise, calls the book "less an 'historical novel' in conventional terms than *a meditation on history*" (emphasis added).[26] The difficulty of finding appropriate terms with which to comment on "a meditation on history" and its generic status, even at the level of book reviewing, led one journal of opinion to commission two reviews of the book. One reviewer was to regard the book as a literary work of art, the other to discuss it as history. Both were published in the same issue.[27] This critical schizophrenia is symptomatic of the bipolar theories of fiction—the crude division of all prose narrative into the fictional and factual.

In its attempt to retrieve the facts of the past events, *The Confessions of Nat Turner* resembles some of the prose narratives referred to in this study as nonfiction novels. A few critics, relying on the superficial similarities, have mentioned such books as Mailer's *The Armies of the Night* and Capote's *In Cold Blood* in connection with Styron's work.[28] Melvin J. Friedman, in his review essay, *"The Confessions of Nat Turner:* The Convergence of 'Nonfiction Novel' and 'Meditation on History,' "* asserts that Styron "might have used, with some appropriateness, Capote's coinage 'nonfiction novel.' "[29] Friedman's reasons for such a comparison, however, are critically unconvincing: the two books are similar, he argues, because Styron has done his homework and has "scrupulously consulted his sources as Capote did before him."[30]

26. William Styron, *The Confessions of Nat Turner* (New York: Random House, 1968), p. xi.

27. See *The Nation,* Oct. 16, 1967, pp. 373–74 and pp. 375–76.

28. David D. Galloway, *The Absurd Hero in American Fiction,* rev. ed. (Austin: University of Texas Press, 1970), p. xix.

29. Melvin J. Friedman, *"The Confessions of Nat Turner:* The Convergence of 'Nonfiction Novel' and 'Meditation on History,' "* *Journal of Popular Culture,* 1 (1967), 168.

30. Ibid.

The generic identity of a nonfiction novel is not deter-mined by mere effort in retrieving past events or examining sources; these are interests which some fictive novels and factual narratives share with the exegetical nonfiction novel. The important factor—to repeat the point again—is the manner in which facts are used in a narrative, and not the mere presence of facts in a narrative. Styron has tried to write a modally complex work to deal with the inherent complexity of his subject, but the result is a book very close to a mono-referential narrative—a fictive novel which is based on an historical happening. In terms of the poetics outlined above, *The Confessions of Nat Turner* does not have the "right angle" of reference; its angle of internal refer-ence is obtuse to the degree of turning the whole narrative into a single field of fiction. Styron himself seems to be aware of the nature of his work when, in an interview, he explains: ". . . the book is an actual happening. There were guide lines I could follow all the way. *I had to flesh the mate-rial out . . .*" (emphasis added).[31] He has carried this pro-cess of "fleshing out" to an extreme, since *The Confessions* (especially section II, "Old Times Past," and section III, "Sunday War") is essentially a mono-referential fictive novel. In its "fictionalization" of events, it is not unlike Jo-seph Wambaugh's *The Onion Field* (1973), although the lat-ter, perhaps partly because of its temporal proximity with its subject, is closer to the actualities.

Like other fictive novels, *The Confessions of Nat Turner* tries to impose upon the events of the past a private vision or in-terpretation: the view that slavery in the United States was essentially a benevolent institution. To support such a view, Styron turns the *person* of Nat Turner into a *character* and a "stock" one at that. Nat is made to be the product of a "typi-cal" unstable Negro family who, in order to grow up men-tally, needs the help of the "significant others"—the whites, generous Marse Samuel and his family. Nat has a twisted sexual life: in the narrative Styron fails to mention his slave wife but instead attributes to him homosexual tendencies on

31. Interviewed by Phyllis Mears, *Saturday Review*, Oct. 7, 1967, p. 30.

one hand and lust for the white flesh of a southern belle on the other. In a curious way, the repressed desires of Nat for Margaret Whitehead, the only person that Nat finds himself capable of killing, are related to his social rebellion, which is primarily explained away by psychologism. My intention here is not to list historical inaccuracies or to comment on the loaded incidents invented by what Ernest Kaiser calls Styron's "vile racist imagination" to support the white liberals' view of slavery.[32] And the crucial question is not whether Styron has distorted a few "facts" here and there (as, according to Philip K. Tompkins, Truman Capote has done in *In Cold Blood*).[33] Styron has conceived the whole history of the revolt of Nat Turner within a totalizing frame and then has used scattered facts to support that total vision. As a result, a fictional logic dominates the book. The obtuse angle of internal reference and lack of balanced focusing deprive *The Confessions of Nat Turner* of the existential inevitability of a nonfiction novel. This judgment, of course, does not exclude the possibility of reading the book as a successful historical novel or a fictive narrative.

An essentially right angle of reference is maintained between two zones of experience in Truman Capote's *In Cold Blood,* one of the achieved nonfiction novels written in the postwar years. The book evokes, through an exploration of the actual, the myths shaping contemporary consciousness. By mapping the visible surfaces, Capote sustains the tension between the factual and the fictional, and manages to capture in the modal ambiguity of the narrative the inherent complexity of contemporary reality. In Capote's book, the blurring of boundaries and its agonizing effects on communal consciousness in a small American town are formalized with such intensity and precision that the actual reverberates with and echoes the mythic. Holcomb, Kansas, is ex-

32. Ernest Kaiser, "The Failure of William Styron," in *William Styron's Nat Turner: Ten Black Writers Respond,* ed. J. H. Clarke (Boston: Beacon Press, 1967), p. 57. See also Seymour L. Gross and Eileen Bender, "History, Politics and Literature: The Myth of Nat Turner," *American Quarterly* 23 (1971), 487–518.

33. See Philip K. Tompkins, "In Cold Fact," *Esquire,* June 1966, pp. 125, 127, 166–71; and William Stafford's poem, "Holcomb, Kansas," in *Allegiances* (New York: Harper and Row, 1970), p. 6.

plored so thoroughly that the smallest details of everyday life begin to reveal their interior space and complexity until each sign becomes a symbol, and the usual distinction between the literal and the metaphorical, the happened and the imagined, the fact and fiction, vanishes. The town itself gradually loses its geographical solidity and becomes an emblem of quintessential America, where what happens is less a random murder than a collision between the forces and ideas which have shaped the American Dream and "a certain [amount of nothing]" in the "dream deferred." The narrative energy of the book is generated by that formative force which Capote thinks is "so awfully inevitable about what is going to happen: the people in the book are completely beyond their own control." [34]

In Cold Blood opens with a graphic description of "out there"—a lonesome area on the high wheat plains of Kansas that forms the topography of the narrative. Although the area has a literal existence outside the book, it also becomes a metaphorical place where the facts of this bizarre event assume a universal resonance. Holcomb lies about seventy miles east of the Colorado border, home to people who are "quite content to exist inside ordinary life—to work, to hunt, to watch television, to attend school socials, choir practice, meetings of the 4-H club." The first part of the book, "The Last to See Them Alive," is, in essence, a testing of the thinness of the security and contentment of those who lack the inner resources to confront untamed reality.

An alien reality, symbolized by the two strangers who stealthily enter the village in the darkness of the night, shatters the life routine of the village and creates an almost communal psychosis. The rural innocence of the people, evoking the lost innocence of America, is violated by the urban experience of the two strangers who finally kill Mr. Clutter—the epitome of the values and attitudes of the community—and his entire family. The shotgun blasts echo the collision of "desperate, savage, violent America" with "sane, safe, insular, even smug America," of "people who have

34. George Plimpton, "The Story behind a Nonfiction Novel," *New York Times Book Review*, Jan. 16, 1966, p. 43.

every chance" and "people who have none."[35] The incident is so bizarre that, as Paul Levine observes, it seems to come straight out of the world of contemporary fiction.[36] The trust, confidence, and assurance of the small community is so destroyed that "old neighbors" are now viewed as "strangers" and people cannot look at each other "without kind of wondering!" Fear paralyzes people's self-confidence and upsets their life pattern. In the village, at night, one now sees: "windows ablaze, almost every window in almost every house, and, in the brightly lit rooms, fully clothed people, even entire families, who had sat the whole night wide awake, watchful, listening." Holcomb has become a crisis city: a state of existence reflecting contemporary America, which, having failed to cope with emerging urban reality, is immersed in a total communal fear, estrangement, and paranoia.

The force of the collision and the subsequent emotional paralysis of the village are captured by the technique of "synchronic narration." After a short topographical description of Holcomb in the first section, the next sixteen sections of Part I focus alternately on the last day of the Clutters and on the progress of the killers toward their home. The intermingling of the two systems of actemes continues throughout the narrative and, consequently, sustains an inscriptional suspense. Moreover, the "synchronic narration" in *In Cold Blood,* as well as in other nonfiction novels, permits measurable, chronological clock time, not the dramatically heightened interior time of Modernist fiction, to be the main organizing device. In these early sections, Capote narrates the events in a chronological order. The intercutting of actemes enacts the contingency of experience, the unsuspected collision of events. While the Clutters prepare for the Thanksgiving reunion and their daughter Beverly's approaching wedding, Perry Smith and Richard Hickock contemplate the type of rope and tape most suitable for tying and gagging them.

35. Truman Capote, quoted by George Garrett, in "Crime and Punishment in Kansas: Truman Capote's *In Cold Blood," Hollins Critic,* 3 (Feb. 1966), 4.

36. Paul Levine, "Reality and Fiction," *Hudson Review,* 19 (1966), 135.

The last day in the life of the Clutters, a retrieving of events which actually took place on November 14, 1959, bears an uncanny resemblance to June 16, 1904, the day in *Ulysses* in which Joyce condensed a whole universe. In Joyce's narrative, the human condition is totalized through the invention of a fictive paradigm; in Capote's book, the actuality itself is registered, and the visible surface reveals the fictuality of a day's life. Details of the Clutter family life during this day are subjected to an exegesis, which reveals, without any intervention from the writer's inventive imagination, the symbolic resonance of each act. Nancy helps a little girl bake a cherry pie; Mrs. Clutter, during a conversation with the little girl, reveals her deeply troubled mind; Kenyon goes about his routine life of making things, and Mr. Clutter, among other things, provides for the family's future by purchasing "a forty-thousand-dollar policy that in the event of death by accidental means, paid double indemnity." These actions are typical of the family which, according to one town resident, "represented everything people hereabouts really value and respect." The annihilation of such a family creates a vacuum: "It's like being told there is no God," says one local observer.

Mr. Clutter is a prosperous farmer, familiar with the latest technological advancements in his field, practical-minded, an active participant in community affairs, with deep social and religious commitments. He has served as a member of the Federal Farm Credit Board, although, tied to home and the soil as he is, he has not actually lived in Washington, D.C. The city is the fearful unknown. Physically he cuts a "man's man figure," with broad shoulders and a confident face which "retains a healthy youthfulness." He enjoys harmonious relations with his children, who are happy and have either settled down or are preparing to do so. Nancy, his youngest daughter, is the "town darling." He hopes that his son, Kenyon, who presently "leans toward being an engineer or a scientist," will eventually prove a "born rancher" and run the River Valley Farm. He is "real proud" of his children.

The happiness of the Clutters, as it turns out, is more a

veneer than a deep, richly rooted, inner peace. Mrs. Clutter almost symbolically represents the sensitive soul estranged, unable to conform with the stiff-necked culture all around her. Her dissatisfaction with purely materialistic and pragmatic values is reflected in an inward rebellion which manifests itself in the form of what the Clutter family and their friends euphemistically refer to as "little nervous spells." Tellingly enough, the source of her difficulty in adjusting to the surrounding life is believed to be not in her "head" but in her "spine"—in the physical. However, in order to regain her "old self," she must undergo an "operation." Adjustment has brought her a social "maturity" which has "reduced her voice to a single tone, that of apology," and a personality now nothing but "a series of gestures blurred by the fear that she might give offense." Husband and wife have two different paths: his is "a public route, a march of satisfying conquests," but hers "a private one that eventually [winds] through hospital corridors."

Fear and inner tension are by no means characteristic of only Mrs. Clutter. To the amazement of her close friend Susan, Nancy Clutter implies in a telephone conversation that Mr. Clutter himself is "finding secret solace in tobacco." The human indifference hidden in the work ethic so zealously adhered to by Mr. Clutter is exposed by Mrs. Clutter's remark that her husband "cares more for those trees than he does for his children." The unjustified rigidity of such a morality is graphically commented upon by Lynn Russell, a friend of Mr. Clutter, when discussing his attitudes toward hired hands: "You've got no mercy. I swear, Herb, if you caught a hired man drinking, out he'd go. And you wouldn't care if his family was starving."

Mr. Clutter, who publicly stands for family life, is himself denied the private sharing of any nourishing emotional intimacy. The gnawing contraries of his seemingly fulfilled life surface when we learn that he does not share the same bedroom with his wife. There is some speculation that another woman might have been involved in his private life. His affection for his family is, one suspects, more a matter of public respect than felt personal attachment.

Nancy reveals a facile mind satisfied with excuses rather than reasons. She professes love for her boyfriend Bobby, but is more than willing to give him up just because her father thinks that Bobby's different religion is incompatible with a happy marriage. She too suffers inward anxiety which becomes visible in her habit of biting her fingernails.

After the first part of *In Cold Blood* examines the lives of the Clutters, the remaining three parts register the lives and backgrounds of the actants, Perry Smith and Richard Hickock. The registration takes various forms: letters, confessions, autobiographical sketches, and interviews during which they talk about themselves to an "acquaintance" or a "journalist"—a device Capote uses to keep himself out of the main flow of the narrative.

The very values which have shaped the Clutter family life of public fulfillment and interior emptiness have also shaped the life-style of their killers. They are in a real sense the incarnation of the darker side of the Middle American psyche, the side inhibited and exiled from the consciousness which perceives and reacts to everyday reality. They represent the unacknowledged inner anxieties which, like canker, eat up the private life of the Clutters. The same cultural values which endow the Clutters with wealth and public security prevent the human development of the abilities of Perry and Richard, and deny them any personal fulfillment. The antagonism, if one may describe the relationship between the Clutters and their murderers as such, is quite impersonal, more the result of unresolved problems of a culture in its totality than a conscious effort by two outsiders to eliminate those who symbolize the oppressive forces. Perry perhaps refers to this impersonal clash of eruptive forces when, in a conversation with Donald Cullivan, his only visitor at the prison, he emphasizes that: "They [the Clutters] never hurt me. . . . Maybe it's just that the Clutters were the ones who had to pay for it." The collision is so tragically inevitable: "I thought he was a very nice gentleman. Soft spoken. I thought so right up to the moment I cut his throat."

Unlike Herb Clutter and his family, Perry Smith is

marked with spontaneity, intuition, and an emotional response to life. The dream of freedom and escape activates
his life, which is otherwise "an ugly and lonely progress
toward one mirage and then another." He is "an incessant
conceiver of voyages," a collector of maps of faraway lands,
a man whose recurring dream is that of the journey back, "a
dream of drifting downward through strange waters, of
plunging toward a green sea-dusk, sliding past scaly,
savage-eyed protectors—a drowned cargo of diamonds and
pearls, heaping caskets of gold." He is the Knight of the
Seas who is maimed. Despite his underwater reveries and
much talk about skin-diving, he has never entered the water
and cannot swim; his short legs were badly injured in a motorcycle accident. Perry is the man-child outsider; a half-
breed Cherokee; a bed-wetter, with legs too short for his
torso: "when he stood up he was no taller than a twelve year
old child." He is arational in his reaction to outside reality
and works his way through life by hunches and intuitions.

The dream of escape from anonymity, poverty, and loneliness fantasized in locating sunken treasures, searching for
his father, and being rescued by the "big yellow bird" are
all manifestations of the suppressed forces in the public
dream of the Clutters—the successful, homebound, prosperous, and rational citizens. Perry's private dream vanishes
in the blinding light of the realities recalled by Richard:
". . . wake up, little boy. There ain't caskets of gold. No
sunken ship. And even if there was—hell, you can't even
swim," but another method of escape, suicide, replaces them
in his musings. His frustrations have turned him into an ap-
athetic person, fascinated by Richard because of his own
self-hatred.

Richard is Perry's anti-self. Perry is the poet, conceiving
of the outside world in terms of a network of metaphors
and dreams; Richard is "very literal-minded," having "no
understanding of music or poetry." Richard's very pragma-
tism and literalness make him seem the authentically tough
and "totally masculine" person to Perry. Richard likes to
think of himself as a quite normal person looking for a
" 'regular life' with a business of his own, a house, a horse to

ride, a new car and 'plenty of blonde chicken.' " His preoccupation with normality creates fear and guilt that his sexual predilection for little girls may be found out. He is callous and also brutalized by his life experiences; he runs
down dogs as a hobby. Both Perry and Richard are smashed
in accidents on the road—roads which were supposed to
take them "away, away from here." They are the refugees
of the American Dream.

Perry's inner life, his background, and his attitude toward
the external world are all conveyed in the narrative through
a number of documents. Capote shuns internal analysis and
such Modernist techniques as interior monologue. The
method of informing the reader is similar to the way the
reader as a real person in his or her own life gathers information about other people: external observations and statements made by the people themselves or their friends, relatives, and acquaintances. We learn about Perry's life from
his father's letter to the State of Kansas,[37] his sister's letter
to him in prison (pp. 138–42), comments on this letter made
by Willie-Jay (pp. 143–45), Don Cullivan's letter (pp.
260–61), Perry's own autobiographical sketch (pp. 273–76),
and Dr. Jones's psychiatric evaluation (pp. 296–98). The author refrains from any analysis himself; he merely acquires
the appropriate documents and inserts them in the narrative. The same method is employed in discussing the life
and ideas of the Clutter family and Richard. There are
numerous interviews, testimonies, and statements in the
book, but documentation in *In Cold Blood* is mostly covert in
the text.

Through documentation and the insertion of such verifiable information as the names of persons, cities, hotels, or
references to publications (the paper by Dr. Satten in *The
American Journal of Psychiatry*, July 1960), Capote authenti-
cates his narrative. The documents, which are the self-
verifying apparatus of the narrative, form a pole of external
reference in the book and point outside the narrative to the
actual world. But what emerges from the registration of

37. Truman Capote, *In Cold Blood* (New York: Random House, 1966), pp.
125–30. Subsequent page references to this edition will appear in the text.

facts is a narrative charged with fictive resonance. The relationship between Perry, the dark-skinned half-Indian, and Richard, the white male devoid of any mature and sustained heterosexual love, the obsession of at least one of them with death, and the latent, innocent homosexuality embedded in their friendship echoes the archetypal pattern which Leslie Fiedler has discovered in American fiction.[38] Of the archetypal pattern in *In Cold Blood,* Fiedler has said: ". . . a white man and an Indian are walking down the road together. There's a gun someplace in the picture and one beast or another is going to get killed, the two favorite beasts of America, a grizzly bear and a white woman, a clean white girl in the case of Truman Capote's book." [39] The pattern of the killers' relationship in *In Cold Blood,* a transcription of an actual friendship between two persons, bears an unmistakable resemblance not only to the fictive patterning of relationships in such contemporary novels as Mailer's *Why Are We in Vietnam?* but also to such classic American fictions as *The Adventures of Huckleberry Finn.* In Capote's bi-referential narrative, the fictive and the factual are no longer valid categories. The mythos develops out of actemes and points to an area of experience which is meta-fictional, meta-factual.

The writer of a nonfiction novel, unlike the fictionist, does not "father" a fictional universe, but is merely the "midwife" of experiential reality: he or she attempts to find the appropriate technical means to assist the verbal birth of a segment of reality, However, as I have written in Chapter 1, the nature of man's perception of the outside world and the nonfiction novelist's need to use language, which is the depository of communal values, inevitably create in the nonfiction novel a view of reality. Such a view is "local" and is epistemologically different from the "global" *Weltanschauung* of the totalizing novel. Capote cannot transcribe everything which has happened; the necessities of his me-

38. Leslie Fiedler, *Love and Death in the American Novel,* rev. ed. (New York: Stein and Day, 1966).

39. Leslie Fiedler, "Wrestling (American Style) with Proteus," *Novel,* 3 (1970), 206. See also Fiedler's *The Return of the Vanishing American* (New York: Stein and Day, 1968), p. 14.

dium, which prevent durational realism, force him to select.

The type of distortions that the limitations of the medium impose on the nonfiction novel is illustrated by the ending of *In Cold Blood*. Part of the fault in the ending, of course, is Capote's. Faced with the necessity of bringing the narrative to an end, he falls back on his habits as a novelist. Tony Tanner has observed that the ending would have been "regarded as pretty cheap and sentimental" if the book were a "plain novel." [40] Vladimir Nabokov has also objected to the ending: "I like some of Truman Capote's stuff, particularly *In Cold Blood*. Except for that impossible ending, so sentimental, so false." [41] My point is that the falseness of the ending of *In Cold Blood,* as of other nonfiction novels, including Norman Mailer's *The Armies of the Night,* goes beyond the clumsy handling of a technical problem by a particular author. It is more "ontological" than "compositional" and is connected to the all-important question of closure in the nonfiction novel. Any ending in such narratives will be to a certain degree "false," since an ending is an arbitrary and artificial but required imposition of a medium on the uninterruptable flow of life, whose movements the nonfiction novel follows.[42] The closing of such unimagined narratives, in other words, works against the open-endedness which informs the body of the narrative and life itself.

One of the important elements of the "imaginal" component of Capote's nonfiction novel is its narrative point of view, which is largely responsible for the narrative's "architectonics." An examination of the narrative point of view in *In Cold Blood* will clarify the manner in which the nonfiction novelist transcribes reality without imposing a personal vision upon it, since point of view is basically a variable of the writer's relationship with reality in his narrative. The point of view in *In Cold Blood* corresponds to what is traditionally referred to as "omniscient." A contradiction seems to arise between the intention of the nonfiction novel and the point

---

40. Tony Tanner, "Death in Kansas," *The Spectator*, March 18, 1966, p. 332.

41. "Checking in with Vladimir Nabokov," *Esquire*, July 1975, p. 133.

42. I am not dealing here with "closure" in the totalizing fictive novel, which is a function of a completely different set of variants.

of view adopted in *In Cold Blood:* what is the legitimacy of the use of the seemingly totalizing omniscient point of view in a nontotalizing narrative? Early in the narrative, when Capote relates the events of the Clutters' last day, he quotes Mr. Clutter's talk with the pheasant hunters from Oklahoma who are offering him hunting fees. Mr. Clutter refuses the money: "I'm not as poor as I look. Go ahead, get all you can." Then we hear the voice of the omniscient narrator interrupting the flow of narrative to add: "Then touching the brim of his cap, he headed for home and the day's work, *unaware that it would be his last*" (p. 13, emphasis added). When speaking of Nancy Clutter, Capote mentions in parentheses that the dress he is describing will later be the dress she is buried in. The question here is, of course, the question of authority: how does the nonfiction novelist, who records events as they unfold, know that a particular day is the last day in a person's life or that a certain dress will later be the burial dress? A Dickens knows such facts because he is the god of his universe. Though the point of view used in *In Cold Blood* resembles the omniscient point of view employed in *Our Mutual Friend, Middlemarch,* and many other fictive novels, the omniscience which informs a nonfiction novel is based on the writer's thorough research, rather than on his or her imaginative authority. In other words, the omniscient point of view of *In Cold Blood* is an "empirical omniscience." Truman Capote knows that Nancy Clutter will be buried in a particular dress, and so informs his reader, because he has learned it through his research.

While the fictive novelist's authority for shaping and presenting his reality through his control of the point of view is his totalization of the experiential *donnée,* the authority of the nonfiction novelist is obtained through exegesis of his *données.* In using "empirical omniscience" in *In Cold Blood,* the all-knowing author substantiates his authority by weaving the narrative web from interviews, official documents, autobiographical sketches, and even the article in the learned journal.

Ironically enough, the source of concern for the reader of *In Cold Blood* is less the intrusive voice of the author than some of the events recorded in the book. Mr. Clutter, for example, buys an insurance policy with double indemnity on the day which proves to be his last. Perry and Richard are arrested just after withdrawing from the post office the box containing the boots that matched the footprints left at the Clutter house. Such events seem contrived, but life is the contriver; it hands the author coincidences no fictive novelists would dare invent today. Can one be critical of "plot" probabilities for true events? The very concept of "plot," as I have suggested earlier, will have to be replaced by the concept of "acteme."

The events of a nonfiction novel are known beforehand, so the nonfiction novelist has very little use for the conventional "situational suspense" which sustains a fictive novel. Instead of "situational suspense" (suspense based on unknown events and new turns of the story), the nonfiction novel offers "inscriptional suspense." To build such suspense, Capote does not invent new incidents but dwells on the details of the existing ones. The "irony" in *In Cold Blood* is also derived from the bizarre permutations of events and not from the writer's imagination. When, in recording the last day of Mr. Clutter, Capote mentions Clutter's conversation with Mr. Johnson, the insurance man, and quotes Johnson's remark, "Why, Herb, you're a *young* man. Forty-eight. And from the looks of you, from what the medical reports tell us, we're likely to have you around a couple of weeks more," he is recording such an empirical irony.

In Cold Blood uses a modally complex narrative to capture an event which is inherently ambiguous and so bizarre that it cannot be categorized as either factual or fictional by our current epistemological standards. The event has occurred and thus qualifies as factual, but the factual is enveloped by the atmosphere and ambiance of the fictional. The sense of wonder and puzzlement is clearly reflected in the behavior of the experienced chief detective, Alvin Dewey, who in many ways represents the common sense of the community. Having heard the confessions of Perry and Richard, he is disappointed because "the confessions failed to satisfy his sense of meaningful design."

A factual or a fictional solution would have distorted the event by simplifying it. The actemes can be revealed, not resolved. Capote has combined the power of art with the authority of facts to write an anti-illusionist narrative about what Norman Mailer in *The Presidential Papers* calls the double life of the Americans, "one visible, the other underground." On one level, the life is "concrete, factual, practical, and unbelievably dull." But also present is "a subterranean river of untapped, ferocious, lonely and romantic desire, that concentration of ecstasy and violence which is the dream life of the nation." [43] Capote refuses a fictional logic, and forces the reader to confront these two zones of experience through his fictual narrative.

Hersey, Capote, and the other exegetical nonfiction novelists, haunted by the stubborn facts of a past event which does not yield itself to a fictional treatment and is not energetically mapped by a factual retelling, try to restore the inner tension and ambiguity of the event by employing a narrative with dual mode. Rejecting an illusionist concept of art, they write narratives of judgment which remind the reader of their authenticity by documentation and force the reader to confront the fictuality of experiential reality.

43. Norman Mailer, *The Presidential Papers* (New York: G. P. Putnam's Sons, 1963), p. 38.

five
The Contingent *Donnée:*
The Testimonial
Nonfiction Novel

The "monumental disproportions" of events—to use
Norman Mailer's comment on his own eyewitness stance in
The Armies of the Night—have aroused suspicions about the
epistemological authority of any omniscient interpreter of
reality. In contemporary writing, "The literary tones are
those of voices paying witness to the fantastic." [1] The dominance of the testimonial narrative situation in recent American literature manifests a "common sense of crisis and a
common feeling of having been conned about it." [2] The
witness stance assumes that the only authority on appearance and existence is the witness himself—a kind of solipsism imposed on the contemporary consciousness by fabulous reality. By adopting this narrative posture, the
nonfiction novelist further rejects the very notion of a monolithic, separable reality beyond sense experience which
might be discovered through the patterning of life impressions or the exercise of the fictive imagination. The testimonial nonfiction novel, in other words, enacts the epistemological belief that in an extreme situation the only
authentic way to deal with outside phenomena is to report
them as they register themselves on one's participating
senses.

This participation has seemed to many critics an active,
personal interference with events and an implicit, private
totalization of reality which charges the neutral actuality

1. Jack Hicks, *Cutting Edges: Young American Fiction for the 70's* (New York: Holt,
Rinehart and Winston, 1973), p. xix.
2. See Theodore Solotaroff's editorial in *New American Review,* No. 5 (1969), pp.
1–2, 271.

with values and meaning. However, the nature of the involvement of the witness participant in this type of nonfiction novel differs from the conventional fictive eyewitness narrative situation. In the testimonial nonfiction novel, the participation is "instrumental," not "projectional": although a person participates in events and reports in his own individual voice from the inside circle of action, the ensuing subjectivity is that of the involved people themselves, not a "projection" of the writer's personal feeling onto them for the purpose of totalizing the experience. The witness-participant-narrator is more a medium, an instrument, an articulating voice through which the interiority of events experienced by people is registered. Tom Wolfe compares such a participant narrator to a "method actor"—one who gets inside the emotions and passions of people, rather than projecting his own emotions into them. "It is a matter," he maintains, "not of projecting your emotions into the story but of getting inside the emotions, inside the subjective reality of the people you are writing about." [3] The witness-narrator usually maps the interior landscape of the psyche by means of intensive "saturation reporting" and long periods of living with, talking to, and observing his subjects. Chapter XXI of Tom Wolfe's *The Electric Kool-Aid Acid Test* is an extended "interior monologue." The interiority, however, is Ken Kesey's. The witness-narrator Tom Wolfe serves only as an instrument through which Kesey's mind registers its feelings, fears, and flow of sensations. The chapter is "constructed completely from diaries, letters, tapes, and interviews with Kesey." [4] John Sack's *m* is a nonfictive narrative almost entirely in the form of "interior monologue" which follows a company through its tour of duty in Vietnam. Sack also serves as a reflecting instrument which registers the soldiers emotions.

3. Tom Wolfe, in the *Bulletin of the American Society of Newspaper Editors* (Sept. 1970), p. 22.
4. Quoted from a letter by Tom Wolfe to the author. See also the interview with Tom Wolfe in *The New Fiction*, ed. Joe David Bellamy (Urbana: University of Illinois Press, 1974), p. 85; and "Author's Note" in *The Electric Kool-Aid Acid Test* (New York: Farrar, Straus and Giroux, 1968) in which Wolfe explains his method of composition.

The degree of participation of the witness in the actions he registers varies from total immersion (*The Armies of the Night*) to detached observation (*The Electric Kool-Aid Acid Test*): in briefer terms, from "generator" to "reflector" of feelings. The two roles are closely related in *Armies*, where Mailer is both "generator" and "reflector" of reported actions and emotions. Significantly, the ideas and acts of Mailer the "generator" of events are registered by Mailer the "reflector" of events from a third-person point of view. This narrational schizophrenia of *Armies* is in itself a direct acting out of the schizoid nature of the actualities in which Mailer is trapped. Here we see another instance of the differences between modernist and supramodernist aesthetics. Modernist poetics requires that the schizophrenic reality be stylized from a proper aesthetic distance: you do not behave like a schizophrenic if you are trying to write about the schizoid behavior of reality or its agents. In supramodern literature, Yvor Winters's "imitative fallacy" is in fact an operative aesthetic principle.[5] What most critics have found objectionable in Wolfe's stylistic devices are aspects of this principle of imitative form: attempts to approximate the haze that envelops the mental atmosphere in which persons of the book receive actuality.

The testimonial nonfiction novel, then, is the narrative of encounter between the author—the historical person whose name appears on the title page, not a fictional "second self"—and the brute psychic or physical facts. Like other types of nonfiction novel, the testimonial too relies on public records, documents, interviews, and other information sources, but, unlike the exegetical nonfiction novel, the voice of the narrator-participant-witness is one important constituent of the narrative axis of the book. Indeed in some cases the author's participation in and witnessing of the events forms in itself a kind of public document. The involvement of Norman Mailer in the March on the Pentagon, the culmination in the late 1960s of dissenting voices gathering momentum since the Civil War, is now an insepa-

---

5. Yvor Winters, "The Experimental School in American Poetry" in *In Defense of Reason* (Denver: University of Denver Press, 1947), p. 41.

rable part of the history of the March. Historians will utilize the active protest of writers such as Mailer and Lowell to describe and evaluate the postwar American public consciousness. The testimonial nonfiction novel may emphasize essentially public occurrences or the primarily private domain of experience. In either case, the belief that only the reality-tested part of actuality can be trusted by the individual informs the narrative.

Ken Kesey's bus trip across the United States in 1964 (which, as Tony Tanner observes, is in a sense his third novel,[6] an attempt like Mailer's New York City mayoral campaign "to move beyond writing" [7]) forms the central episode of Wolfe's nonfiction novel, *The Electric Kool-Aid Acid Test* (1968). Wolfe's transcription of Kesey's trip represents an attempt to deal with that zone of consciousness which emerges from the tension between the "factual" and the "fictional" levels of experience. In order to liberate themselves from the fictions imposed on their minds in the name of reality, the Merry Pranksters, as Kesey and his followers call themselves, attempt to construct a counter-reality. They neutralize a fictitious reality by releasing their wildest fantasies. The official reality in which contemporary man tries to relate to his fellows and society at large cannot endure the pressures of the live sur-fiction invented by the Pranksters. Once tested by their planned fiction, official reality collapses into fragments no less fictitious than that invented by the Pranksters. Kesey and his cohorts are aware of the nature of their actions and of the fiction they externalize with their actions. Their intention is to bring everybody into their "movie"—their own fiction—or, put another way, their own reading of reality. Once a person is brought into the "movie," he realizes the fictitiousness of the more encompassing assumptions accepted in the outside world as real-

6. Tony Tanner, *City of Words* (London: Jonathan Cape, 1971), p. 390. Kesey's latest book, *Kesey's Garage Sale* (1973), consists of reflections, poems, letters, sketches, photographs, and a screenplay. It is not a fictive novel, but an eyewitness account of Kesey's adventures during the 1960s.

7. Wolfe, *The Electric Kool-Aid Acid Test*, p. 366. Subsequent page references to this edition will appear in the text.

ity. The two "fictions" clash, the mind is freed, and the individual nears "Edge City"—the ever-expanding frontiers of consciousness. Out of the tension between the two versions of reality, the "on the bus" and "off the bus" versions, the "fictual" zone of experience emerges. Wolfe captures this area of experience in his book, which Elizabeth Hardwick calls an "extraordinary, imaginative achievement . . . one of those rare, strange books that is not like any other book." [8]

> Then I pick up my telephone and he picks up his—and this is truly Modern Times. We are all of twenty-four inches apart, but there is a piece of plate glass as thick as a telephone directory between us. We might as well be in different continents, talking over Videophone. [p. 9]

Here Tom Wolfe himself, not his fictional persona, registers his first meeting with Ken Kesey, the historical man who up to the time of this conversation had written *One Flew over the Cuckoo's Nest* (1962) and *Sometimes a Great Notion* (1964), set up an acid commune in La Honda, California, been arrested twice for possession of marijuana (April, 1965, and January, 1966), and, at the time of the phone conversation, following capture by the FBI on the Bayshore Freeway south of San Francisco, was jailed in Redwood City, San Mateo County, California. The glass-partitioned, phone-connected, first meeting of Wolfe and Kesey gradually loses its literalness and gains a metaphorical significance. Strangely charged with the horror associated with political polemics-caricature-propaganda, the scene captures in a single visual image the life of contemporary caged man, his attempt to reach out, and his final subjugation and abandonment. It could have been lifted from plays by Adamov, Ionesco, or van Itallie. Wolfe merely records the scene, and the transcription reads like an energized fiction—an absurd playlet.

Wolfe recalls this scene while waiting at the Warehouse, the Pranksters' headquarters, for the "Chief's" release. The

8. Interview by Philip Rahv with Elizabeth Hardwick, *Modern Occasions*, 2 (Spring 1972), 165.

double layer of surrounding reality is signaled here by
Wolfe's disclosure that Kesey has two names: "Chief," when
traveling to "Edge City," and "Kesey," when operating
within the circle of ordinary life. The two names are used
according to the *niveau* of meaning he is involved in. Kesey,
the "straight" successful man, and "Chief," the spiritual
guru, work like two terms of the dialects of an identity fad-
ing into a flow of actions-thoughts-feelings, partly man,
partly the projection of a mythical figure. In one of the acid
festivals Kesey appears as the "Space Man" in a silver space
suit complete with a big bubble space helmet.

The Warehouse, situated on Harriet Street, between
Howard and Folsom, is a storehouse of objects as well as
projected images and masks, a collage of the factual and fictional, a reverse image of a middle-class house, a place in
which people wearing white coveralls sewn over with American flag patches do their own things. Theater scaffolding,
curtainlike blankets, and "whole rows of uprooted theater
seats" line the walls. As the newly arrived Wolfe tries to
orient himself to this scene, a blanket curtain moves, and a
little man wearing a sort of World War 1 aviator's helmet
vaults down from a platform about nine feet high. He tells
Wolfe: "I just had an eight-year-old-boy up there." Wolfe's
new acquaintance is the "Hermit." All the Pranksters have
allegorical names, like characters in medieval morality plays.
Wolfe also meets Mountain Girl, Cool Breeze, Black Maria,
and, as if to complete the range of fictual personages, Neal
Cassady, who behaves as though he has just walked out of
On the Road. The solidity of identity begins to crack, and the
sense of "reality" recedes and merges with some version of
fantasy as Wolfe discovers in the center of the room-garage
a curious *objet d'art*: "A school bus . . . glowing orange,
green, magenta, lavender, chlorine blue, every fluorescent
pastel imaginable in thousands of designs, both large and
small, like a cross between Fernand Leger and Dr. Strange,
roaring together and vibrating off each other as if somebody had given Hieronymous Bosch fifty buckets of Day-
Glo paint and a 1939 International Harvester school bus

and told him to go to it" (p. 15). This is the bus used by the Pranksters to invade towns and cities all over the country to disturb the deep sleep of the citizens.

The registration of the trip is one of the main blocks of narrative in the book. The destination sign on the bus reads: "Furthur." From the outside, the bus looks "freaking lurid"; inside it possesses a sophisticated communications system to proclaim its message, verbally as well as visually, to the outside world (p. 69). The journey acquires the form and significance of an initiation rite into a "separate reality," a "nonordinary reality" to use Castaneda's term. An element of playfulness, however, redeems the counter-reality of the Pranksters from becoming a self-righteous, substitute reality. The Pranksters know their version of "reality" is only another "game"; although a dynamic and flowing "movie," their counter-reality is a "fiction"—another reading of reality and, as such, an imposition of a model of values on the experiential continuum. The ultimate objective is to "transcend the bullshit"—to attain self-liberation and emancipate the consciousness of others by juxtaposing charged levels of reality.

The trip moves toward the de-totalization of commonly accepted models of reality, but Wolfe's recording of this ongoing "movie" refuses to enter and totalize its de-totalization. *The Electric Kool-Aid Acid Test* maintains a complex relationship with the experiential world. Ostensibly an intimate mapping of the contours of a particular gesture by a group of people toward accepted reality, its actual informing theme is not the Pranksters' "movie" but the fictuality of contemporary experience. In the book, the two basic approaches to the external world mentioned in Chapter 1 are combined. Kesey's "movie"—his nonverbal, action novel—is an "over-totalization" of reality, a parallel fiction very much like the transfictions of Barthelme, Nabokov, Barth, Pynchon, and others. Wolfe's approach to Kesey's "movie," on the other hand, is nontotalizing. Wolfe's methodology is often similar to that of the exegetical nonfiction novel. He supplements his actual witnessing of parts of the "group adventure and personal exploration" of the Pranksters, such as the acid graduation ceremonies, with a forty-hour movie, tapes, written statements, and other records kept in the "Prankster Archives." As the book opens, the events of the past are retrieved, then the present is registered directly by Tom Wolfe, the testifier.

Through meticulous recording, the book reveals how Kesey and the Pranksters transform the trip into a collective parable. As the parable progresses, the bus, its riders, the space in which they move, all become metaphorical components of an "action allegory." Each person is fully aware of his part in a parable—not only have they gone through a baptismal rite of adopting new names, but they behave and talk as actors of the ongoing movie, literally shot by Hagen "like this was some crazed adventure in cinema verite." Kesey is the psychic force which animates the Pranksters' counter-environment. His statements, as the events unfold, become more cryptic, metaphorical, and aphoristic: "You're either on the bus or off the bus," "feed the hungry bee," "Nothing lasts," "See with your ears and hear with your eyes." Gradually they form an elaborate interpretative pattern for a metaphorical ordering of reality approaching the complexity of Yeats's extended metaphor, *A Vision.* The key concept in Kesey's thought system is "fantasy." The aim of the "fantasy" is to actualize the allegory of the trip to reach Edge City. One of the Merry Prankster signs reads: "Hail to the Edges." It symbolizes the quest for the absolute NOW which the Pranksters are trying to achieve through drugs. The only authentic mode of being is existence in the moment itself, for "any attempt to plan, compose, orchestrate, write a script, only locked you out of the moment, back in the world of conditioning and training where the brain was a reductive value." But Kesey admits there is always a sensory lag, the lag between the time your senses receive something and your reaction—one thirtieth of a second, if you're the most alert person alive—and he acknowledges that ". . . we are all of us doomed to spend our lives watching a *movie* of our lives—we are always acting on what has just finished happening." He accepts that NOW is always a movie of the past, but sees the destination as "Furthur," toward a liberated consciousness, away from one's own "snug-harbor dead center, out of the plump little game of being ersatz alive, the middle-class intellectual's game, and move out to . . . Edge City . . . where it was scary, but people were whole people." [9]

Those moving toward Edge City are "on the bus"; those trapped in what Kesey has called (in *One Flew over the Cuckoo's Nest*) the "combine" or "system" are "off the bus." The last phrase need not be taken literally. Sandy, one of the Pranksters, is physically on the bus but reserved, detached, not "out front," and therefore "off the bus." The allegorical quality of the trip and the significance of the bus metaphors are most clearly revealed in what might be called "The Boy and the Bus" exemplum:

> And in Boise they cut through a funeral or wedding or something . . . and a kid—they have tootled *his song,* and he likes it, and he runs for the bus and they all pile on and pull out, just ahead of him, and he keeps running for the bus, and Kesey keeps slowing down and then pulling out just out of his reach, six or eight blocks this way, and then they speed up for good, and they can still see him floating away in the background, his legs still running, like a preview—
> —allegory of life—
> —of the multitudes who very shortly will want to get on the bus . . . themselves. . . . [p. 114]

Those "on the bus" can formulate their own version of reality and protect themselves from other people's "movies." The term "movie" refers both to the literal forty-hour film shot by the Pranksters on their trans-American trip and to various metaphorical readings of reality. The collective parable works here too: the Pranksters try to absorb all America into their movie (the literal-metaphorical movie) before America puts them in its movie (the metaphorical movie). The refusal to play other people's games, to let them entrap him in their movies lies behind Kesey's "foul-

9. As Tony Tanner observes, the fascination of Kesey and the Pranksters with "Edge City" echoes the yearning for the edges of Hank Stamper, a fictional figure in Kesey's *Sometimes a Great Notion.* Tanner, *London Magazine,* n.s. 9 (1969), 11.

ing up" of a Vietnam rally held at Berkeley. While awaiting his turn to speak, Kesey becomes convinced that the antiwar rally is modeled on a war rally, and that the rhetoric of the pacifist is patterned after the rhetoric of the warmonger. He decides that the peace people are actors in the military's movie and, once on the platform, urges them to free themselves: "You know, you're not gonna stop this war with this rally, by marching. . . . That's what they do. . . . They hold rallies and they march . . . and that's the same game you're playing . . . their game" (p. 222). And he takes out his harmonica and plays "Home on the Range."

To invent one's own "fantasy" and to shoot one's own "movie" is the route to "Edge City," an expedition into the innermost circle of one's unique reality—to move with its "flow." "Going with the flow" is the ability to "transcend the bullshit," to see through the surfaces and discover the movement of reality behind appearance. The Pranksters are reluctant to verbalize the meaning of "flow" and other concepts for fear of limiting their meaning: Mountain Girl at the annual California Unitarian Church Conference at Asilomar shouts at the minister: "Do It!" She expresses the basic Prankster outlook—don't explain it; do it!

This firmly rooted belief in action rather than explanation is embodied in the Pranksters' most famous reality-disturbing device—the Prank. The idea behind the Prank is to perform great public put-ons to dislodge the established official reality and project a liberating fiction, which will enlarge people's concept of the real. The Pranksters' clothes, their Day-Glo colors, their behavior at the Vietnam rally and the Beatles performance, are all part of this great public put-on. The Pranks should shock and free observers and actors, since the very process of performing pranks is in itself emancipating. This double liberation of observer and actor is one of the differences between the Prank and the Modernist efforts to shock the dull middle-class, *épater le bourgeois.* The latter is usually a one-way affair, with the artist firmly convinced of the superiority of his own values. The Pranks reveal how much the consciousness is inhibited by societal conditioning, and how much Blakean innocence has been lost. To overcome the damage, one must act, be "out front," confess "hang-ups." To remain inhibited and to think rather than to act is to go with the old middle-class intellectual game, to continue one's existence as a "shit kicker"—a state of consciousness not dissimilar to acting with "bad faith." To overcome the "bad faith" and live "out front" with absolute self-transparency, the Pranksters undertake a series of almost ritualistic acts, aimed at dislodging the mind from its habitual mode of thinking and transposing it to a higher order of reality. These rituals, like most tribal rites, are performed with some consciousness-expanding, mind-opening potion (pp. 140–41). Drugs and multimedia manipulation of ordinary experience expand, if not completely annihilate, the boundaries of the uptight ego, and *"Ego* and *Non-Ego* start to merge." Sense impressions also merge: "a sound became . . . a color! blue . . . colors became smells, walls began to breathe like the underside of a leaf. A curtain became a column of concrete and yet it began rippling . . . the entire harmonies of the universe . . . all flowing together in this very moment." More startling is the cultivation of "intersubjectivity," the crushing of the private, individual reality by collective reality. One way the Pranksters try to achieve this is through "rapping"—a kind of surreal monologue—which Wolfe describes as a "form of free association conversation, like a jazz conversation, or even a monologue, with everyone, or whoever, catching hold of words, symbols, ideas, sounds, and winging them back and forth and beyond . . . the walls of conventional logic." The emerging verbal flow creates a surreal reality, as though the Prankster consciousnesses open up and flow together. In one of the "briefing" sessions we hear Cassady speaking about "Blue noses, red eyes . . ."; the phrase is modulated to "God is red," and then, "God is dead," and finally, into a flow of mystical contemplation that "God is not dead, God is red, God is the bottled-up red animal inside all of us, whole, all feeling, complete, out front, only it is made dead by all the lags. . . ."

The Pranksters see themselves as liberators. They want to extend the range of their projected fiction and bring everyone else into their movie: "Suddenly it seemed like the Pranksters could draw the whole universe into . . . the movie." To accomplish this, they organize their Acid Test festivals. The typical Acid Test offered music, Prankster movies, acid, and *the strobe!* "To people standing under the mighty strobe everything seemed to fragment. Ecstatic dancers—their hands flew off their arms, frozen in the air —their glistening faces came apart—a gleaming ellipse of teeth here, a pair of buffered highlit cheekbones there—all flacking and fragmenting into images as in an old flicker movie—a man in slices!" The strobes, projectors, mikes, tapes, amplifiers, the variable-lag Ampex are all part of the arsenal of technological gadgetry the Pranksters employ to further subvert the official reality with their private, empirical sur-fiction. The acceptance of the "gadget" as an inseparable element of present-day experience endows the Pranksters' "trip" with a quality uniquely American and unmistakably "technetronic"; it also sharply contrasts Kesey and Timothy Leary, another guru figure in the book, who advocates a trip from the technological reality of contemporary America to an agrarian dreamland. The Acid Tests are a head-on confrontation with contemporary experience in what Mailer disparagingly calls "technology land." The participants in these sacraments, by means of the resistance-crushing pressures generated by drugs, decompose and neutralize the seemingly solid reality through which society has shaped their vision of themselves and the outside world. *The Electric Kool-Aid Acid Test,* however, is not a study of the nature of psychedelic experience. The narrative, like Warhol's *a,* takes the drug experience as its *donnée* and registers the pressures of a fictual reality as it is translated in the actions and thoughts of people attempting to reestablish contact with reality through drugs. The fictivity of the sur-fiction generated by means of chemicals, in other words, is part of the larger fictional reality of postwar America, which has made drugs necessary for finding an epistemological anchor for the self in a discontinuous culture.[10]

10. See Malden G. Bishop, *The Discovery of Love: A Psychedelic Experience with LSD-25* (New York: Dodd, Mead, 1963); Timothy Leary and W. H. Clark, "Religious Implications of Consciousness-Expanding Drugs," *Religious Education* (May–

When Kesey's drug quest for "super identity" in an alternative reality encounters opposition from the law, he accepts a new identity as an outlaw. In a mock ritual of death by water, Kesey leaves a note mixed in tone and hallucinatory (p. 266), and disappears into Mexico—"the land of competent Outlaws." But the "Acid Tests" continue, culminating in an unusual Acid Festival in Watts on Lincoln's Birthday, February 12, 1966. The evening begins with films of Furthur, the bus, and its riders. Then some slides of flowers and patterns. Afterward everyone is invited to help themselves to Kool-Aid in a large, plastic trash can. Clair Brush, a "novice," describes her initiation:

> . . . it was being served in paper cups, and since Kool-Aid is a staple in the homes of . . . friends of mine, I thought it quite a natural thing to serve . . . had a cup, and another, wandered and talked for a while, had another . . . suddenly I began to laugh . . . and laugh . . . and the laugh was more primitive, more gut-tearing, than anything I had ever known. It came from somewhere so deep inside that I never felt it before . . . and it continued . . . and it was uncontrollable . . . and wonderful. Something snapped me back and I realized that there was nothing funny . . . nothing to laugh about . . . someone came up to me and I shut my eyes and with a machine he projected images on the back of my eyelids . . . and nothing was in perspective, nothing had any touch of normalcy or reality. . . . [pp. 274–75]

In Mexico, Kesey gradually develops the idea of going beyond the drug-induced state of consciousness toward a permanent alternative reality attainable without the help of external agents. "There is no use opening the door and going through it and then always going back out again," Kesey says of the drug experience. "We've got to move on to the next step." The drug-aided projected fiction of the

June, 1963); Charles Savage and others, "LSD, Transcendence and the New Beginning," *Journal of Nervous and Mental Diseases,* 135 (1962); Sanford Unger, "Mescaline, LSD, Psilocybin, and Personality Change: A Review," *Psychiatry: Journal for the Study of Interpersonal Processes,* 26 (1963); Alan Watts, *The Joyous Cosmology: Adventures in the Chemistry of Consciousness* (New York: Random House, 1962); and B. S. Aronson and H. Osmond, eds., *Psychedelics* (Garden City, N.Y.: Doubleday, 1970).

Pranksters, originally an anti-environment created to neutralize the official reality, has now become a static reality, almost another ordinary environment. Kesey now wants to project an anti-reality into the reality which was originally an anti-reality itself. The technetronic culture's power to absorb counter-environments into the matrix environment has transformed the Prankster's drug-induced, counter-environment into an accepted part of public reality.

After returning to California, Kesey announces plans for a public ceremony and reveals his vision of a new sur-fiction with which to go beyond the official reality and keep the anti-environment vibrant and dynamic. The "current Fantasy" is to be a Prankster Fugitive Extraordinaire—the bringer of the message on the run. But he is in the cops' movie now, and the acid heads regard his new vision as a betrayal of the psychedelic cause, rather than a further step toward nonordinary reality. Kesey finds himself alienated from both the police, the guardians of the agreed values, and the acid people, the guardians of the now-emaciated projected fiction. Convinced of the creativity of his "current fantasy," Kesey schedules the Acid Test Graduation for Winterland on Halloween night. The Prankster bus, bearing a sign reading ACID TEST GRADUATION, wheels through Haight-Ashbury, downtown San Francisco, North Beach, and Berkeley, advertising the world's biggest convocation of all the heads. The ceremony is promoted in prankish tones:

> Kesey for Governor!
> A man of convictions!
> He stands on his record!
> The idiot's choice!
> A joint in every stash!
> No hope without dope! [p. 383]

Mountain Girl's shouts from the touring bus create a Prankster version of the Brown-Reagan gubernatorial campaign. Prevented from having the festival at Winterland, Kesey holds it in the Pranksters' Warehouse on the same Halloween night. The Pranksters, dressed in American Flag coveralls, dance under a "huge orange-and-white parachute," which is "the very same parachute . . . that astronauts use on reentry for the splashdown." Kesey appears, "bare chested, wearing only white leotards, a white satin cape tied at the neck, and a red, white, and blue sash running diagonally across his chest. It's . . . Captain America! The Flash! Captain Marvel!" (p. 394). At the height of the frenzy, the lights go out, the music stops, and a single spotlight glares on the center of the floor. Kesey steps into the light and describes his new sur-fiction. But from now on Kesey's trip toward supra-reality is a lonely one; most friends stay behind, trapped in what originally was a fiction invented to cancel the official reality. The final celebration in The Bar, a psychedelic nightspot in Scotts Valley, ten miles from Santa Cruz, is, as Hagen says, more like a "wake." The juncture of realities—the agreed reality, the tamed fiction of the acid heads, and the new supra-reality toward which Kesey is groping—proves unsuccessful. The fear of the new supra-reality moves even the Pranksters who have followed Kesey to The Barn to drift off. Finally, only Kesey (on electric guitar) and Babbs (on the electric bass) remain in the center of the vast gloom of the barn singing a "song" which ends in the incantatory refrain, "WE BLEW IT."

In *The Electric Kool-Aid Acid Test,* Wolfe ostensibly transcribes the projected live fiction of the Merry Pranksters, but the actual area of experience reflected in the book is the zone of consciousness created in contemporary America by the pressure of the technetronic culture and the bizarre, baffling behavior of its various sub-cults. Wolfe's narrative strategies are all aimed at capturing the live fiction of the Pranksters not only in terms of its heterogeneous elements but also, to use Wolfe's own words, its "mental atmosphere" and "subjective reality." The concept of "subjectivity" should not be understood in its conventional sense—the writer's private reading of reality and the projection of his own emotions. "Subjectivity" here is Wolfe's attempt to transcribe the inwardness and feel of events as they register themselves on the minds of people whose lives or actions he is recording. Of *The Electric Kool-Aid Acid Test,* Wolfe has said: "I was not at all interested in presenting *my* subjective state when confronted with the Pranksters or whatever they had done. It was rather to try to get Kesey's completely" (emphasis is Wolfe's).[11] Wolfe's book is a registration of the Pranksters' emotional involvement in their actions and of the emotive layer of their experience, which seems for them to be the only reliable reality.

To register the Pranksters' adventures, Wolfe employs an imitative form in a supramodernist manner. Robert Scholes's comment that "Wolfe's chameleon styles are more reflective of his material than himself" [12] sums up the characteristics of Wolfe's linguistic style and his overall narrational strategies. *The Electric Kool-Aid Acid Test* is one of the most technically rich and innovative nonfiction novels written in the postwar years. Its narrative methods vary from a mostly discursive section on the nature of religious vision and "the experience of the holy," with density of reference to authorities and comparative religion (Chapter XI, "The Unspoken Thing"), to a type of extended interior monologue (Chapter XXI, "The Fugitive").

The book combines the retrieved past and the experienced present. The most important source for the recovery of the past is the Pranksters' Archives, which contain tapes, diaries, letters, photographs, and the forty-hour movie of the bus trip. The recaptured past is framed between two narrative blocks which are a direct registration of the present. The first segment, told from a witness stance by Wolfe, registers his first contact with Kesey, the Pranksters, and the Warehouse. Then follows his record of the past, based on the Archives as well as oral and written testimony from various participants.[13] The third narrative block is an eyewitness account of the acid graduation ceremony. Wolfe first thinks of Kesey in terms of conventional reality categories and decides to do a piece on him entitled "Young Novelist, Real-Life Fugitive." But, when he finds himself

11. Interview with Tom Wolfe in *The New Fiction*, ed. Bellamy, p. 85.

12. Robert Scholes, "Double Perspective on Hysteria," *Saturday Review*, Aug. 24, 1968, p. 37.

13. Wolfe identifies them and his sources in his "Author's Note" on the composition of the book, pp. 415–16.

within the centripetal movement of the Pranksters' circle, he realizes the inadequacy of his approach and, abandoning his original project, becomes instead the scribe of past and present events which are constituents of a myth in formation.

Wolfe's witnessing is usually signaled by the use of the first person pronoun; although sometimes the pronoun acknowledges private feelings ("That hurt, Doris Delay, but I know you meant it as a kindly suggestion"), it primarily reports, without intervention, the sense data to testify to what has been observed by the reporter. The epistemological effect of the typographical presence of the "I" is the owning of a "self," and thus a warning to the reader that everything is told by a single man with his unique, acknowledged limitations. The book opens with Tom Wolfe's shy voice talking from the back of a pickup truck which is "Bouncing along. Dipping and rising and rolling on these rotten springs like a boat." He is being given a lift to the Warehouse, where he will see the "Chief." The contrast between his own clothing style and that of the Pranksters makes him aware of the difference in their attitudes toward life in general and toward the projected fiction of the Pranksters in particular. He becomes self-conscious, and the tone of narration curves toward apology for his "Black Shiny FBI Shoes." This tone reinforces the presence of a feeling person whose testimony of events will be presented in the book. The owning of the "ego" becomes clearer in the exchange between Wolfe and Black Maria:

> "When is your birthday?
> "March 2."
> "Pisces," she says. And then: "I would never take you for a Pisces."
> "Why?"
> "You seem too . . . *solid* for a Pisces." [p. 5]

Wolfe adds: "But I know she means stolid. I am beginning to feel stolid" (p. 5). Wolfe records his own reactions to the situations—a technique developed to its full potentialities by Mailer in *The Armies of the Night*. This voice sometimes becomes more obviously reflexive: "Oh christ, Tom, the thing was fantastic, a freaking mind-blower . . ." (p. 367). But in most cases, the "I" is used to report what Wolfe has seen or heard: "Kesey stares at a spiral notebook he has and then starts talking in a voice so soft I can hardly hear him at first . . ." (p. 388). Though frequently typographically visible, the "I" is sometimes not foregrounded: "Late in the afternoon in the Warehouse—Christ, it's dismal in here!" (p. 387). When Wolfe uses someone else's testimony to recover the past, Wolfe's voice becomes a linking device between the original witness, Wolfe, and the reader. For example, Wolfe quotes Clair Brush on her acid experience: " 'I think what decided me'—Clair is recalling it for me—" (p. 272). Sometimes the "I" informs the reader of events yet to take place: "Nobody ever knew his real name at all until a few months later when, as I say, the police would get technical about it . . ." (p. 133). This use of "I" to tell the reader about future events is similar to Capote's use of the omniscient narrator, since it is based on research, not the imaginative authority of the writer.

The Electric Kool-Aid Acid Test is based on a dual perspective or a double mode of narration which counterpoints the "factual" with the "fictional," and releases the "fictuality" of the total experience. The counterpointing in the book takes a complex form, because the book deals with two layers or circles of "reality." The immediate "reality" which Wolfe depicts is itself a cultivated fiction which attempts to reveal and discredit the thinness of the accepted common reality. In Truman Capote's *In Cold Blood*, the depicted "reality" was the circle of the common reality (albeit a reality so charged with fictivity that its mere transcription produced a strange fictual narrative). The counterpointing in Capote's book was between the experiential reality (facts) and the inherent fiction (bizarreness of facts) in that "reality." In Wolfe's book, the counterpointing is more complicated. Wolfe records a layer of reality which is deliberately "fictional" in the traditional sense of the word. But this fiction, projected by the Pranksters, is located in the tangible reality—which the Pranksters consider a deceptive public fan-

tasy. Both circles of "reality" are part of the recordable outside world and thus form the axis of external reference in
The Electric Kool-Aid Acid Test. The fictuality which emerges
from Wolfe's book, therefore, results from a complex interaction between experiential reality and the invented fiction of the Pranksters on one hand, and the factual registration of this dialectic on the other. Something close to this
interaction among layers of experience is present in *The
Armies of the Night* where Mailer, the Scribe, records the actions of Mailer, the Beast (Prankster of intellect?) in a book
which is a factual registration of both.

The function of the core of documentation in the book,
like that of any other nonfiction novel, is to authenticate the
events as actual occurrences, not invented components of
an interpretation of reality in the narrative. In *The Electric
Kool-Aid Acid Test* the core of documents establishes the
"facts" about the "fiction" of the Pranksters and thus makes
the two components of the external field (the Pranksters'
fiction and daily reality) a unified field of external reference whose constituent events have, at various levels of reality, "happened," and, therefore, become "verifiable." Such
events as the trans-American bus trip of the Pranksters are
easily verifiable, because they drew a great deal of attention
and are now matters of public record. Less publicly known
events, such as details of a particular "rap session" or an
"acid party," are related in full detail and usually tied to a
well-known person (Allen Ginsburg, Timothy Leary,
Hunter Thompson) for further possible verification. Such
incidents as the Pranksters' visit to Esalen Institute and its
director, Gestalt psychologist Fritz Perls, as well as Kesey's
appearance, while still a fugitive, on San Francisco television
station KGO, the local ABC outlet, also serve as elements of
the verifiable out-referential field.

The blurring of "fact" and "fiction"—the cracking up of
the seemingly solid reality and the release of its inner fictivity—is much more obvious in *The Electric Kool-Aid Acid Test*
than in the nonfiction novels discussed before. But within
the book there are moments when the emerging fictuality is
so heightened that it transcends its immediate context and
gathers a prototypical resonance for contemporary experi-

ence. The disappearance of rational markers for locating
the self under the pressure of a new force of reality
emerges from Wolfe's record of the trans-sensory experience of Beauty Witch on the bus trip. Her going "stark raving mad" embodies in itself the condition of her generation,
for whom the only authentic means for finding a real interior space in which to achieve a sense of self has become the
experience of madness and nervous breakdown. The scene
of the take-over by the developers of the Bohemian living
quarters at Stanford is another case of the clash between
two orders of actuality which heightens itself into a mythical
pattern of the displacement of contemporary man. Like
other aspects of contemporary experience, the "tragic" is
embedded in the "comic" and an undertone of black humor
pervades the whole episode, which has a deep psychic resonance to it:

> The papers turned up to write about the last night on Perry
> Lane, noble old Perry Lane, and had the old cliche at the
> ready, End of an Era, expecting to find some deep-thinking
> latter-day Thorstein Veblen intellectuals on hand with so-
> norous bitter statements about this machine civilization de-
> vouring its own past.
>
> Instead, there were some kind of *nuts* out here. They were
> up in a tree lying on a mattress, all high as coons, and they
> kept offering everybody, all the reporters and photog-
> raphers, some kind of venison chili, but there was something
> about the whole setup . . . and it was hard as hell to make
> the End of an Era story come out right in the papers, with
> nothing but this kind of freaking Olsen & Johnson material
> to work with,
>
> but they managed to go back with the story they came
> with, End of an Era, the cliche intact, if they could only blot
> out the cries in their ears of *Ve-ni-son Chi-li—*

The acid graduation festival in the Warehouse has the overtones of a pagan feast tinged with a Kafkaesque sense of
persecution and, with the appearance of the police, assumes
the extra dimension of a ritual of chase such as one finds in
a modern detective story.

Some of the sketches of persons in the book read so much
like fiction that some readers have approached Wolfe's book

as a "novel" and criticized him for not "developing" his "characters." [14] If real people seem to behave as fictional characters, it is because they are actors in the extended allegory of their own life style. They have adopted a new life pattern and symbolically rebaptized themselves with allegorical names in response to the pressures of the freakish current reality. Like allegorical characters, they are frozen in their single role in parody of the roles they had to play in their "actual" lives: "They were all now characters in their own movies or the Big Movie. They took on new names and used them. Steve Lambrecht was Zonker. Cassady was Speed Limit. Kesey was Swashbuckler. Babbs was Intrepid Traveler . . . George Walker was Hardly Visible. And Paula Sundsten became . . . Gretchen Fetchin the Slime Queen . . ." (p. 78). Neal Cassady, the Dean Moriarity, Denver Kid, of *On the Road*, consciously behaves as a person who has walked out of one fiction into another. His new name, Speed Limit (with a pun), refers to his new function as the Driver of the Bus, destination "Furthur." They all deliberately suppress other aspects of their personalities and act as two-dimensional, "flat characters" in order to parody the very flatness imposed by common reality on the multifarious, spontaneous human life.

The Electric Kool-Aid Acid Test, like other nonfiction novels, contains a great deal of "discursive" discourse. It brings into the narrative conceptual modes of discourse and incorporates what conventional aesthetics rejects as "chunks of raw life." Chapter XI, "The Unspoken Thing," is a good example of this mixed mode used throughout the book.

The most controversial aspect of *The Electric Kool-Aid Acid Test* as a nonfiction novel, a book which purports to be a registration of happened events, is its style and linguistic maneuvering. The main question is not whether Wolfe's style is "affected," but whether his linguistic pyrotechnics are epistemologically appropriate to the task they undertake. As Robert Scholes has demonstrated in his review

14. Ralph Thrift, "Esquire and the New Nonfiction," in *The Magic Writing Machine*, ed. Everett E. Dennis (Eugene: University of Oregon School of Journalism, 1971), p. 14.

of the book, Wolfe succeeds. Describing Wolfe's style as "chameleon," Scholes sees it as "more reflective of his material than of himself." [15] The style of the book is based on what the Modernist aesthetics would denounce as the "imitative fallacy." Tom Wolfe's linguistic transcendences capture the psychic transcendences of the Pranksters' extended trip; their immediate medium is "drugs," Wolfe's is language.

What first strikes the reader about Wolfe's style is, of course, its visual aspect; its iconic typography tries to mimic the ambience of the events. The most visible elements of this typographical concretism are the unexpected use of dashes, periods, exclamation marks, and question marks, nonsense lexical items, punctuation points rarely used in the language (for example ::::::) and onomatopoeic words. Such use of the print medium tries to revivify the experience of a "history cut up in slices" by the Pranksters. To do so, Wolfe seems to be aiming at the stylistic equivalent of what the Pranksters call "Sura-Medium." In describing the early experiments with drugs at Perry Lane, Wolfe uses the layout of his page to convey the feel of a "high":

But then—soar. Perry Lane, Perry Lane.
Miles
     Miles
          Miles
               Miles
                    Miles
                         Miles
                              under all that good
vegetation from Morris Orchids and having visions of
Faces
     Faces
          Faces
               Faces
                    Faces
                        Faces
                         Faces
                            so many faces

15. Scholes, "Double Perspective on Hysteria," p. 37.

rolling up behind the eyelids, faces he has never seen
before. . . . [p. 48]

Or to describe Beauty Witch—the girl who went mad on the
bus:

> She keeps coming up to somebody who isn't saying a god-
> damn thing and looking into his eyes with the all-embracing
> look of total acid understanding, our brains are one brain, so
> let's *visit,* you and I, and she says: "Oooooooh, you really
> *think* that, I know what you mean, but do you-u-u-u-u-u-u-u-
> ueeeeeeeeeeeeeeeeeeeeee"—finishing off in a sailing tre-
> molo laugh as if she has just read your brain and it is the
> weirdest of the weird shit ever, your brain eeeeeeeeeeeeee
> eeeeeeeeeeeeeeeeeeeee— [p. 84]

The total impact of all these devices in conveying a moment
can be seen in "The Fugitive" chapter where Wolfe describes Kesey's growing paranoia (pp. 289–99). The tribal
consciousness present in a "rap" is captured by internal and
end rhymes and staccato rhythm. To combine images,
Wolfe may write them together: "Unfreakingbelievable" (p.
270), or use a recurring phrase (p. 90).

The most innovative section of the narrative is the
chapter entitled "The Fugitive." Here Wolfe expands the
range of technical possibilities of the in-referential axis of
the narrative so the nonfiction novel can contain the most
bizarre cacophonies of reality. The dominant narrative device in the chapter is "interior monologue" with suggestions
of "stream of consciousness." The technical rationale for the
use of such narrational devices in the nonfiction novel is the
treatment of the subjectivity of the situation or person portrayed, as distinguished from the projected subjectivity (em-
pathy) of the fictive novelist. The consciousness transcribed
in this chapter is the layer of awareness experienced and articulated by Kesey. The techniques for obtaining such interior information are essentially those used in the exegetical
nonfiction novel—interviews and documents. The interviewing, however, is directed less at the subject's opinions
and ideas than at his "thoughts and emotions." [16] Elaborat-

---

16. Tom Wolfe, "Why they aren't writing the Great American Novel anymore,"
Esquire, Dec. 1972, p. 158.

ing on this type of interviewing, another observer adds: "If I were interviewing Tom Wolfe, I would ask him what he *thought* in every situation where I might have asked him in the past what he did and said. I'm not so interested in what he did and said as I am interested in what he *thought*. And I would quote him in the way I was writing as that he *thought* something." [17]

The voice that speaks in the opening "Interior monologue" is reflexive: Kesey addressing Kesey, remembering the past. Gradually the voice modulates. The typography signals the movements of the voice of a man who is going through an acute phase of paranoia, half seeing, half imagining police coming to arrest him. Kesey's voice is then contextualized by a straightforward description of the room in which he is sitting:

> . . . with his elbow on a table and his forearm standing up perpendicular and in the palm of his hand a little mirror, so that his forearm and the mirror are like a big rear-view mirror stanchion on the side of a truck and thus he can look out the window and see them but they can't see him. [p. 288]

The description is then punctured by Kesey's hysterical voice:

> COME ON, MAN, DO YOU NEED A COPY OF THE SCRIPT TO SEE HOW THIS MOVIE GOES? YOU HAVE MAYBE 40 SECONDS LEFT BEFORE THEY COME GET YOU [p. 288]

The time then corresponds to the rhythm of Kesey's movements and is echoed in the pace of the narrative. The chronometric movement is a countdown:

> 40 seconds left . . .
> You have maybe 35 seconds left . . .

so on down to:

> ZERO:::::::000000000::::::::RUN!

And Kesey, with one mad dash, jumps out the window and runs into the jungle. The scene is indeed fictitious, even em-

---

17. Transcript of a panel discussion conducted by Leonard Wallace Robinson at Columbia University as printed in *Writer's Digest*, Jan. 1970, p. 34.

bellished with the "surprise ending" element (Black Maria appears on the scene. The reader realizes that Kesey had taken her footsteps for those of the FBI agents!). But the events have actually happened.

Through the use of "interior monologue" and empirical omniscient point of view, Chapter XXI blends three levels of "reality." All three are clearly distinguished on the first page, but the first two (the inner world of the paranoid Kesey and his interpretation of the outside events) blend into one level which is contrasted with the researched reality the omniscient author brings into the chapter. The omniscient author is at all times alert to the minutest details. Through him we learn about Kesey's state of mind—how he has "hooked down five dexedrines," how he was hidden "in the back of Boise's old panel truck" while crossing into Mexico. The Mexican landscape is carefully depicted. To convey this, Wolfe, like Capote, uses flashback, and this brings to the texture of the prose two tenses: the past and the historical or actual present. This flexibility of tense operates as a very effective mimesis of the fluidity of the "real" in the mind of Kesey and the other Pranksters who somehow participate in the journey to Mexico.

The chronometric rhythm continues to the middle of the chapter, then gives way to a series of interjectory markers to signal the rhythm of Kesey's movement:

WHAZZAT? . . .
PLUNGE—
SHHHHHHHHHHHWAAAAAAAAAP—
WHOP! . . .

When Kesey's movements slow, the rhythm of the mimetic style slows and acquires a meditative mood:

. . . the rush lowers in his ears, he can concentrate, pay total attention, an even, even, even world, flowing into *now*, no past terrors, no anticipation of the future horror, only *now*, *this* movie. . . . [p. 305]

Wolfe employs a range of narrative techniques whose sophistication enables him to render the current fictuality.

Any other approach, such as the dramatic treatment of a fictive novelist, would be reductive.

In reviewing one of Tom Wolfe's earlier books, Richard Hoggart, using the famous typology of American writers first formulated by Philip Rahv, refers to Wolfe as "substantially a Paleface pretending to be a Redskin." [18] Norman Mailer is a Redskin through and through who, for reasons discussed at the opening of this chapter, sounds like a self-searching Paleface in *The Armies of the Night*. In many instances, his voice is indistinguishable from the Paleface Robert Lowell whom he portrays in the book. It is no coincidence that the sudden spread of "confessional poetry" after Lowell's *Life Studies* (1959) should parallel the development of the testimonial nonfiction novel. The two literary kinds seek to reestablish a direct relationship between man and experience. Like other supramodern works, both types reject the concepts of "aesthetic distance" and "fictional persona" and try to become transparent media for people eager to talk to other people about the places they have been and the experiences they have suffered. In a culture lacking in externally reliable frames of reference for verifying individual experience, sensory data become the ultimate authority, and sincerity and confession the last act of regaining elusive selfhood.

Philip Rieff in *The Triumph of the Therapeutic* notes the changing sensibility in postwar America: "We are, I fear, getting to know one another. Reticence, secrecy, concealment of self have been transformed into social problems. . . ." [19] Mailer's so-called egotism and exhibitionism—the observation has been made that he thinks even his bowel movement has a national significance—relates to this changing sensibility. The publicization of the private is not an empty, playful gesture but the last attempt of the

18. Richard Hoggart, "The Dance of the Long-Legged Fly," *Encounter,* Aug. 1966, p. 68; see also Philip Rahv, "Paleface and Redskin," in *Literature and the Sixth Sense* (Boston: Houghton Mifflin Co., 1969), pp. 1–6.

19. Philip Rieff, *The Triumph of the Therapeutic* (New York: Harper and Row, 1966), p. 22.

pressured self to retain contact with the outside world. In a society with moral and valuational consensus rooted in established and shared norms, the individual feels little need to validate cultural realities by testing them against his or her own perceptions and experiences. But the individual engulfed in the ever enclosing and splintering technetronic culture must discover reality by himself for himself. The glaring "I" in testimonial nonfiction novels and confessional poetry, far from being the result of an arrogant personality, is the cry of a lonely, anguished man who must be his own Columbus without any value markers or cultural compasses. Stephen Stephanchev sees this fragmentation of sensibility dominating the works of postwar American poets: "Feeling secure only when dealing with personally tested facts, they render the loneliness and terror of contemporary life with the terseness and immediacy of a diary record. They permit no evil of 'objective correlatives' to hang between them and their readers, they distrust 'aesthetic distance' and 'anonymity'. . . ." [20] The artist no longer orders the sensory world; rather, the sensory world shapes the work of art.

Nowhere is the schizoid nature of the contemporary sensibility and the need for absolute transparency, both caused by the pressure of the crisis situation in contemporary America, more powerfully enacted than in Mailer's *The Armies of the Night*—a puzzling book both in its generic status and in its aesthetic mode of being. Most critics, reading the book in terms of its surface patterns and the interpretation which seems present in the foreground, have considered *Armies* an extended private reading of recent American reality.[21] From such a point of view the book is, of course, anything but a nonfiction novel. That there is "interpretation" and an attempt to understand, synthesize, and reach

20. Stephen Stephanchev, *American Poetry since 1945* (New York: Harper and Row, 1966), pp. 4–5.

21. See, for example, Barry H. Leeds, *The Structured Vision of Norman Mailer* (New York: New York University Press, 1969), pp. 247–62; Richard Poirier, *Norman Mailer* (New York: Viking, 1972), pp. 77–106; Robert Solotaroff, *Down Mailer's Way* (Urbana: University of Illinois Press, 1974), pp. 212–37; and Kingsley Widmer, "The Post-Modernist Art of Protest: Kesey and Mailer as American Expressions of Rebellion," *Centennial Review*, 19 (1975), 121–35.

conclusions about American experience in the book is beyond question. Every page piles metaphor upon metaphor—the main carriers of personal vision and value-markers—and scrutinizes the experiential *données* received by the narrator. But the ultimate determination of the generic status of the book will depend not merely on the presence or absence of "interpretation," but on the way in which that "interpretation" is used. The question is not unlike the relationship between the use of empirical reality (facts) in a naturalistic novel (e.g., *An American Tragedy*) and their use in a nonfiction novel. The mere presence of empirical data in a naturalistic novel does not make it a nonfiction novel; it remains a fictive conception of reality which uses the commonly known set of facts to solidify its conclusions and interpretations. Mailer's use of "interpretation" in *Armies* transforms its very nature so that even calling his rumination "interpretation" would be misleading. He employs a type of discourse which reads on the surface like "interpretation" but is in fact "meta-interpretation." It brings out the absurdity and arbitrariness of the usual "interpretation," and thus transcends its meaning-imposing function to reach a state in which interpretations are interpreted. Thus the ostensible interpretation is turned into an anti-interpretation; a negation of the proposed reading of reality.

The transformation of one state into meta-state, verbally or actionally, occurs throughout the book. The Ambassador Theater incident represents such an actional change: Mailer compulsively scrutinizes in public his "forty-five second" piss in the darkness of the men's room, and, in the process, he and the audience transcend the conventions of a political rally and reach a meta-rally, which is a curious fictual combination of politics, vaudeville, and an acknowledgment of the helplessness of the individual confronted with a baffling reality. The political rally from that moment is no longer a means of a redefinition of reality; it is a recognition of the impenetrability of reality. A similar transformation takes place with Mailer's verbal "interpretations" of the reality he is dealing with. Analysis of isolated passages is pointless, because the verbal transcendence is a cumulative process, each instance of interpretation building on previous instances so that by the end, "The Metaphor Delivered," the whole string of "interpretations" is transformed into meta-interpretation.

An example of a single verbal "interpretation" which approaches such transcendence is the section entitled, "Grandma with Orange Hair." Mailer gazes into the faces of the Federal Marshals, seeing them collectively as an index of American reality which he then starts to analyze. The analysis, however, cannot stand the pressure of the fictual reality which gradually emerges from Mailer's own probing of America. The "interpretation" disintegrates into a bizarre tableau which transforms the whole episode into a meta-interpretation, a transformation which acknowledges the impossibility of a coherent and sustained decoding of reality or a total patterning of it. Mailer seems like a surgeon who is himself affected by the anaesthetic he is using for his operation. A brooding immobility accompanies the unfolding analysis, and his "interpretation" not only fails to clarify the "meaning" of contemporary reality, but even envelops the particular incident under scrutiny in a haze. The Private Scribe in the book acknowledges this loss of focus by pointing out the lack of correspondence between the interpretation and the data being interpreted.

The meta-interpretation (or meta-situation) can therefore be characterized as an interpretation which ostensibly aims at providing a pattern of meaning, but its aim is undermined by the tension which develops between the data to be interpreted and the conceptual model imposed on them to yield meaning. Mailer's strategy is to let his "actant" Participating self interpret the data of American reality and his "actee" Scribal self acknowledge the untenability of his reading of reality. The confusion caused by a bewildering reality is acknowledged and, as Gerald Graff observes, is built "into the texture of the work." [22] The split point of view is the narrative correlative of the schizophrenic reality. These transformations of commentary into anti-comments

22. Gerald Graff, "Babbitt at the Abyss: The Social Context of Postmodern American Fiction," *TriQuarterly*, No. 33 (1975), p. 316.

by acts of transcendence—reaching a meta-state—are performed by the book's narrative point of view—the use of the third person vantage point by the first person actee.

Armies is the narrative of a narrativist, and what is narrated should not be confused with what is narratively conceived. The book reflects an agonizingly pressured self under an exacting situation and registers minute by minute the confrontation of that self, bewilderingly divided into an actant and an actee, with the ongoing events. The actant, Mailer the public man, acts to bring about changes in the outside world as the only authentic means of existential cognition. Through deeds, he will achieve an existential coherence which will lead to a vision—a view or a totalization of the reality surrounding him. This is the man who in *Armies* willfully superinduces metaphysical attributes to his experience; develops theories about America, past, present, and future; and conveys his message through elaborate networks of metaphors. Side by side with Mailer the actant, the omniscient interpreter of American experience, exists Mailer the Scribe, who passively records the acts, ideas, and dreams of the performer. The book presents the Mailer who performs and yearns to grasp the overall pattern of the behavior of reality, but it also presents the narrational device which enacts Mailer's complete awareness of the futility of his yearnings and the arbitrariness of his interpretations. The scribe who records the interpretations of the performer is recording Mailer's surrender to the actual and his self-mockery of his ambitions to reach an all-inclusive reading of reality. The existence of the Performer and the Scribe signals a gap between "yearning" and "getting," "wanting" and "achieving." The gap reveals that the most ardent interpreter of American reality over the last two decades is beginning to acknowledge the untenability of superimposing meaning on the emerging reality of an America in which even he finds himself somewhat disoriented. By registering the confrontation between Mailer's will to totalize and the defiant, emerging actualities, *Armies* enacts Mailer's awareness of the futility of reductive superimposition of grand patterns of meaning on the actual.

In *The Naked and the Dead* (1948), Mailer, like most members of his generation, had a good grasp of the outside reality, and was in command of that segment of it that he was putting into his novels. The world seemed to follow an understandable course, and the narrative techniques he had learned from the Big Brothers such as Dos Passos were quite adequate to depict this reality and its occasional eccentricities. By the time he was writing *An American Dream* (1964), the eccentricities had become the rule rather than the exception, but Mailer refused to accept the obsoleteness of meaning-mongering. Instead he tried to give unruly reality an order by imposing an aesthetic pattern on it in his "novel." [23] One can even argue that the feeling that American reality was no longer available to the fictive novel had dawned on Mailer as far back as the late 1950s, when he was putting together his generically curious book, *Advertisements for Myself* (1959). This book purported to tame American reality by an amalgamation of all literary genres. The very form of the book is a commentary on the impossibility of squeezing American experience into a fictive novel. But Mailer did not take his *Advertisements* very seriously and continued to write fictive novels because, as Richard Gilman suggests, his antiquated conception of the fictive novel prevented him from thinking of any other form of literary art as powerful and as capable of dealing with reality as the novel. "Beginning with a fundamentally bourgeois idea of fiction," Gilman believes, Mailer's "idea has always been of the novelist as someone whose gift of intuition and prophecy enable him to see more deeply than other men into society and human organizations." [24] Carrying the old romantic notion of the novelist within him, Mailer puts that concept to the test in *Armies*. By articulating his divided loyalties in the actant and the actee, he transcends the limitations of his fictive vision, and mocks his own effort to view the actual through his fictive imagination. *Armies,* through its double

23. See also Ihab Hassan's comment on *An American Dream* in *The Literature of Silence* (New York: Knopf, 1967), p. 13.

24. Richard Gilman, *The Confusion of Realms* (New York: Random House, 1969), p. 150.

narrational perspectives, registers both the brute facts of the world outside and the changing perception of Mailer. He abandons both realistic portrayal of an orderly reality and aesthetic ordering of the lawless actualities. In his "commentary," Mailer longs for the old grand pattern of meaning, and by recording that desire through his alter ego, the Scribe, he mocks it, "comments" on it, and transforms it into meta-commentary. "Commentary," he now sees, is an act of will; and throughout the book, Mailer parodies and ridicules his willful, meaning-seeking self. Mailer's posture as "clown" in *Armies* is not as innocent a gesture as most critics would have us believe. The "clown" is the seer who, like another "clown," Ken Kesey at the end of *The Electric Kool-Aid Acid Test,* seeks the meaning of America and admits that he "blew" it.

Mailer's growing awareness of the complexity of reality and the impossibility of rendering it in a conventional, realistic manner can be seen in his earlier writing and comments. In "The Man Who Studied Yoga," Sam has given up writing his novel "temporarily," because he cannot find a form. "He does not want to write a realistic novel because *reality is no longer realistic"* (emphasis added).[25] In a speech given at the Modern Language Association of America and printed in *Commentary,* Mailer again expressed his doubts about the authenticity of the conventions of the fictive novel for dealing with contemporary reality: "The realistic literature had never caught up with the rate of change in American life, indeed it had fallen further and further behind, and the novel gave up any desire to be a creation equal to the phenomenon of the country itself; it settled for being a metaphor." [26] The incorporation of these "ideas" into his writing two years later produces *Armies,* an attempt at "a creation equal to the phenomenon of the country itself."

Armies is an odyssey of a self yearning for a grand pattern of meaning behind its fragmentary experience but aware of the futility of such hungering. This awareness, signaled by a

25. Norman Mailer, *Advertisements for Myself* (New York: G. P. Putnam's, 1959), p. 179.
26. Norman Mailer, "Modes and Mutations," *Commentary,* March 1966, p. 39.

split point of view similar to the strategic use of the split screen in films to represent contradictory impulses, creates in the book a sub-text that effectively undercuts and negates the text. In the text, Mailer clearly commits himself to the metaphysical search; in the sub-text, Mailer the Scribe consciously mocks his commitment. The resulting book is a registration of his "lonely odyssey into the land of the witches." [27] The separation between the Performer, the quester for and projector of meaning, and the Scribe, the receptor of the actual, is so great that Mailer himself is bewildered by his own actions. He acknowledges that it seems to him "as if he were watching himself in a film." The book should be read not in terms of the surface comments and ruminations of the public man, but as the recording of those comments and ruminations by the private Scribe, who observes from the outside and registers the desire for coherence and the frustration of that desire by the engulfing chaos and confusion that befog the consciousness. The witness narrative stance of the book, then, operates at two levels: Mailer the public man witnessing the public events as clues to the meaning of American experience, and Mailer the private Scribe witnessing the public man haunted, like Poe's fictional figure of Arthur Gordon Pym, by the white phantom of meaning. But the phantom is elusive; and coherence, solidity, and meaningfulness are only dim memories of the past (the "voice" is that of the private Scribe):

> He is awakening Friday morning in his room at the Hay-Adams after his night on the stage of the Ambassador and the party thereafter. One may wonder if the Adams in the name of his hotel bore any relation to Henry; we need not be concerned with Hay who was a memorable and accomplished gentleman from the nineteenth century (then Secretary of State to McKinley and Roosevelt) other than to say that the hotel looked like its name, and was indeed the staunchest advocate of that happy if heavy style in Washington architecture which spoke of *a time when men and events were solid, comprehensible, often obedient to a code of values*. . . . [p. 54; emphasis added]

27. Norman Mailer, *The Armies of the Night* (New York: New American Library, 1968), p. 123. Subsequent page references to this edition will appear in the text.

The witness stance of the private Scribe in relation to the public performer is reflected in the image of the book as a "house of mirrors," as if there are always two persons surprised at each other's vastly different existence. The split self has its counterpart in the split nation—the book is full of references to the schizophrenia of America. The narrative is indeed a literalization of a metaphor—Mailer acting out his interpretations and comments—not a metaphorization of the literal, which is the strategy used in the fictive novel. There is nothing metaphoric in the registration of events. The events themselves are charged with metaphors. The book is a demonstration in its very narrative apparatus of the untamability of contemporary "reality" which, to use Mailer's own phrasing, is "an intersection between history and the comic book, between legend and television, Biblical archetypes and the movies."

In his reading of *Armies,* Warner Berthoff maintains that the "formal precedent" of the book is Thoreau's *Walden.*[28] But Berthoff's comparison is not supportable. In *Walden,* a voice *directly* records his own actions and responses in a very serious tone. Thoreau presents his own experience as a paradigm of a mode of life he would like to see universalized. No double perspective exists in the book and, consequently, no tension. The reality Thoreau depicts requires no such dual vision; the dual vision, with its implications of crippling doubt, is detrimental to his utopian views. But in Mailer's book a utopian model—the remnant of Mailer's past search persisting into the present—joins a voice which constantly undercuts that search, reminding the reader that the quest, in the face of the enormity of contemporary reality, is being turned into a mock-quest. Thoreau writes as the "future leader," while Mailer is the "future victim."

Armies, significantly enough, opens with Mailer looking at himself from the outside—from the point of a *Time* magazine reporter. Such focusing on self from without, through alien eyes, signals the emergence of the private Scribe who will examine Mailer the performer. The mode of what

28. Warner Berthoff, "Witness and Testament: Two Contemporary Classics," *New Literary History,* 2 (1971), 322.

Richard Poirier calls "self-watchfulness" is thus established. The difference between Wolfe's testimonial narrative stance and Mailer's is that while Wolfe witnesses other people's activities, Mailer is a self-witness; his *données* are Brownian motions of his "ego" caused by the bombardment of the actual events. In *Armies,* the counterpointing of the "factual" and the "fictional" is done on various thematic and structural levels: "ego" and "events," "the actor" and "the scribe," and "History as a Novel" and "The Novel as History."

External observation of the self at the opening of the book is an indication of the Performer's awareness of the tension which exists between the ego and actuality: two components of his "image." The private Scribe is quick to note the sensitivity of the performer to his image, which is essentially a carry-over from the past when the performer was searching for the all-embracing concept of the real:

> Mailer had the most developed sense of image; if not, he would have been a figure of deficiency, for people had been regarding him by his public image since he was twenty-five years old. He had in fact learned to live in the sarcophagus of his image—at night, in his sleep, he might dart out, and paint improvements on the sarcophagus. During the day, while he was helpless, newspapermen and other assorted bravos of the media and the literary world would carve ugly pictures on the living tomb of his legend. Of necessity, part of Mailer's remaining funds of sensitivity went right into the war of supporting his image and working for it. Sometimes he thought his relation to his image was not unlike some poor fellow who strains his very testicles to bring in emoluments for his wife yet is never favored with carnal knowledge of her. [pp. 5–6]

The "image" is that of the fictive novelist who, by some mysterious ritual, is aware of the workings of reality and possesses the all-embracing metaphor which leads to a total reading of reality. But Mailer is also aware of the difference between the "image" and the "person." The fictive novelist's squeezing of reality to yield meaning is not unlike the straining of testicles to lead to "carnal knowledge," since the fulfillment, the knowledge of the body of the real, is too complex to be related to a simple act of will. The consciousness of "image" on another level is a consciousness of all the people whom he names and whose bias and prejudice distort his image until the image generator, the real Mailer, cannot recognize it. The substantial difference between the projected image and the received image generates a paranoia about the very core of his identity which at the beginning was the spring and source of his image.

Part of the paranoia is created by the intense life that the Participant lives. To be on the frontiers of contemporary American reality means to live in excitement, confusion, and chaos. *Armies* reports from such outposts of American reality, where the preestablished norms fail to order life and reality. The book is an extended enactment of Keats's concept of "negative capability," the development of the ability to live in organic disorder and to check the desire for imposing a wished-for order on the ambiguous, thus falsifying it. Mailer, more than most contemporary American writers, is cultivating this ability to accept chaos as the norm, because he has been more committed to the search for order. His first commitment was to the recognizable order without, then to the order generated within and projected to the outside world. In *Armies,* he acknowledges the futility, the sheer unviability, and the falsehood of such an anthropomorphic ordering of life.

His journey to the frontiers of reality starts with a border crossing—leaving the familiar Brooklyn and traveling to Washington, a city which makes Mailer feel "small." Washington is the focal point of confrontation between established reality and the new forms of actualities. This urge to seek the edges of experience has earned Mailer, the Participant, such titles as the "whitest Negro," and "the oldest Hippie"; his position on the edge provides him with a vision alien to the insiders. The border crossing is another attempt on Mailer's part to literalize his metaphors—to actualize his outsider's views and to project his views of reality into the actual. His micro-politics is a form of "prank," and he himself operates as a Merry Prankster of neo-politics.

Mailer's odyssey begins at a party given by a liberal couple in a house so "oversecure" as to smell of "the scent of the void which comes off the pages of a Xerox copy." The secure, sheltered, and tamed mode of middle-class life is joltingly followed by the bizarre, Dadaistic sense of the Ambassador Theater, where the political pep-rally before the March is turned into a "happening," in itself a miniature of the surprising concatenations of events in the outside world. Mailer's actions here are rather ambivalent: they are the acts of a man who, like the youths in the audience, has taken up political activism as a clue to understanding the workings of the body politic of his country, but, at the same time, by his irreverent behavior is intimating that such undertakings in a post-political, post-humanist society, whose frames of references and values are shaped by a technology-generated reality, are no more than evening amusement for middle-class children. The scene enacts Mailer's transformation of commitment (the search for clues to reality) into a meditation on commitment, and thus exposes the complexity and difficulty of distinguishing "the dancer from the dance," the establishment from the anti-establishment, selfishness from selflessness, and the "actual" from the "fictional." What he does in the Ambassador Theater resembles the projected fiction of the Pranksters; it heightens the unreality of the purported solid reality of the rally. The deliberately fictive scene that Mailer arranges hints at the "bad faith" with which the middle-class youths dull their senses to the "smell of the void" which exudes from their lives in suburban homes. They are:

the Freud-ridden embers of Marxism, good old American anxiety strata—the urban middle-class with their proliferated monumental adenoidal resentments, their secret slavish love for the oncoming hegemony of the computer and the suburb, yes, they and their children, by the sheer ironies, the sheer ineptitude, the *kinks* of history, were now being compressed into more and more militant stands, their resistance to the war some hopeless melange, somehow firmed, of Pacifism and closet Communism. And their children—on a freak-out from the suburbs to a love-in on the Pentagon wall. [p. 34]

Mailer angers everyone. The leaders of the March "depose" him from his role of Master of Ceremonies. The audience treats him more as an entertainer than an American "provo"—a self in search of an anchor. Nevertheless, the "provo" regards himself as the General of the army about to attack the bastion of capitalism and smash the machinery of technology-land. "The Beast" (one of many epithets the Scribe uses for the Performer) is "in a good mood." Before speaking, he goes to the men's room:

> [He] stepped off into the darkness of the top balcony floor, went through a door into a pitch-black men's room, and was alone with his need. No chance to find the light switch for he had no matches, he did not smoke. It was therefore a matter of locating what's what with the probing of his toes. He found something finally which seemed appropriate, and pleased with the precision of these generally unused senses in his feet, took aim between them and a point twelve inches ahead, and heard in the darkness the sound of his water striking the floor. Some damn mistake had been made, an assault from the side doubtless instead of the front, the bowl was relocated now, and Master of Ceremonies breathed deep of the great reveries of this utterly non-Sisyphian release—at last!!—and thoroughly enjoyed the next forty-five seconds, being left on the aftermath not a note depressed by the condition of the premises. No, he was off on the Romantic's great military dream, which is: seize defeat, convert it to triumph. [p. 31]

The performer's projected image as general of the dissenter army is mimicked by the military images used in describing the scene. He "locates" and "probes" as if in a dark night of assault, and expresses satisfaction with the "precision" of his senses. He takes "aim" and the water "strikes" the floor. Missing the right goal is an errant "assault" so he has to "relocate" the bowl. The duration of the act is exactly "forty-five" seconds, and the tactic for converting "defeat" to "victory" is a "military" dream. The same language is used by the private Scribe to put the image of General Mailer in the total context of his quest. The Performer thinks of the March as a "Civil War"; he develops a theory that every man in a war should dress as he pleases as long as the dress makes him "ready for assault"; he decides the middle-class runaways are "crusaders" going out to "attack" the hard core of technology-land with "less training than armies were once offered by a medieval assembly ground." The overall tone conveys a relentless assault against chaos and confusion. The man in command hopes to put an end to the disarray and discover the pattern of meaning and order.

Mailer's subsequent confession of his washroom adventure to the audience intensifies the fictivity of all the evening's activities. Political rally and vaudeville merge. The reality resists the nice ordering planned by the rally's leaders. Mailer emerges from the "experience" and its retelling as a half-fictional, half over-real person; the performer gradually assumes dimensions larger than life, and the private Scribe registers the growth of the fictive-factual dimension with such precision and clarity that one critic felt "as if the techniques and faculties of fiction were invented for such a penetration of real life." [29] The manner in which the Scribe registers the welling up of fictuality in the scene reminds the reader that he is reading a factual account. In this sense, the split point of view of the book—one part of Mailer looking at his other part—has an alienating effect on the reader. It prevents the reader from losing himself in the "illusion" of reality. The Scribe keeps him aware of the factuality of the situation and forces him to use his critical judgment about the fictive reality of the world he inhabits.

After the Ambassador Theater incident, Mailer goes to another party, drinks more, and eventually ends up in his hotel. He is tired, baffled, and caught in the confusions of his own actions. Pressured by the fictual experience he has gone through, he compares the harsh actuality of registering one's bewilderment in dealing with reality and the fictive novelist's reassuring solutions: "Sometime in the early morning, or not so early, Mailer got to bed at the Hay-Adams and fell asleep to dream no doubt of fancy parties in

29. Alan Trachtenberg, "Mailer on the Steps of the Pentagon," *The Nation*, May 27, 1968, p. 701.

Georgetown when the Federal period in architecture was young. Of course if this were a novel, Mailer would spend the rest of the night with a lady" (p. 52). But the book is rooted in facts, so Mailer must sleep alone. Indeed his preoccupation with facts is so intense that he, the old fictive novelist, the co-founder of *The Village Voice,* and the sponsor and supporter of many underground newspapers and magazines, at one point finds himself mocking one such underground publication: "Since this interview was printed in the *East Village Other,* one cannot be certain it exists; psychedelic underground papers consider themselves removed from any fetish with factology" (p. 256).

On Friday morning, he wakes up with a hangover. The comment of the Scribe is another undercutting of Mailer's commitments: "Revolutionaries-for-a-weekend should not get hangovers." The day drags on and eventually, after the rallies, demonstrations, draft-card surrenders, and speeches, the March begins, with Mailer "stationed between Lens and Lowell." Being so positioned he feels "the separate halves of his nature well-represented, which gave little pleasure, for no American citizen likes to link arms at once with the two ends of his practical working-day good American schizophrenia" (p. 107). General Mailer, under the scrutiny of a camera crew from the BBC, heads the March with assistance from such other notables as Robert Lowell and Dwight Macdonald. The presence of a camera enhances Mailer's preoccupation with his "image." The camera watches Mailer who also watches Mailer who participates in the March. Reality is filtered through so many reflectors a Chinese-box structure seems to surround the core of the alleged real.

As he marches, the sense of America "divided on this day" suddenly releases in him "an undiscovered patriotism." Contradictory feelings attack him from every sensory direction, and, as he nears the Pentagon, the mystery and incomprehensibility of events increase. The Novelist ponders "what a mysterious country" America is. By now, he is "virtually in love with the helicopters not because the metaphors of his mind had swollen large enough to embrace even them!"—another comment on the nature of his metaphor-searching guest—but "he loved helicopters because they were the nearest manifestation of the enemy." Gradually Mailer finds himself dissolving the harsh and untamable actual into a more controllable private fantasy, a defense strategy he also uses in other episodes recording his encounter with unyielding and stubborn reality. Whenever the real defies his totalizing metaphors, he retreats to the fantastic, over which he has total control:

> . . . Mailer, General Mailer, now had a vision of another battle, the next big battle, and these helicopters, press, television and assorted media helicopters hovering overhead with CIA-FBI-all others of the alphabet in helicopters—and into the swarm of the choppers would come a Rebel Chopper in black, or in Kustom-Kar Red, leave it to the talent of the West Coast to prepare the wild helicopter; it would be loaded with guns to shoot pellets of paint at the enemy helicopters, smearing and daubing, dripping them, dropping cans of paint from overhead to smash on the blades of the chopper like early air combat in World War I, and Fourth of July rockets to fire past their Plexiglas canopies. That was the way, Mailer told himself, that was the way. The media would scream at the violence of those dissenters who attacked innocent helicopters with paint. . . . [pp. 114–15]

The March ends at the Pentagon's North Parking Lot, where Mailer listens to the music of the Fugs. The members of the band are dressed in "orange and yellow and rose colored capes and looked at once like Hindu gurus, French musketeers and Southern cavalry captains." Then the most bizarre act begins: the ritual exorcism of the Pentagon. To the accompanying sounds of an Indian triangle, cymbal, trumpet, finger bells, and drums, the Marchers engage in the "Holy Ritual of Exorcism" to cast out the evil. Then a solemn voice intones:

> In the name of the amulets of touching, seeing, groping, hearing and loving, we call upon the powers of the cosmos to protect our ceremonies in the name of Zeus, in the name of Anubis, god of the dead, in the name of all those killed because they do not comprehend, in the name of the lives of

the soldiers in Vietnam who were killed because of a bad karma, in the name of sea-born Aphrodite, in the name of Magna Mater, in the name of Dionysus, Zagreus, Jesus, Yahweh, the unnamable, the quintessent finality of the Zoroastrian fire, in the name of Hermes, in the name of the Beak of Sok, in the name of scarab, in the name, in the name, in the name of the Tyrone Power Pound Cake Society in the Sky, in the name of Rah, Osiris, Horus, Nepta, Isis, in the name of the flowing living universe, in the name of the mouth of the river, we call upon the spirit . . . to raise the Pentagon from its destiny and preserve it. [p. 121; ellipses in original]

And the voices join in the climax of incantation:

"Out, demons, out—back to darkness, ye servants of Satan—out, demons, out! Out, demons, out!"
    Voices from the back cried: "Out! . . . Out! . . . Out! . . . Out!" mournful as the wind of a cave. Now the music went up louder and louder, and voices chanting, "Out, demons, out! Out, demons, out! Out, demons, out!" [p. 122]

The reality is so heightened that a fiction oozes out of it; the two merge. The rite of exorcism, as one critic suggests, echoes the supernatural of traditional epic narratives with the difference, of course, that in *Armies,* which is more a meta-epic, the supernatural is generated by the actual and the natural itself.[30] The supernatural agent is technology, which is the matrix of the entire registered experience.

After the arrest, Mailer and the other demonstrators are taken to a makeshift courthouse in a post office. Hours pass, and Mailer's thoughts move from public issues to his relationship with his wife, and the ultimate unknowability of other people, leading him to think again about the function of the fictive novelist. His wife of four years is still a "stranger"; this outrages the novelist in him. As a fictive novelist, he regards himself as a kind of "seer," a penetrator into the psyches of other people, a reader of minds. Now, confronted with the opacity of today's people—who, exposed to a complex reality, have learned to internalize their sophisticated environment, banish their true feelings, and

30. K. A. Seib, "Mailer's March: The Epic Structure of *The Armies of the Night,*" *Essays in Literature,* 1, No. 1 (1974), 89–95.

develop a surface life of social roles in the overcrowded, ur-banized culture—Mailer feels that his imagination no longer helps. This is particularly annoying because, like all fictive novelists, "he prided himself on his knowledge of women." Once more he confronts the stubborn, untamable, descrip-tion-defying reality, this time on the level of family life and marriage. He draws a parallel between his wife and America and implicitly acknowledges the realization that both elude his habitual and learned categories of knowing and connecting. The sense of living in an impenetrable world—on both public and private levels—leaves Mailer the Performer estranged and deeply hurt.

Mailer's release from prison ends the first part of the book, the part narrated from the eyewitness stance. In the second part, Mailer the *histor* tries to retrieve the events he did not personally observe by use of the techniques of the exegetical nonfiction novel. He likes to think of the second book as a kind of "collective novel" which is "scrupulous to the welter of a hundred confusing and opposing facts," as the first book was "scrupulous to fact and therefore a docu-mentary." The March on the Pentagon was an enactment of America's schizophrenia, and he wanted to be an eyewitness to it all. His existential confrontation with the events did not give him a solid sense of the present-day American reality, because, the Scribe whispers, he was looking for what was no longer there. He could not identify with any of his fellow marchers or take more than symbolic interest in his arrest and imprisonment; he showed a kind of world-weariness in facing the events. For the Knight of Meaning, all problems and questions were, if not solved, at least categorized. In Book Two, he wants to investigate what happened when he was not present, and to discover if others have managed to find the America he was seeking. Of course, that America does not exist. This is why Mailer finds himself moving from one source to another like a lost child seeking his parents. He finds all accounts contradictory and confusing and talks about using "the strange lights and intuitive spec-ulation which is the novel" to capture the elusive America. As the heading of the sixth part of Book Two indicates,

Mailer is using all his resources, a complete "palette of tactics," to reach the white phantom of meaning. Failing in this, he settles for a metaphor and turns away from embracing the vibrant actuality.

As a quest for the grand informing pattern of meaning behind the facade of chaotic reality, *Armies* is a failure, but as an enactment of the tension between "interpretive" frames of reference and the untamable flow of actualities, it is a great triumph. It does not proclaim the inability of totalizing models to decode current fictuality, but it enacts such inability on a split screen on which we see simultaneously the Old Quest and the New Actuality. Whether one reads the last part of the book, "The Metaphor Delivered," with an alien ear, as does Conor Cruise O'Brien,[31] or an American ear, as does Warner Berthoff,[32] the ending fails to achieve Mailer's conception of the novelist's task: to create something "equal to the phenomenon of the country itself." [33] It is "settling for a metaphor," [34] an evasion rather than a formulation. But that is the essential point: *Armies* is a nonfiction novel of self-exposure. The actual acting out, verbally and actionally, reveals the impossibility of overall formulations. Only by rejecting the antiquated ambitions of the fictive novelist can the writer, confronted with an event like the March on the Pentagon—in Mailer's words, "a paradigm of the disproportions and contradictions of the twentieth century itself"—create something equal to that event by permitting the inner dimension of facts to become visible through techniques of registration and by allowing the complexity of the real to find its resonance in the mythic pattern of the factual. The rhetoric of "The Metaphor Delivered,"

31. Conor Cruise O'Brien, " 'The Metaphor Delivered' . . . reads like the reverie of a patriotic adman, on reading of Yeats's The Second Coming," *New York Review of Books,* June 20, 1968, p. 18. See also O'Brien's *Albert Camus* (New York: Viking, 1970), p. 67.

32. "The great Blakean metaphors of parturition and ambiguous new birth with which the book ends are treacherous to reawaken . . . to my American ear they have the heart-sinking beauty of an entire fitness to this fearful, intimately American occasion; it is hard not to feel that they form a climax which has been fully earned." Berthoff, "Witness and Testament," p. 327.

33. Mailer, "Modes and Mutations," p. 39.

34. Ibid.

which is a *coup de theatre* by the fictive novelist, is a warning to questers for grand patterns of the informing meaning of reality. Such questers, the Scribe implies, will be reduced to sermonizing. The tension throughout the book between the seeker and the observer culminates in this finale: the gap between the solipsistic, meaning-imposing self and actualities opens wider, and the metaphor is delivered in this chasm. The actualities elude the metaphor and, uncaught, move on. If "totalitarianese," like "technologese," is a language stripped "of any moral content," then the language of "The Metaphor Delivered" (Mailerese) is stripped of any earthly, secular, and terrestrial substance. Both "technologese" and "Mailerese" fail to grasp the mythic dimension of contemporary experience. "Technologese" imposes a mechanical order on the unruly experience, and "Mailerese" superinduces a rhetorical order; neither is equal to the ambiguous nature of the fictual.

The book, however, uses the rhetoric of the final sermon as a concrete example of the "bad faith" of the fictive novelist's falsifying self-assurance, not as an escape from complexity. *Armies* ends with the sermon, but behind the sermon are silhouettes of:

> . . . naked Quakers on the cold floor of a dark isolation cell in D.C. jail, wandering down the hours in the fever of dehydration, the cells of the brain contracting to the crystals of their thought, essence of one thought so close to the essence of another—all separations of water gone—that madness is near, madness can now be no more than the acceleration of thought. [p. 287]

The book retains its complexity through the private Scribe, who exposes the impossibility of a fictive patterning of actualities in current America by registering Mailer's will to totalize and, at the same time, the nontotalizable experiences he undergoes.

Like other nonfiction novels, *Armies* is based on a double perspective on reality: the empirical facts of the outside world and the inner fiction released by registration of the apocalyptic facts. The out-referential dimension of the book, the March on the Pentagon, is the external field of reference and the empirical data of the book. Within this larger field of external reference are the mental processes of Mailer's reactions to the outer circle of actualities. The performer immediately brings to the narrative that larger ring of the actual, while the private scribe registers the inner circle of subjective reality. The outer and inner circles continually mingle and provide the basis for a transcendence of interpretation to meta-interpretation.

The out-referential dimension contains the verifiable facts and the core of documentation—references to people, places, events, publications—for authenticating these facts. One of the most challenging problems in the out-referential field is the introduction of actual living people. Here problems of terminology arise. The word "character," as I have suggested before, is quite misleading in discussing living people who appear in a nonfiction novel. In a fictive novel, there are criteria (for example, "flat" and "round"), no matter how arbitrary, for measuring the degree of the writer's success or failure in delineating his characters. By definition, all "persons" in a nonfiction novel are "round" characters. On the jacket of *Armies*, Robert Lowell, a well-known poet, is pictured arm in arm with Mailer, Dr. Benjamin Spock, Noam Chomsky, Dwight Macdonald, and other protesters. While it is true that no two eyewitness accounts of Robert Lowell on the March or at the pre-March party would be identical, the degree of "distortion" in the presentation of his character is limited (if only because of legal considerations). The difficulty added to the problem of "characterization" is that all leading people in the book (Paul Goodman, Macdonald, Lowell) are well-known citizens. All these notables appear in the book both as people whose identity can be verified and as people who have an extrafactual dimension. The tension between the Lowell who has a file with the FBI and who may hold a driver's license, and the person who appears in *Armies* with "languid grandeurs of that slouch" creates both a living human being and an embodiment of something meta-factual. Lowell is both a person and an archetype: "Robert Lowell gave off at times the unwilling haunted saintliness of a man who was repaying the moral debts of ten generations of ancestors." The out-referential dimension tries to bring the solid facts of the outside world into the narrative, but under scrutiny that factual dimension is sooner or later enveloped by the fiction it releases. The barriers, as Alfred Alvarez has observed in his essay on *Armies,* between fact and fiction, life and art, are thus broken down. According to him, Mailer "has written a full-scale imaginative work in which almost every detail can be verified." [35]

The in-referential axis of the narrative facilitates the release of the hidden mythic dimension of the factual and demonstrates what I have called the ultimate "fictuality" of experience. The "Microlanguage" of the book, one of the elements of the in-referential dimension, provides a tight network of military images and battle words, giving General Mailer a context of operation and implying the Civil War–like division of America. The "Microlanguage" of the narrative also releases the mythic undertone of the visible; an example of this is the use of the word "white" in a pre-March episode in the book. Mailer is not the user of the word—he is not playing a linguistic trick here. The meanings of the word are released by the facts themselves. Initially the word has a literal meaning, but gradually it becomes an emblem of not just present American crises but the past as well:

> . . . he [Harris, the Negro leader] now stared out at the listening onlookers, picked up the bread and said, "Anyone like some food? It's . . . uh . . . ." he pretended to look at it, "it's . . . uh . . . *white* bread." The sliced loaf half-collapsed in its wax wrapper was the comic embodiment now of a dozen little ideas, of corporation-land which took the taste and crust out of bread and wrapped the remains in wax paper . . . the white bread was the infiltrated enemy who had a grip on them everywhere, forced them to collaborate if only by imbibing the bread (and substance) of that enemy with his food processing, enriched flours, vitamin supplements, added nu-

35. Alfred Alvarez, "Reflections in a Bloodshot Eye," *New Statesman,* Sept. 20, 1968, p. 352.

trients; finally, and this probably was why Harris chuckled when he said it, the bread was *white* bread, not black bread—a way to remind them all that he was one of the very few Negroes here. Who knew what it might have cost him in wonder about his own allegiances not to be out there somewhere now agitating for Black Power. Here he was instead with White bread—White money, White methods, even White illegalities. [pp. 62–63]

In his analysis of contemporary American narratives, Tony Tanner observes that "a writer seeking to get at American reality might do well to combine the documentary and the demonic modes, to develop a sense of magic without losing the empirical eye, and to admit his own relationship to the material he is handling and the interpretation he is offering." [36] Tanner then labels Mailer's novels "demonized documentary," which, though not a correct description of *Armies,* is certainly a suggestive one. The label points to the complexity of the book and especially its movement between the dark side of the novelist's quest (Tanner's *demonic*) and the pressure of actualities (Tanner's *documentary*). Such a reading could become simplifying outside the context of the testimonial stance described in this chapter. The schizophrenia, which is not just stated in the book but enacted in its very narrative fabric and point of view, is ´a manifestation of the brute facts of contemporary experience and the agonies of the "isolated self, the multifaceted and complex 'I' " which "rises above the communal, historical and extra-rational events, and assumes mythic proportions of its own," and loudly asserts "I am my own myth." [37]

Such tension between the public reality and the private consciousness—and also the inadequacies of the narrative techniques devised by fictive novelists to map this ever-increasing gap—is surely at the heart of *Armies.* In this book, as one reviewer observes, Mailer "gives the impression of a writer so disoriented from his art that he is perhaps consciously writing the equivalent of Fitzgerald's

36. Tanner, *City of Words,* p. 348.
37. A. Poulin, Jr., "Contemporary American Poetry: The Radical Tradition," in *Contemporary American Poetry,* ed. Poulin (Boston: Houghton Mifflin, 1971), p. 393.

Crack-up; the idea being that if he shows his mind with complete honesty the public will understand why he cannot write the great novel which is expected of him." [38] Norman Mailer himself has summed up the predicament of the contemporary fictionist: "The nature of existence cannot be felt any more. As novelists, we cannot locate our center of values." [39]

38. Mario Puzo, "Generalissimo Mailer: Hero of His Own Dispatches," *Book World,* April 28, 1968, pp. 2–3.
39. *New York Times Book Review,* March 14, 1976, p. 37.

six

The Austere Actuality:
The Notational
Nonfiction Novel

The notational nonfiction novel is the narrative of total transparency. With the aid of sophisticated technological devices, its narrative stance acts out the contemporary mistrust of totalizing fiction. As in the exegetical nonfiction novel, the "author" of this kind of narrative rarely participates in the actual events himself, but the content of his book, as in the testimonial nonfiction novel, consists of the tested experiences of its narrators, and the narrative axis of the book revolves around their testifying voices. This apparently paradoxical situation—the existence of a narrative which seems to have no "author" and many "authors" at the same time—has developed because of the manipulation in literature of current technological devices such as the tape recorder which eliminate the conventional "author" and bring into being a type of narrative in which the testimony of the "narrator" reaches the reader without being filtered through the mind of an official "author." The epistemological authority of the interpreter of reality therefore is undermined, and the "author" becomes a sensitive device for faithfully capturing and transmitting the realities as they are generated. The raw experience itself, not its codification according to an interpretive scheme, constitutes the narrative. Such a stance differs radically from the traditional modernist position which, in Henry James's words, believes that life is all inclusion and confusion while art is all discrimination and selection. As I have mentioned before, one of the main thrusts of supramodernist aesthetics is the elimination of such partitions and the creation of works of art which operate as whole open systems, energized by a dialectical tension derived from an active connection with life. These open systems, for the most part, are based on the principle of total registration and on a rejection of conventional artistic selectivity. The notational nonfiction novel, like other forms of supramodern literature and art, aims at complete inclusiveness, but, because of the limitations imposed by the medium of literature, rarely achieves it.

Through an unselective, total observation of the surface of experience, the notational nonfiction novel reveals the truth of Oscar Wilde's statement that "the true mystery of the world is the visible, not the invisible." The quotidian, the "trivial," and the "banal," registered from this narrative stance, gradually lose their familiar crust and reveal their unsuspected preternatural existence—a process not unlike looking through the lenses of a compound microscope at minute objects and discovering their hidden, monumental, and vibrant life. This unselectivity is a manifestation of the untenability of fixed and preestablished sets of values from which the conventional criteria for selecting the significant derive.

The use of devices produced by an advanced technology has paradoxically taken narrative art to its primitive origins, rediscovering in the form of the notational nonfiction novel the lost oral-aural dimensions. In Andy Warhol's *a;* Oscar Lewis's *Five Families, The Children of Sanchez,* and *La Vida;* in such experiments as Bruce Kaplan's "Convention Coverage"; [1] or even in less ambitious works such as Studs Terkel's *Division Street, Hard Times,* and *Working,* or Theodore Rosengarten's *All God's Dangers: The Life of Nate Shaw,* prose narrative seems to have come full circle: from the oral yarns of the tribal hunters to the spoken urban sagas of the denizens of the megalopolis. Narrative once more becomes not so much the expression of the totalization of experience by an individual writer as the articulation of the deep, dark,

1. Bruce Kaplan, "Convention Coverage," printed in a special issue for "Fantastic Literature" in *Chicago Review,* 20, No. 4, and 21, No. 1 (May 1969), 124–73, rpt. in part as "Talking" in *Experiments in Prose,* ed. Eugene Wildman (Chicago: Swallow Press, 1969), pp. 3–22.

and unmediated forces which agitate the consciousness of the group.

In notational nonfiction novels, the colorful, expressive, and powerful idioms of ordinary people are heard directly, calling into question another widely held aesthetic dictum that the "author" is the articulator of the mind of the inarticulate, the one who forges in the "smithy" of his soul the "uncreated conscience" of his race and its charged idiom. The notational nonfiction novel, by its uninhibited use of the available technology, frees the suppressed voices. The traditionally "inarticulate" may not be able to manipulate the medium of written language in which the traditional critic is most at home, but in his spoken idiom he matches the products of the smithies of the more established modes of expression. The new technological devices have liberated the "artist" in exile, suppressed within the inhibited. In reference to such an emancipation and to an abolition of the concept of the chosen "author" of images, Andy Warhol talks about anonymity in supramodern art: "Everybody's always being creative . . . and how many painters are there? Millions of painters and all pretty good . . . I'm using silk-screens now. I think somebody should be able to do all my paintings for me. . . . I think it would be so great if more people took up silk screen so that no one would know whether my picture was mine or somebody else's." [2] Silk-screen techniques, tape recorders, small movie cameras, and sound synthesizers end the dichotomy of artist/layman, art/life. The notational nonfiction novel, like some forms of supramodern art, embraces the current technology. Warhol's enthusiasm for technology is evident in his references to his studio as the Factory—a name inspired by the assembly line.

The use of new technological devices is another step toward the elimination of willed commentary on the multifaceted, ambiguous, and elusive contemporary experience. The replacement of the "author" by technological devices

2. "Andy Warhol: Interview with G. R. Swenson," in *Pop Art Redefined,* ed. John Russell and Suzi Gablik (New York: Praeger, 1969), pp. 116–17.

helps to prevent the imposition of meanings and the extraction of order from the flow of chaotic experience. In this type of narrative, "insight" is out, and meaning mongering, that symptom of man's terror of facing his arbitrary destiny, is impersonally and ruthlessly prevented. Of course, such a narrative does embody a view of life. But the "view" or "vision" lies in the experiential situation itself and is not projected onto the neutral experience by the "author." Ondine expresses this point clearly when he talks to Warhol in *a* about "a vision I don't see." In other words, the notational nonfiction novel, although testimonial in its content, is non-relational as far as the "author" and the book are concerned. The persons in the narrative bypass the "author" and connect directly to the reader. This type of narrative has the unpredictability for its "author" that the conventional forms of prose narrative have for their reader. Like "Action Painting," in which shapes and masses come into existence in front of the eyes of the "painter" without his foreknowledge of their existence, the narrative line of the notational nonfiction novel and the components of its experiential situation unfold before the "author" as he listens to the "narrators" depict their own fictual world. This makes the notational nonfiction novel a kind of aleatory narrative. Unlike the two types previously discussed, the notational nonfiction novel is "authored" as time progresses. *In Cold Blood* is composed mainly to "re-cover" the experience; *The Armies of the Night* aims at "covering" the experience; *a* is in fact "discovering" the experience. During this process of "dis-covery," the "reader," the "author," and the "narrator" are all simultaneously hurled, to quote Sartre, "into the midst of a universe where there are no witnesses." [3] The notational nonfiction novel, therefore, through a minute-by-minute registration of events as they unfold in the course of external measurable time, establishes the "there-ness" of the world and the "other-ness" of the experience of contemporary man. It does this with an august simplicity. An "obviousness" and "transparency" which, in

3. Jean-Paul Sartre, *What Is Literature?* trans. B. Frechtman (New York: Harper and Row, 1965), p. 223.

Robbe-Grillet's words, "preclude the existence of *higher worlds*," [4] allows the presence of the phenomenal world to "prevail over whatever explanatory theory that may try to enclose them in a system of references. . . ." [5] Thus the notational nonfiction novel may be regarded as the narrative of absolute literalness. Instead of a fictive world, the notational nonfiction novel depicts a stubborn phenomenal circle of experience which, when closely examined, proves baffling and mysterious.

The notational nonfiction novel, consequently, contains a great quantity of what Brecht calls "unreworked" raw materials and incorporates chunks of the factual in its own right.[6] This rawness of materials and the method of construction make a notational nonfiction novel the closest form of durational realism in which the rhythm of events inside the book corresponds directly with the movements of actual phenomena. No telescoping, no summarizing, and no metaphorizing occur in such a narrative which, to quote Sartre again, will "exist in the manner of things, of plants, of events and not at first like products of man." [7] If any symbolic dimension pointing beyond the "irreducible truth of appearance" to a scheme of meaning exists in such a narrative, it emerges from the release of the fictivity of the factual and not from any imposition of fictional patterns. The resonance of the grotesque in the disfigured Cruz in *La Vida* is in the person herself. Warhol's statement about himself, its tongue-in-cheek tone notwithstanding, is pertinent to the notational nonfiction novel's attitude toward reality: "If you want to know all about Andy Warhol, just look at the surface of my paintings and films and me, and there I am. There's nothing behind it." [8] Such a statement is indicative of the larger epistemological context of the supramod-

4. Alain Robbe-Grillet, *For a New Novel*, trans. Richard Howard (New York: Grove Press, 1965), p. 87.

5. Ibid., p. 21.

6. Bertolt Brecht, *Notizen uber realistische Schreibweise*, in Rainer Crone, *Andy Warhol*, trans. John W. Gabriel (New York: Praeger, 1970), p. 53.

7. Sartre, *What Is Literature?* p. 223.

8. *Andy Warhol* (published on the occasion of the Andy Warhol Exhibition at Moderna Musset in Stockholm, Feb.–March 1968), n. pag.

ern sensibility—its questioning of the nature of knowledge and of the validity of patterning the meaning which is supposed to underlie the appearance. The notational nonfiction novel is an impersonally executed narrative which hogties the mystique of reality. It shares this aesthetic view with Minimal Art, another supramodern movement which, in the words of Allen Leepa, is "an effort to deal as directly as possible with the nature of experience and its perception. . . ." [9] The Minimalists too practice what I have called a zero degree of interpretation and, like the nonfiction novelist, try to establish contact with the "phenomenal" world.

Such an attitude toward reality is contrary to the position held by the liberal-humanist tradition which defines literature and the arts as an implicit statement about the human condition and thus both a moral exploration of human experience and a resistance against chaos. Elizabeth Hardwick, for example, asks: "Can a work of literature be written by a tape-recorder?" and answers: "It cannot." [10] From the point of view of the liberal-humanist critic, the notational nonfiction novel is morally blank and therefore irresponsible. In reading books like *a* or *La Vida,* most readers experience a moral-aesthetic weightlessness, because there are no valuational and interpretive guidelines toward which their conditioned reflexes can quickly respond. Such a view informs Alfred Kazin's comments on the nonfiction novel in his *Bright Book of Life.* [11] His position is sympathetically summed up by V. S. Pritchett: "The novel of camera, the tape-recorder, the strictly factual document was intended to replace fiction and to be superior to it as contemporary history; but in achieving this it makes our participation in the story narrow and helpless." [12] Kazin maintains that such a work as *In Cold Blood,* where "there is no 'sense' to the crime

9. Allen Leepa, "Minimal Art and Primary Meanings," in *Minimal Art,* ed. Gregory Battcock (New York: E. P. Dutton, 1968), p. 201.

10. Elizabeth Hardwick, *A View of My Own* (New York: Farrar, Straus and Cudahy, 1962), p. 191.

11. Alfred Kazin, *Bright Book of Life* (Boston: Little, Brown, 1973), pp. 209–41.

12. V. S. Pritchett, Review of Alfred Kazin, *Bright Book of Life,* in *New York Times Book Review,* May 20, 1973, pp. 3, 30.

. . . relieves the liberal imagination of responsibility and keeps it as a spectator." [13] He concludes: "In a 'real' novel—one that changes our minds—a single Raskolnikov or Clyde Griffiths commits a singular crime (and is usually pursued by a single law-enforcer who has no other crime to uncover). The resolution of the crime—murder is the primal fault—gave the moral scheme back to us." [14] Indeed, the very act of reading a nonfiction novel, according to these critics, is morally numbing, since we act nothing out; we remain viewers "who can take any amount of shock without changing our habits. We are cut off from the inherent consistency and exhaustive human relationships of the novel. We have become 'apporatchicks.' " [15]

The position taken by Kazin and Pritchett is obviously an Arnoldian one which still considers the function of literature to be criticism of life and the humanizing of the reader. However, as I have argued in Chapter 1, the critical or interpretive power of literature and the arts decreases as their cultural matrix changes from the industrial to the postindustrial environment. We are now in the midst of a historical period which denies us the innocence of the moral or metaphysical certitude which the humanists insist upon. Any attempt to produce works with "the inherent consistency and exhaustive human relationships of the novel" is bound to impose a falsifying order on contemporary experience. That such a falsification is moral as well as aesthetic is easily discovered by reading Malamud's *The Tenants* and Bellow's *Mr. Sammler's Planet,* to mention only the most achieved recent examples of fictive novels striving toward a moral exploration of the current situation. The fear of the actual and the flight into a sterile nonexistent past which underlie the defensive tone of these novels quickly reveal that the humanistic order they propose is the order of a museum rather than a metropolis. The efforts of such novelists as Joyce Carol Oates and Philip Roth, who are turning

13. Kazin, *Bright Book of Life,* p. 219.
14. Ibid.
15. Pritchett, Review of Kazin, p. 30. See also Kazin, *Bright Book of Life,* pp. 220, 234.

more and more openly to entertainment fiction, and the
silence of Ellison are more authentic reactions to the baffling patterns of "city life."

The phenomenological question about reading the nonfiction novel concerns the change in the overall scheme of
behavior and is an index of the depth of contemporary
estrangement. What makes participation in a nonfiction
novel difficult is the "other-ness" of experience; the same
factor, one is tempted to suggest, freezes the bystanders on
a New York sidewalk while a murder takes place before
their eyes. The metaphysical void and the consequent moral
vacuum which permeate contemporary experience cannot
be willed away by enforced, imagined solutions. The intention of the genuine artists of the times, to quote John Cage's
statement again, is "not to bring order out of chaos nor to
suggest improvements in creation, but simply to wake up to
the very life" they are actually living.[16]

Waking up to this life, and getting "one's mind and one's
desires out of its way" so that it can "act out of its own accord," to continue quoting Cage, is what Warhol sets about
doing in his book *a*. *a* is an exhaustive notation of the contours of the sadly comic life of a small community of homosexuals who recoil from orthodox America into a nomadic
life in Bohemian quarters in New York City. The book, a
transcription of the tapes of about twenty-four hours in the
lives of Warhol and his friends, even refuses to juxtapose
this "underground" world with the "uppergound" world
lest an implicit judgment be passed about the ethics of the
"straight" world. Any conclusion about the lives of these
people or the lives of their adjusted countrymen results
from the reader's own reactions—the book itself is neutral.

The key to the book is its particular notational method,
which I shall call "narrative pointillism." The narrative
moves from one acteme to another without trying to sum-
marize, panoramize, or establish any conceptual rela-

16. John Cage, *Silence* (Middletown, Conn.: Wesleyan University Press, 1961),
p. 95.

tionship among them. The book has no single narrator, and the individual actemes are shaped by the experiential situations themselves, which may or may not be related to those preceding or following. Persons in the book move in and out of bars, parties, restaurants, and taxicabs, call other people, and chat in Warhol's studio. The reader must determine who they are, where they are, and what the occasion is. The narrators offer no help. The speakers are not always identified in the text. Unlike a fictive novel, where all "characters" are acting their roles for the benefit of the implied reader, in *a,* people live their lives and feel no need to introduce themselves to one another. If the transcribers happen to recognize the voices on the tape, then the dialogues are attributed to the speakers; otherwise, they are unmarked. From the same transcriber(s), we receive such context markers as "Pause, talking not understandable," "somebody sneezes and giggles," "Door slams"—the closest narrative indicators to the "summary" components of the classic novel in the book.[17] The rest of the book is an unannotated rendering of actuality—acteme following acteme in a strictly chronological order. The events are as new to Warhol, the "author" of the book, as they are to the "narrators" and the "reader." *a* is based on randomness and indeterminacy, taking as its operational aesthetics the "found" rather than the "invented" image. Each image is seen in isolation, non-associatively rather than juxtapositionally, and thus the whole book is "a workshop of chance," to use the surrealists' favorite phrase. But the surrealism which emerges from the book is a surrealism of the daily life lived by Warhol and his friends. Although their life is by no means a Keseyian empirical projected fiction in protest against the limited consciousness of the middle classes, there are close similarities in mode of behavior and approach to reality between the Merry Pranksters and the Velvet Underground people. Such similarities point up an awareness of the fictuality of experience at all levels of con-

17. Andy Warhol, *a* (New York: Grove Press, 1968), pp. 65, 125, 169. Subsequent page references to this edition will appear in the text.

sciousness and all areas of experience, cutting across the geographical as well as personal and ideational boundaries in a technetronic culture.

The bizarre, spastic, and eccentric life registered in *a* is a life broken into its prismatic components. At first glance and from a close distance, Warhol's "narrative pointillism" seems to be nothing but a series of isolated narrative "dots"—actemes. Only after the whole book has been read do these "dots" become the narrative correlative in which various, disparate actemes blend and convey a sense of scale and context and experiential interrelationship. The immediate psychological response that such a narrative pointillism arouses in the reader is, of course, "boredom"— everything in the book seems mechanical, non-engaging, unmotivated. Warhol's narrative pointillism, however, is imitative, not dramatic—it is a "dot" by "dot" notation of the movements, gestures, and speech of a group of actual people in actual situations. The "boredom" which pervades the decomposed lives of these persons is actual: they are indeed swallowed up in their own yawns. *a* is the most vivid example of "durational realism." Paul Morrissey, Warhol's assistant and one of the actants in the book, says: "We're pushing realism to its fullest extent. Fiction is dead. What people are really interested in is autobiography. Confession. Andy's novel does the same thing the films do: record reality all the way." [18]

The attitude toward reality of Warhol's pointillism is that of deadpan factuality. The actuality which emerges from the book is, in Ondine's words, a very "lazy actuality"; it underlines the reluctance of these refugees from the "straight" world to change the course of their lives, and accounts in part for the rage of the humanist critics who refuse to see man fallen and helpless in gradual disintegration. The ambience and mood of the world registered on magnetic bands in *a* has an uncanny resemblance to the desolate world depicted in Samuel Beckett's *The Unnamable*, as if the fiction of yesterday has become the actuality of today. Beckett's image

18. John Leonard, "The Return of Andy Warhol," *New York Times Magazine,* Nov. 10, 1968, p. 145.

for the degradation of man and the loss of all human contact to the point of "Feeling nothing, knowing nothing, capable of nothing, wanting nothing" [19] seems to be incarnated in the persons of *a*. They too suffer from the "inability to speak" and the "inability to be silent." Worm, one of the "characters" in *Unnamable*, who has only a limbless trunk and lives in a jar tended by a woman, seems to be the composite picture of the people who appear in *a*, living in their claustrophobic world with all their limbs effectively cut off by the dominant ethics of the society. One finds an echo of the theme of Beckett's novel in Taxine's statement in *a*: "But I already did die. . . . There's one like I have one step more to go and that's when I give up. But we have to, we just adjust, my dear, that's all. You know what that step is and that is acceptance" (p. 116). Helplessness and cynicism are concretized in the person in *a* who is actually named "Wormgirl." Inertia permeates the atmosphere and a state of sameness—a feeling that people and things have lost their distinctiveness—dominates the book. Nothing actually happens. The entropic de-differentiation and the ensuing chaos, however, are not used metaphorically by Warhol to convey a vision of life. They are embedded in the very situations that he, with the aid of his tape recorder, registers. Beckett, in contrast to Warhol, employs entropic vision as the interpretive matrix of his fiction.

The code of acceptance and the consequent reluctance to explain reality is made even clearer by the gestures and actions as well as the verbal statements of Warhol. In a television interview, Warhol once sat on a high stool, covered his mouth with his fingers, and told the interviewer: "I tell you what. Why don't you give the answers too." When the interviewer protested his ignorance of the answers, Warhol said: "That's all right. Just tell me what to say." [20]

In its brutal directness, *a* demolishes the illusionistic ve-

19. Samuel Beckett, *The Unnamable*, trans. by the author (New York: Grove Press, 1958), p. 85.

20. Alan Solomon, "Introduction" to the catalogue of the exhibition of Warhol's work at the Institute of Contemporary Art, Boston, Oct. 1–Nov. 6, 1966, p. 5.

racity of the fictive novel and substitutes for it an empirical solidity and "other-ness" of its inhabitants. Engagement with this world is total—not a matter of "suspension of disbelief," but of absorbing the life as it is lived. There is always the amazement of the actual. Warhol himself has read *a* at least forty times: "He keeps reading it because it happened: he was there." [21] The reading and re-reading seem to be an effort to remove the alien veil from the experience undergone by the individual himself; an attempt to overcome the self-estrangement. It is ironical however that the gazing at self has been made possible by the very technological instruments that separated the self from the gazer in the first place. Although the supramodernist's re-directed gaze at the exterior of the self and its performances differs in extension and intention from both the introspection of the romantics and the introversion of the modernists, a gaze it is nonetheless. The substitution of mechanical devices for the human observer strips the experience and the self of their metaphysical and personal associations. What Warhol does in *a* and Oscar Lewis in *La Vida* is present a naked image of life so embedded in time it seems uncontaminated by time. In a fictual situation, the distinction between all antithetical constituents of experience vanishes, as does the underlying hierarchy of values which forms the basis for selectivity in the fictive novel. No particular experience is given priority over the others. The result is a recording of the allegedly banal with the same intensity as the supposedly significant.

a opens with Warhol starting a tape recorder and ends when the machine is stopped some twenty-four hours later. The procedures used in producing *a* are very similar to those employed in Warhol's silk-screen portraits of people (Marilyn Monroe), events (race riots), and objects (electric chair), and in his films.[22] The means by which the book is

21. Paul Carroll, "What's a Warhol?" *Playboy,* Sept. 1969, p. 280.
22. "One day in 1964, he asked Henry Geldzahler—curator of contemporary arts at the Metropolitan Museum of Art—to sit on a couch in his studio. Warhol turned a loaded camera on Geldzahler and then walked away, without imparting a hint of direction. 'Andy played a record for an hour or so in the back of the studio'

elicited from actuality are as much a part of its aesthetic semantics as any other element which can, on the traditional scheme, be deduced as "meaning" or "content." The tape recorder is one of the actants in *a*. Like any machine in the daily environment, it affects the behavior of people in the book; they not only acknowledge its presence but also react to it. Numerous references are made to it—some affectionate ("the most insane machine"), some impatient ("how much more do we have of this"), some reflecting sheer boredom ("basta with recording").

The actemes of *a* move on a horizontal axis and have a flat shape—following one after another in a strictly chronological order with no attempt to re-order them for dramatic effect. The narrative has the unpredictability of an open situation, since it unfolds with the same inevitability with which life unravels. The notational nonfiction novel, unlike other forms of narrative, is not set in a compositional context after all other events are known. It is a narrative without "hindsight"—"existential" rather than "meditational."

The book begins with Ondine taking a few amphetamine pills ("Do you need some Obertols?") and ends with his complete exhaustion ("My e yes ar e cl o sing t he l ids are so he av y that—the y have closed—And, I swear I' m asle ep!") What takes place between these two points, which are arbitrary junctures, not determined by any narrative logic, occurs quite by chance. One situation leads to another because of circumstances, not because Warhol or anyone else in the narrative directs it that way.

The 451 pages of taped dialogues and italicized background noises and gestures are a clinical registration of a single routine day which becomes gradually charged with mythic resonance: "Yeah, Bobby, uh, yeah, this is, this is, this is a very weird day; this is a day of uh, twenty-four hours with Ondine and it's uh, on tape . . ." (p. 30).

The "weird day"—twenty-four hours of life for a group

Geldzahler recalls, 'and because I was completely alone, I became a kind of still life. Gradually, I went through my entire vocabulary of gestures as I sat smoking a cigar. That movie,' he claims, 'is the best portrait of me ever done.' " Carroll, "What's a Warhol?" p. 134.

of people in New York City sometime in the summer of 1966—which concludes with a long "soliloquy" by Ondine, inevitably invites comparison with the most celebrated day in modernist literature, June 16, 1904, in James Joyce's *Ulysses*. Joyce structures his "day" in metropolitan Dublin by following the movements of a rootless wandering Jew— Leopold Bloom. The day telescopes all days of Bloom's life, if not all days in the history of his wandering, deracinated race and mankind in general. As a "composite" day, Joyce's day has a highly totalizing perspective. Warhol's recording of Ondine's day, on the contrary, is a literal one. As the most common and universal unit into which human activities can be divided, the day in *a* is a given phenomenon and is experienced in terms of its constituent sense impressions. However, although the day in *a* is a literal day, measured by ordinary chronological time and void of any metaphysical telescoping, it is nonetheless pregnant with resonances of human guests, hopes, and fears. On this literal day, the tape recorder follows a deracinated man—Ondine—bearing the stigma of the homosexual and moving on the margin of his society. The Jew in the fictive *Ulysses*, with his distancing and therapeutic sense of humor, has more than a superficial resemblance to the homosexual in the nonfictive *a,* who also resorts to laughter and nonsensical gestures to distance himself from the surrounding hostile world and its values. The eighteen sections of *Ulysses* are based on Homeric parallels, while *a*'s twenty-four main parts follow the order of reels of tape, each reel having two sides—a segmentation based not on any interpretative stylization of reality but on the operation of a mechanical instrument. The search motif in *Ulysses* for a core of identity (father/son) is paralleled in *a* by Drella's (Warhol's) and Ondine's search for "some cake" and " a little juice" on "Eighty-fifth Street and Madison Avenue." Warhol's conscious intention is not parodic; the parody is inherent in the realities of the metropolitan life that mock the lives and quests of the inhabitants.

The literal, banal day of *a* is a day in the life of the inhabitants of what Ondine calls "the village of the damned"—an underworld to which the persons in *a* are exiled by "straight" America. Psychoanalytical perspectives are not needed to realize how this underworld is the outgrowth of the pathological dread the white, adjusted, heterosexual American male has about his own sexual identity and his ability to meet society's cartoonish norms of masculinity. The strange behavior of the people in this "village," their horseplay and sophomoric pranks, are not unlike the jokes and gestures of prisoners trying to kill long hours. The grotesque world of *a* is a faithful record of the distortion of human values under the pressures of the code of masculinity concocted to protect the sensibility of the fearful majority. Ondine and his friends inhabit the emotional ghetto of America. To survive in this ghetto, they must develop a defense mechanism which, although on the surface unlike the life-style of other minorities, serves the same purpose: to sustain life in a culture of callousness, self-alienation, and atomization to the point of crack-up.

Like a gang in a ghetto, people in this underworld have all baptized themselves with new names which blur, rather than clarify, their personal identities. However, the denizens of the "village of the damned" do not take themselves that seriously—their adopted names parody the norms of the aboveground world and sometimes point to a particular area of experience of personal importance for them. Ondine introduces himself as a person whose first name is "Catherina" while his adopted last name, he is told, means "boredom" in French. The common practice in the gay world of calling men by women's names leads to a confusing blurring of the most visible identity marker—the sex of the named person. Grammatical genders are mixed, and people are referred to as he/she interchangeably, sometimes in the same conversation. Warhol has adopted the name "Drella"; other names include "International Velvet," "Ultra Violet," "Taxine," "Paul Paul," "The Sugar Plum Fairy," "Billy Name," and so forth.

The lives of these people, like all other marginal groups, are characterized by powerlessness and despair. The imposed "masculinity" norm of mainstream life has turned them into schizophrenics who, in a haze of self-estrangement, grope toward some kind of temporary relief from confusion and pain. Most of them numb their senses with drugs. The common bond is fear of the "straight" world rather than a sense of attachment. They are full of hatred, for the "straight" world and for one another. They have internalized shame, self-hatred, and fear and have been conditioned to relate to others in these terms. They also fear the anguish of growing old, becoming less attractive to partners, and thus losing touch even with people within the same circle. The feeling of being "walled-in" and bored dominates *a*.

Boredom has haunted Warhol for a number of years. His treatment of what T. S. Eliot regarded as the most horrifying aspect of technologized life, however, is quite different from that of the modernists. In such movies as *Sleep* (a man sleeps for about six hours), *Empire* (the camera stares at the Empire State Building for about eight hours), *Kiss* (a couple kisses for five hours), or *Eat* (the artist Robert Indiana munches a mushroom for about half an hour), Warhol releases boredom from the very substance of contemporary life by closely registering its various facets with the help of mechanical devices. In his silk-screen paintings he deals with boredom through the technique of the serialization of the image. His method is based on the idea that the only way to deal with boredom—the inseparable essence of contemporary life—is to let the reader/observer/hearer experience it. This aesthetic principle, which Yvor Winters attacked under the label of "imitative form," informs Warhol's art.

Boredom and agitation are inherent in any extreme experience which the involved people attempt unsuccessfully to transcend. In *a*, boredom is enacted in a number of ways. First the lives of the people involved are so minutely registered by the process of durational registration that the routinized, repetitious, and boring qualities are visibly released. The persons in *a* try hard to bring variety and freshness into their lives, but the range of experience they deal with proves to be very limited, partly because the dominant cult of masculinity has turned them into one-dimensional persons. They are, as the earliest painting exercises of Sugar Plum Fairy seem to imply, all "monkeys in a cage" looking at the "green trees" outside the cage. To divert themselves they play games, take drugs, and try to convert the predictable, daily life into an ongoing, open-ended happening. The interview that Ondine and his friends conduct in the Factory to hire a receptionist is one example of the way they play with the actual to distance themselves and lessen its pressures. The interview ends with the successful candidate declaring: "I don't want to come here everyday," and the interviewer advising: "Well, then don't. I don't blame her and I don't think either one of you will want to come here everyday either. I'm serious." Ondine and his friends also play a game for a considerable length of time on side two of reel six. Even text of the book sometimes playfully repeats itself in a manner similar to the serialization of the image in Warhol's silk-screens (pp. 159–60).

Out of the low-definition conversations, repetitious actions, routinized life, and serialized text grows a feeling of inertia, apathy, lethargy, and tiredness: "I'm so tired it's an effort for me to say I'm so tired." But this inertia and seeming passivity is reached after possibilities have been exhausted; it is a nirvana without peace. Commenting on Warhol's life, one of the persons in the book says: "if you ever throw the side he's pointing at, this is the most passive put-on I've ever seen; as a result of having this, Drella doesn't have to participate in life" (p. 145). Most persons in *a* are aware of the nature of their schizophrenic life and the paranoia they live with, but more often than not they choose to joke about it: "Paranoid. I don't even know what the word means," announces Ondine, the most exposed person in the book.

The reality of the outside world is a conventional reality in that the members of the community agree to regard certain events as real: "The *New York Times* has told us so we should know." The lives of people who accept this version of reality and remain insensitive to the pulsations of the times are full of pseudo-questions which Ondine calls "Probloom." The actions of Warhol's friends resemble the projected fiction of the Merry Pranksters to the extent that both groups, in rejecting the falsifying versions of reality, try to establish a connection with the actuality. This usually results in the adoption of an attitude of mockery and ridicule toward the world outside. Some of the doings of the Velvet Underground are post-Dadaistic in their counterpointing of one-dimensional reality with a more complex human actuality.

The outside world, in defense of its values, attempts to turn the Velvet Underground into a big joke, using it as a source of entertainment, and thus adds to the alienation and frustration of the people who refuse to accept the communal reality. The pressure of the agreed reality of the outside world so drastically distorts the situation that one can no longer decide with any certainty to what extent the announced code is a mocking of the moral hypocrisy of the aboveground world and to what extent a "serious" announcement of a moral position in its own right. The fictuality of the situation intensifies and the ambiguity of the code becomes even more paralyzing when Ondine comments on the Vietnam war: "Anyway. Anybody tells me about peace and doesn't give up their US citizenship is a liar. Simple and honest," but he adds: "I believe in WAR. any war. Its usually essential for the economy of the country" (p. 439). In one statement, the patriotism of the world outside is admired, mocked, commented upon, and mixed with a partly Marxist reading of the fate of a Capitalist society, but the reader is kept in a state of intellectual weightlessness, not knowing how to take these statements. The actuality of the lived life has forced upon Ondine an ability to both hold and mock ideas. He is responsibly irresponsible or irresponsibly responsible.

The nervous preoccupation with sex in *a* is the direct result of the pressure of the "straight" world, which refuses to recognize these people as anything but "queer"—an anomaly. The stigma, naturally, focuses the attention of the "queer" on his "queerness," and this obsession in turn is regarded as evidence of immaturity. The so-called promiscuity among homosexuals becomes a justification for perpetuating pressures on sexually unorthodox persons. If the behavior of people in *a* seems occasionally "childish," it reflects the cruelty the aboveground world has inflicted; because they have been forced to concentrate on their "oddness," full development of their human abilities has been blocked. No wonder the informing image of the book, reflected in the title, is "asshole." Most of the experiments with sex, therefore, are motivated by the sudden eruption of the "id"—the removal of the tyrannous, synthetic superego forged by the aboveground world. The sudden release of pent-up feelings is violent and disquieting to the self-righteous, "straight" reader (pp. 21–22). The one-dimensional personality visible in *a* is an arrested anal personality. The slightest mention of things related to bodily functions sparks a debate or raises a question about sex. When somebody mentions a hair cream, for example, someone asks, "How does it feel up your ass?" And they heatedly debate the comparative physiology of girls' and boys' assholes (p. 27).

An anti-female undertone exists in *a*. The male homosexuals blame women for the formulation and perpetuation of the tough masculinity code. They consider women to be insecure in their own female sexual identity, and prone to see acts of tenderness and love among men as a direct threat to their own position in a relationship. Women are seen as a source of unhappiness at all levels: "And so I, I called mummy and I said: 'You, I'm doing this because uh I'm trying to say what I really think and believe and and you've twisted me basically ever since I was born and I've made mistakes. . . .' " Ondine admonishes a friend: "And get those fucking girls from around your knees. The streets are just full of eligible men. . . ." The presence of "straight" females always painfully reminds the inhabitants of the "village of the damned" of their own sexual estrangement: "Aah! Diana says she's not allowed up here and I said and you would be if you wouldn't bring all those fucky girls with you I said because we uh, we don't, we don't like feeling like freaks" (p. 55). But the anti-female attitude is not a simple either/or proposition; alongside this attitude one finds paradoxically an intense desire to become a "woman" and push aside the male code. The persons in *a* reject the established norms associated with femaleness but cherish the lyricism of vision closely connected with it. One is reminded of Soledad's statement in *La Vida:* "I'm sorry for the effeminate men. They think they're women but they never can be as we are." Ambivalence also marks the homosexuals' attitude toward "male" persons. They admire the strength and generosity of mind associated with the male, but institutions representing male dominance and authority—teachers, policemen, churches, and the like—are bitterly hated.

This ambivalent attitude toward maleness and femaleness is only one manifestation of the homosexuals' deep desire to create a new sex. This new sex, dreamed with the intensity of a mythographic imagination, seems to embody the lyricism and tenderness of the female with the strength and magnanimity of the male. The new sex, however, is not a figure patterned after Aristophanes' concept.[23] It is more an androgynous state of mind—a way of approaching sex in human relationships—than of achieving the self-sufficiency that Plato seems to attribute to the primary sex.

The lack of a spiritual center in the lives of Warhol and his friends in *a* is compensated for by a geographical focus: Warhol's studio. Like the people, the studio has an emblematic name, "Factory." The Factory symbolizes Warhol's anti-romantic attitudes toward art as self-expression ("All right, if he wants to be a poet, let him suffer. There's no poetry without suffering") and provides him with a working philosophy. The Factory is a loft, a kind of village green, which provides for the persons around Warhol the only stable center in their lives. Geographically, it is located in Union Square, New York City, and serves as the focal point of the external field of reference in *a*. Through the Factory—a verifiable center—the reader is constantly reminded that the events registered in the book, and the people mentioned are all real, easily identifiable, and sometimes quite famous (notorious) in artistic circles.

23. See Plato's "Symposium" in *The Dialogues of Plato*, 4th ed., trans. B. Jowett (Oxford: Clarendon Press, 1953), I, 521.

The most disturbed and disturbing person in *a* is Ondine. He is one of those whom Eugene O'Neill describes as "fog people." Rotten Rita, the Velvet Underground candidate for mayor of New York City, himself one of the most eccentric persons in the book, warns Ondine: "When this thing [tape] gets played back, Ondine, you'll realize how CRAzy you are." Throughout the book, he is on the edge of reality and the end-beginning of a dream from which he awakes only to retreat into it immediately by swallowing more amphetamine. Talking under the stimulus of amphetamine is, for Ondine, the equivalent of action in the "straight" world. In a sense, he is the seismograph of the vibrations in this eerie situation; in his confusion, he registers the confusion of the community of which he is a member. He is not the "main character"—the author surrogate—since there is no main character in a nonfiction novel, but certainly he is the most exposed actant. In his talks, he does not try to establish a critical distance between himself and his experience; he is too sophisticatedly naïve to believe that such distancing devices are tenable in extreme situations. He meets the actuality of the situation head-on. Like most other persons in the book, he has learned to use a campy manner in order to survive the hostility of the "straight" world. "Camp," for him, is the conversion of the "seriousness" of the aboveground world into impotent solemnity. He has learned the common device of self-mockery and self-deflation, and keeps reminding everybody: "I 'm no brain—and I never have had a brain—and I don't want one."

Ondine's actual name is Robert Oliva. He has appeared in such Warhol movies as *The Chelsea Girls,* in which he played the role of the Pope—listening to confessions and getting angry at the girl who confesses. But he has re-named and re-gendered himself: "My last name is Olivo. My first name is Catherina," and he uses drugs heavily: "I love amphetamine I love amphetamine I love a mphetamine." Ondine's ancestry and offspring are invented as part of the empirical fiction which is his life: "my life is so much my dick is my life my balls are my husband and myass is my mother in law Now you have the whole family tree my tits are 2 children."

His language reveals a Swiftian preoccupation with images of excretory functions. For him, the tenderest word in the English language is "SH-SH-SH-SHITHOUSE," and he has an obsession with "pissing" in public and/or semi-public places. He is passionately interested in noninterpretive, abstract arts—especially music—but is incapable of reading novels:

> I mean, I mean, I don't mind reading documentaries or Schwann catalogs or lists of one sort or another. I don't mind that. I really don't mind reading biographies if they're, you know, fairly well-written, but I can't take reading novels or anything like that when they're . . . I just can't do it. Anyways, isn't that, isn't that heartbreaking news? I was shocked when I found out that I wasn't reading novels. [p. 9]

The "shock" is the recognition of the loss of comfort that the fictive novel brings with its aesthetic order and artistic coherence imposed on chaotic sensory experience. Ondine's inability to read novels is the inability of the inhabitants of the "village of the damned" to suspend disbelief and step into the imaginative, orderly, and organized world of the fictive novel. The "Schwann catalogs" at least reflect with typographical sincerity the hodge-podge of objects and object-generated experiences which form the matrix of contemporary culture.

Like a shadow, Drella, the quiet carrier of the tape recorder, follows Ondine. Andy Warhol's reflection is seen in the title of the book, whose significance also includes "*all* woman," and "*all* witch." He is the embodiment, for the Ondine circle, of the mythical tenderness, care, and love offered by the female and the protection, authority, and creative toughness associated with the male—the ideal, uncreated third sex. He is unpretentious and quiet: "I'm not more intelligent than I appear" and his appearance is anything but that of an intelligent person.

Although some of the things Warhol does in *a* are similar to the pranks of people like Tzara, Breton, and Jarry, his mode of approach to experience is quite different from that of the avant-garde artists of the early part of the twentieth century. The very idea of avant-garde in the supramodern era is untenable; the avant-garde of yesterday is the most reactionary core of the present literary and artistic establishment. The avant-garde has been replaced by a protean underground, which purges itself of wider respect by constantly contradicting and negating its previous positions. The avant-garde movement sought new modes through which it could integrate the unruly modern experience into forms of expression which were recognized and defined as "artistic." The supramodern counterpart of the modernist avant-garde—the underground—is more interested in the discovery than the taming of experience. Avant-garde art is a "cooked" art, while that of the underground is "raw." Warhol's parties, his avoiding of privacy, and his constant socialization is in sharp contrast with the romantic idea of the avant-garde artist who believed in contemplation and isolation. Warhol tries to find his interior space amid the crowd. The technologized mass society has canceled such romantic views as meditation in privacy: "everybody looks alike and acts alike, and we're getting more and more that way. I think everybody should be a machine." [24] Little privacy can exist in the Factory and there is no moment of individual meditation in *a*—meditation is replaced by thinking aloud. Each person in *a* has his/her own way to find interior space amid the crowd. The Duchess, for example, takes refuge in a hospital, where she manages to obtain three thousand Librium pills and a blood-pressure gauge, and, in a stolen white doctor's coat, wanders ghostlike around the hospital. Her presence in *a* is felt by her absence, and the longest "appearance" she makes is over the telephone as a disembodied voice. Others scarcely amount to anything more than dismembered persons; none of them possesses or strives to possess the old solid self—it is regarded more as a drag than an illuminating center of reference. [25] This changed view of self runs through most supramodern literary works. Behind this new approach to self lies the convic-

24. "Andy Warhol: Interview with G. R. Swenson," *Pop Art Redeemed,* p. 116.
25. See Warhol's comments on his emotional life in *The Philosophy of Andy Warhol* (New York: Harcourt Brace Jovanovich, 1975), p. 26. The book concerns the impossibility of having a philosophy.

tion that in our times, "particularly in the past two decades, the self as a veritable, definable, even possible, entity has vanished in the ironic acceptance of a world without metaphysical center, one fragmented into multiple realities."[26]

Unlike the conventional fictive novel, *a* is not directed to an audience. This stance results in certain formal features which a fictive novelist would regard as awkward. For example, when Ondine is on the phone talking to Duchess and Drella wants him to convey his message to her, the reader reads the message twice: once as uttered by Drella, the second time when Ondine actually conveys it. When Sugar Plum Fairy says of Ondine's life: "He hasn't progressed from anything to anything," his statement is also true about the book. *a* has no sense of movement or progress except that of the passing of chronological time and the slow turning of reels of tape. The book operates, with the aid of its technical devices, like a machine which swallows up anything and everything which happens to be within its operational range. Warhol (?) explains the mechanics of the book to a friend by warning him: "Yeah, Bobby, uh, yeah, this is, this is, this is a very weird day: this is a day of uh, twenty-four hours with Ondine and it's uh on tape *and so are you right now*" (p. 30, emphasis added). The moment Bobby starts talking within the recording range of the tape recorder he's in the book—it gobbles him down. The machine's total registration acquires such a frighteningly totalitarian control that even Ondine begins to get scared: "How much more do we have of this?"

The composition of the taped book is frequently discussed: "this this this is the, this is a novel. It's a uh, so far it's gonna b uh, 18 hours . . ." or:

> DOUGIE—What are you gonna do with this?   O—We're gonna write a novel. It's a novel.
>
> It's being transcribed by three girls.   DOUGIE—What is it all about?
>
> O—Me! [p. 357]

---

26. Max F. Schulz, *Black Humor Fiction of the Sixties* (Athens: Ohio University Press, 1973), p. 52.

And the significance of the project is also discussed:

> How come you're recording his voice?
> Cause cause it's it's you heard what I say darling.
> (D) Not really, that's how he says it. I'm doing a
> a 12 hour uhhh a 12 hour novel.
> (O) On me and my time.
>   What's interesting about Ondine?
> Ondine?
> (O) More than you'll ever see sir. [p. 76]

There are discussions about making the book a tape, "We can make a tape book y'know so that, so that you can only play it on a taper," which would extend the range and fullness of the oral-aural dimensions of the narrative. The naming of the book is discussed with the same casualness:

> O—. . . I think Ondine would be fine.
> D—Ondine sounds, it could be uh
> O—It could be but it isn't gonna be. I mean what else can it
>   be called, Sunday at the Races?, what, A Day At Stark's?
> D—a.
> O—A. (*Laughs.*) Then we'll go on to B, right? oh perfect.
> D—What?
> O—Then we'll go right on to B.
> D—Yeah.
> O—Why call it A?
> D—Well there is no B, but A.
> O—Well we can't, A, B, C, D, E, F, G, H. . . . . certainly.
>   You can't give them more than a sixth of the whole
>   thing. . . . . role as teacher. [p. 257]

These references to the tape identity and title of the book prevent the readers from dropping into a fictional world and reading the book as a fantasy, but, at the same time, the factual account is so fantastic that they cannot read it as a case history of a community or marginal people. The book, in its pushings and pullings into and out of the fictional and factual worlds, requires a reading as a fictual narrative.

The awareness of the persons in *a* of the impossibility in the current age of a "suspension of disbelief"—the *sine qua non* of the phenomenology of reading fictive novels—is shown not only in direct statements but also in a number of subtle parodies and jokes based on the stock in trade of fictive novels. When Warhol and friends prepare to visit Irving du Ball at his apartment, Ondine announces, with the tone of a Victorian novelist, "We are going to visit our hero." The drug-induced "OND INE SO LILIQUY," the only "chapter" of the book which bears a title, is a fictual stream of consciousness which recalls the eighteenth episode of Joyce's *Ulysses:*

> O—I feel li ke a mi llion bu cks!.! I s aid. We ll, whe rever
> they're going, I'll be so mewhe h e else! The y've always
> be en so meo ne. All—t ho se— t h i ngs. I s aw th e m
> in my t ime when I was a child, a long time ago, in a por ch
> so mewh e r e in red clay. Re d clay No rthwes t
> Nebr aska. Po h nny twe lr th—twel fth th i r te en
> miles from f a thering A—is th is is tr ue! H i s true. I was
> ve r y y ou n g at th e time of course but—I sti ll kn e w
> en ou gh—then—that I cou ld decipher what was what!
> What? It was whatit always ie? whate ver it is. Eh, what is
> t h at? What i s th i s? What is th o. Whachowhat. Public
> aaclamati o n—it came to me e ar ly. Ye s, t h at's ri ght.
> People s tarted cheer ing when I we nt to scho ol.
> Scr e aming an d cheer ing— Hur r ay! Ray! Xay! Ray!
> I'll n e ver for get t h e r inging—of—their voices in my
> hair.
> . . .
> th i s is t h e mo st i n ane t ape I' ve e ve r taped. I feel
> h um an ly r e spon si ble f or it! Alt h ough I don't
> l ike th e id e a o f bei ng all too h u man. I st i ll
> res e nt the fact o f be i ng human at all. [p. 446–47]

In a sense, Ondine's soliloquy is another way of revealing that in an extreme situation quotation of the content of the mind is enough. There is no need for the made-up. Warhol is not parodying Joyce in the conventional sense; he is quoting the content of Ondine's consciousness. Any parodic effects are created by the experiential situation itself and not the manipulation of that situation by the producer of *a*. In other words, it is the fictual density of life which is changing the perspective on Joyce's work, not the imagination of Andy Warhol.

The merging of the factual and the fictional, the experiential world and the inner shape of the narrative, create many moments of pataphysical fictuality, during which the familiar is transformed into the monumental and mythical. The relationship between art and life is put in a new context, not by the imagination of the artist or the argumentation of the critic, but by the fictual contemporary reality. When Andy Warhol was shot by Valerie Solanas (B.S. in psychology, University of Maryland, 1958, organizer of SCUM—Society for Cutting Up Men), her sympathizers in Greenwich Village distributed a broadside which read:

ANDY WARHOL SHOT BY VALERIE SOLANAS. PLASTIC MAN VS. THE SWEET ASSASSIN . . . NON-MAN SHOT BY THE REALITY OF HIS DREAM.

The two terms of the dialectic of reality here seem to have been displaced to create a synthesis which grows out of neither.[27] A new category of reality, referred to in *a* as "real and nonsense," emerges in the game Ondine plays with friends; the new reality becomes visible when Ondine paints himself "white from head to toe" and is conveyed in its essence when he excuses himself, because he is "talking to the potato chip." The bizarre experience, however, as Ondine puts it, "has a bit of reality about it somewhere that's scary."

a, like other nonfiction novels, has a self-verifying system which can show that the recorded fictual events have actually occurred. One basic constituent of this checking system is the persons who appear in the book. All the people in *a* appear under names which differ from their real names in life, but there are enough clues in the book to allow for the verification. Ondine is Robert Oliva; Drella is Andy Warhol. They are photographed by a third person, appearing under the name of Billy Name, who in real life is William Linich, the "foreman of the Factory" [28] (in the language of the Velvet Underground), and a competent photographer.[29] Sugar

27. See Warhol's own comments on his conception of reality before and after being shot in *The Philosophy of Andy Warhol*, p. 91.
28. The reference is to the credit on the Grove Press publicity photograph.
29. *Current Biography* (New York: H. W. Wilson, 1968), p. 414.

Plum Fairy is James Beam; Paul is Paul Morrissey, "Warhol's prime minister, major-domo and factotum"; [30] International Velvet is Susan Bottley; and Gerard, the suffering
poet in *a,* is actually the poet Gerard Malanga.[31]

Like other nonfiction novels, *a* has a dual mode of narration. In addition to the in-referential, a discursive mode
leads to the out-referential field of the narrative. Discussions and arguments occur, for example, about human behavior (pp. 359–60). The heated discussions on war (pp.
439–42) are part of this discursive mode, as are discussions
about music (e.g., p. 57) and the arts in general throughout
the book.

The layout of the book comprises three basic "styles":
double-column, block, and what I shall call dented style (the
three styles can be seen on pages 54, 3, and 361 respectively). The dialogues in these three printing styles may or
may not be attributed to an identifiable person. There are
also a number of combinations of styles with labeled and
unlabeled speeches. Scenes with a number of persons carrying on two or three different lines of conversation simultaneously are usually printed in block form with unlabeled
speeches. Such a group situation quickly develops a character of its own, obliterating the identities of individual
members of the group. The block layout with unattributed
lines sums up the personality of the crowd. As the group
identity vanishes, and individual people become more visible, the layout changes (p. 90).

a preserves all the typographical mistakes made in the
process of transcribing to enact the faulty relationship that
usually exists between the message and the receiver of the
message as well as the degree of print literacy of contemporary persons. The language is usually incoherent and prac-
tically one-third of the sentences are not understandable. *a*
is a book of broken sentences, incomplete thoughts, and
stops and repetitions. O'Neill's observation that "stammering is the native eloquence" of the "fog people" seems to

30. Leonard, "The Return of Andy Warhol," p. 143.
31. Malanga's latest collection of poems is *Incarnations* (Los Angeles: Black
Sparrow Press, 1974).

have found an experiential incarnation in the microlanguage of *a*. This stammering, which reaches the point of a disintegration of language, is captured on reel 13/2 (especially pp. 300–301), a scene which resembles the last segment of Ionesco's fictive *The Bald Soprano,* and is, to use Ondine's words, a "hallucinating on words." Ondine's own final soliloquy is mimetically printed in a fractured manner, with letters attached to words not because they belong to those words, but because Ondine pronounces them with a different style of emphasis and stress.

Billy Name has devised running heads, usually taken from the body of the page above which they appear. Some are complete sentences ("I'd like to lay her, I said"); some mere phrases ("mean big paper,") or just a word ("Norma"). The running heads function as a reversed "catch-word" of the old books—rather than directing the eyes from the bottom of one page to the top of the next, they distract the reader, bringing his reading rhythm to a momentary halt, an equivalent to the false starts in daily talking and thinking.

The world which emerges from *a* is a strange, bizarrely passive world in which the raw chaos is registered through imitative form and durational realism. The horror and boredom of contemporary experience is not talked about but iconographically captured so the reader himself is bored, frustrated, confused in the very process of reading. Such an approach to experience in art has outraged the liberal humanists, who look at literature as an agent "resisting brutalization of man by his machine instead of embracing it." [32] It is a total abdication of the traditional responsibilities of the artist as the creator of order out of chaos and the shaper of experience. The artistic talent, for the humanist, is defined as a faculty through which personality is revealed by perception and selection, not acceptance and registration. For the humanist, Warhol is "a mythical beast" who feeds "on the refuse of a civilized society," [33] and *a* is

32. Leonard, "The Return of Andy Warhol," p. 150.
33. Robert Scholes, "The Tape-Recorded Unreality," *Saturday Review,* Dec. 21, 1968, p. 41.

"405 pages of homosexual gossip, inconsequential phone calls, petty squabbles, hours of flittish flutter," [34] which is "haphazardly recorded, sloppily typed, irresponsibly printed." [35] The reality registered in *a* is so different from the network of relationships espoused as "reality" by the fictive novel that humanist critics, confronted with *a*, experience an epistemological disorientation and weightlessness.[36] *a* is indeed "a concentrated mirror of actuality, and the closer we get to it the more frightening it is." [37] The disorienting realization that reality may be quite different from what one is taught by interpretive literature scares the humanists and causes the recoil. *a* is regarded as an act of treachery to the cause of art, which in Ondine's facetious remarks must deal with "the degradation, dishonor and *renewal*" (emphasis added). But, as Ondine suggests, the moral struggle is no longer viable. *a* registers the post-humanist sensibility by putting on the page what Hugh Kenner calls "unweighted facts." [38] In *a*, the facts, which are called (with an eye to the Proustian "privileged moment") "privileged facts," point not to a monolithic, interpretable reality but to a fragmented actuality which indeed the title of the book enacts: the "a" of the title stands not only for *Andy*, and *asshole*, but also for *abominable, amphetamine, acid, amateur*, and, of course, the first letter of the alphabet—the initiator into the secrets and mysteries of experience.

Some narratives bear a superficial resemblance to the notational nonfiction novel in their method and materials. With the widespread use of technological devices by writers, the number of books based on the recording of events will no doubt increase. Most attempt to make sense of incoherent actualities and offer, implicitly or explicitly, commen-

34. Richard A. Ogar, "A Package of Inert Gases," *San Francisco Chronicle*, Feb. 16, 1969, p. 12.

35. Scholes, "The Tape-Recorded Unreality," p. 41.

36. See, for example, Robert Mazzocco, "aaaaaa . . . ," *New York Review of Books*, April 24, 1969, pp. 34–37.

37. Toby Mussman, "The Chelsea Girls," in *The New Consciousness*, ed. A. J. La Volley (Cambridge, Mass.: Winthrop, 1972), p. 464.

38. Hugh Kenner, *The Counterfeiters: An Historical Comedy* (Bloomington: Indiana University Press, 1968), p. 13.

taries on the human condition. The technological devices
used by writers to produce such books more often than not
are put at the service of their own preconceived notions
about human life and reality: the function of technical devices in their work is not to strip away the anthropomorphic
layer of interpretation imposed on reality by established
beliefs, but to support their own theses about that reality.
Like the fictive novelist, they use recorded facts in an endorsive manner to buttress a view of reality. Through the
questions put to them, the interviewees are manipulated to
solidify the private view of the "author," who retains control
of the tape recorder.

The editor of *Chicago Review,* in a special issue devoted to
"Fantastic Literature," announced that "Some of the selec-
tions represent a personal and introspective fantastic, writings that give the landmarks of an inner world. Other selec-
tions represent the 'modernist' tradition of departure from
convention, original fantasy, sound and fury, in various
media. A third category burst upon us with the Chicago
Democratic Convention, the fantastic of the actual events,
what is commonly known as reality." [39] After acknowledging that "it is impossible to pin down the mass of actions
and motivations to a simple interpretation," he offers the
reader "the raw transcript of a fantastic tape made in Lincoln Park during the convention." [40] The fifty-page transcript of the tape is indeed in places an incarnation of "the
fantastic of the actual events"—what Eugene Wildman calls
"pure contemporary oral epic" in which we find *"people . . .*
bewildered and caught by their own now, and glorifying
themselves with their own selves, with their own bodies,
with their own words, with their own acts." [41] But, on the
whole, the tape is a mono-referential narrative collage
which is closer to precision and advocacy journalism than to
the notational nonfiction novel. Bruce Kaplan, the producer
of the piece, shapes the responses of his interviewees by his
direct questions, which narrow the range of response and

39. *Chicago Review,* 20–21, p. 120.
40. Ibid., p. 123.
41. *Experiments in Prose,* ed. Wildman, p. vii.

relate to his interpretation of events. The formulaic and therefore partial approach to the "fantastic actuality" can be seen in his questions, which are repeated with only slight variations in wording ("Why did you come to Chicago?" "What do you think of this?" or most awkwardly, "Have you anything to say about this?"). Like other writers of fact novels or New Journalistic feature articles, he seeks the "truth" allegedly discoverable behind the facade of the chaotic, baffling actuality if one does enough probing with the right kind of techniques. The ultimate allegiance of Kaplan's tape narrative is to the informing, albeit hidden, metaphysics behind the puzzling actualities. The "fantastic" and "strange" appearance of actuality is treated more as an eccentricity, a temporary departure from an otherwise recognizable reality, than as an index of the fusion of fact and fiction caused by the inner tension of various constituents of reality. The duality of experience—the fictuality of the situation—is willfully simplified to a linear, propagandistic interpretation.

Studs Terkel's less ambitious but widely acclaimed books, *Division Street: America, Hard Times,* and *Working,* are tape-recorded accounts of life in Chicago, memories of the Depression years, and modes and moods of working in the United States in the early 1970s.[42] On the surface, they resemble the notational nonfiction novel in their use of tape recorders and narrators who connect to the reader without the mediation of the author. The similarities between Terkel's books and *a* or *La Vida,* however, end here, since, like Kaplan, Terkel approaches his subjects with a well-established frame of reality and literally uses his interviewees to support his reading of American reality past and present. The three books are a series of "portraits" with a great deal of "human interest." Although Terkel is aware that "in unbalanced times, balance is as difficult to come by as Parsifal's Grail," he admits that he was "seeking some balance in the wildlife of the city." [43] Despite some occasions,

---

42. Studs Terkel, *Division Street: America* (New York: Pantheon, 1967); *Hard Times* (New York: Pantheon, 1970); *Working* (New York: Pantheon, 1974).
43. Terkel, *Division Street: America,* p. xix.

especially in *Working*, where they reach a degree of fictuality and become collections of "nonfiction short stories," [44] his books are on the whole mono-referential narratives in search of the ultimate truth whose possession is presumed to liberate the reader. Terkel's preoccupation with a humanistic hunt for the lost order of reality is also evident in his attitude toward the technological devices he uses. He only *tolerates* his tape recorder and is apologetic about using it. For him, the technological device is an "inhibiting factor" to be "kicked" and tamed by "clowning." [45] He jokes about its presence in a human situation—that of interviewer and subject. *a* enacts the befogged sensibility of the contemporary man and is in a sense "a manifesto of our time." [46] Narratives such as *Working* or *All God's Dangers,* on the other hand, are efforts to find the "whole man" whose life and deeds are "the very fiber of the nation's history," probings of individual lives to discover the metaphysics of collective reality which is today's America.[47]

The numbing effects of an extreme situation in which the traditional boundaries between the real and the fictitious disappear in the emerging fictuality are most comprehensively registered in the pioneering works of Oscar Lewis. His writings have had a shaping influence not only on the works of such American authors as Truman Capote, Norman Mailer, Tom Wolfe, and other lesser talents, but also, as Marc Saporta, the French experimental novelist and critic points out, on writers all over the world.[48] Paul Bodin's *Une Jeune Femme* (1966) and Alain Prevost's *Grenadou* (1966) are inspired by the techniques originally developed by Lewis. He has also had a liberating effect on the works of such dramatists as Peter Weiss and Rolf Hochhuth—not to mention the regeneration of the "Theatre of Fact" in the United States itself. George Steiner has emphasized the importance of Lewis's "post-fiction" to contemporary literature: "It seems to me that the language has been most vital,

44. *Rolling Stone,* April 25, 1974, p. 70.
45. Terkel, *Division Street: America,* p. xxii. See also the Introduction to *Working.*
46. *East Village Other,* Nov. 29, 1968, p. 12.
47. *New York Times Book Review,* Oct. 20, 1974, p. 1.
48. Marc Saporta, *Histoire du roman américain* (Paris: Seghers, 1970), pp. 285–86.

most charged with meaning and felt life *not* in the novel, but what one might call 'post-fiction' . . . those works . . . which have inherited the technique, the stylistic vivacity of a great age of fiction but are themselves responsible to the authority of reality." Within this context, Steiner adds, "I would find it difficult to name a recent novel comparable in intensity of rendered life to Oscar Lewis' *Children of Sanchez*." [49]

La Vida, which followed *Children of Sanchez*, registers via tape transcription another extreme situation in which members of a family struggle for their survival when severed from their traditional value roots by the onslaught of brutal urban actualities. The book counterpoints the inner shape of experience associated with "great fiction" with the ultimate "authority of reality" usually reserved for painstakingly factual accounts in such a seamless web that one critic, reviewing the book under the "Recent Fiction" section of a critical journal, found it necessary to preface her remarks by observing: "*La Vida* did win a National Book Award this year; in some future competition it might easily win in both the fiction and nonfiction categories because by then they will have fused under a new label. . . ." [50]

The life of the Ríos family, the subject of *La Vida*, is so mind-boggling in its accumulation of disasters and so complicated in its daily routine that in his lengthy analytical introduction Oscar Lewis, taking (unconsciously?) that life for an ongoing lived fiction, refers to the persons in the book as "characters." The book, nonetheless, is a transcription of tapes made by Lewis and his research assistants. It is, like *a*, a faithful account of events which have actually taken place—a suffered experience which reads like an invented fiction, but whose roots lie in the lives of its many "narrator-authors" rather than in the imagination of one author. The individuals are not constructed types, but real people—sixteen persons from four generations and five households.

The family lives have the harsh nakedness of raw life,

49. *Book Week*, Sept. 26, 1965, p. 5.

50. *Novel: A Forum on Fiction*, 1 (1967), 92. The reviewer, perhaps being deliberately vague, does not mention the actual category in which *La Vida* won an award.

but, like any other fictual situation, enjoy the shape and the curve of the heightened life usually associated with fiction. In one of his earlier works, Lewis himself shows an awareness of such unintended, life-imposed similarities and warns his readers that "Any resemblance between these family portraits and fiction is purely accidental." [51] In reversing the conventional apology of the fictionist, Lewis reveals how much the chemistry of contemporary reality has changed, and how the actual now reads almost like the fictional. He adds: "Indeed, it is difficult to classify these portraits. They are neither fiction nor conventional anthropology." [52] To attempt to formulate the complexity of the Ríos experience into an all-encompassing interpretation is to impose a falsifying pattern on it. Lewis's own lengthy introduction tries to analyze the life of the Ríos family under the rubric of "culture of poverty." But the concept simply leaves out too much that is essential to the very texture of the experience of the family. The bulk of the book itself captures the Ríos multi-dimensional fictual experience.

The overall narrative technique of the book is that of the notational nonfiction novel. Each narrator "authors" his or her own life-story without the mediation of the official author. These stories form the five main parts of *La Vida*. Five sections appear at the beginning of each part, relating— from an omniscient point of view—a "day" or "days" in the life of the household as the subject of that particular section. The book counterpoints the world-directed view, which puts the life of a particular member of the family in an "external" perspective, with the soul-directed view of the persons themselves, who provide an "internal" context for their lives. This double perspective on the lives of the family members is then counterpointed with the actualities of the phenomenal world which exist outside the covers of the book.

The "external" perspective is provided through the five interparts which precede the private, first-person accounts of individual lives. In these sections, as in *a*, the "day" is the

---

51. Oscar Lewis, *Five Families* (New York: Basic Books, 1959), p. 5.
52. Ibid.

unit of duration because a day is an impersonal and universal measurement and has a chronological and established, rather than invented, characteristic. The materials for the "day" or "days" are then reported diachronically, obeying the rhythm of the events as they actually unfold in real life.

The "days" are composed of dialogues and directly recorded scenes, but there are descriptive and explanatory passages which the researchers narrate from a third-person, empirical omniscient point of view. These passages provide a context for understanding the monologues which follow. They give, for example, features of the locale of events:

> The room where she was sitting, the main living and sleeping area, was about nine by twelve feet. With only one small shuttered window facing the sea, it was always dark and damp. . . . A dozen colorful pictures of saints and several bright calendars partially relieved the drab gray color of the room. Finally photographs were tacked on the two-by-fours in the east wall. Below the pictures on a low table were snapshots of Cruz's two children in a handmade wooden frame in the form of two hearts. . . . The kitchen was in complete disorder. Pots which had been used to cook rice and beans, dirty plates and the tin cans from which Cruz and the children drank coffee were strewn over the table and stove. On the table were empty beer and soda bottles, cans of tomato sauce, several jars and a large bag of rice given to Cruz by the welfare agency. She received powdered milk, too, but she didn't like it and sold it or gave it away.[53]

In these interparts, daily routine happenings which provide a context for the Ríos monologues are recorded (pp. 133–35). The "days" are narrated by Rosa, Lewis's research assistant, who rarely tries in these sections to guess the thoughts of the persons or to report on their ideas. Her registration is almost always based on observable behavior. But she herself takes part in some of the dialogues, escorts people to hospitals and welfare offices, teaches English to the children, and serves as a confidante (p. 427). Rosa is the listener and observer; she is not an active participant and

53. Oscar Lewis, *La Vida* (New York: Random House, 1966), pp. 536–38. Subsequent page references to this edition will appear in the text.

exercises no power to shape the course of events or to influence thoughts.

The dialogues in the "days" sections show the person whose story follows in actual daily transactions with his or her friends and relatives. The "days" segments operate as a reality-testing device in which the views of the individual, whose story we hear from a first-person point of view, are seen in the context of his or her interpersonal daily behavior. The reality-testing device is made more reliable by the presence within each part of the views of one or two other persons who are closely related to the main person. In Part V of *La Vida*, for example, we receive two versions of the events which caused Cruz's crippling: her own view (p. 569) and Hortensia's (p. 587). Felicita's recounting of meeting Edmundo (p. 323) is in contrast with Edmundo's account of the same event (p. 335). Erasmo's interpretations of Fernanda's life (pp. 72–86) do not always agree with Fernanda's version (pp. 26–42, 50–72, 87–110, 120–23), and Junior's views of the same events in the same part provide a third perspective on her life (pp. 111–19). These divergent perspectives help to render the complexity of the fictual situation in *La Vida*. The "days" in the lives of the persons involved, the various views of these people on events and on one another's thoughts and actions, create a Rashomon-like technique through which the family is seen through the eyes of each of its members and also through the coolly objective reports of the research assistants. The reader is put in full possession of all available data from all possible points of view.

Such multiple-view accounts of internal and external reality are made possible by the uninhibited use of the tape recorder. Oscar Lewis, a pioneer in the systematic employment of the tape recorder in his work, believed it would help create a new type of literature in which the immediacy of the original experience would be captured intact without being distorted by the inhibitions of the usual middle-class consciousness of an author. Frequently in *La Vida*, a person giving an account of his or her life gets carried away, and the whole story for a considerable length of time takes the form of free-association in which the innermost ideas and feelings of the person are meticulously registered on the tapes. In *La Vida* and in *a*, these moments seem like a plunge outside the conventional reality and a descent to the inward reality of the person. Not surprisingly, Oscar Lewis refers to *La Vida* as an extended account of "unbridled id" (p. xxvi).

"Every day I keep asking the Lord," confides Edmundo in *La Vida*, "to give me more strength and more will and more courage to bear up under all the things that are grinding me down. My life is a novel. If you take a good look at it, it's like a novel." The fictivity that permeates Edmundo's private life—a suffered parable of horror and frustration—is a fiction that oozes out of life itself, a life lived in (to borrow John Calhoun's phrase) a "behavioral sink," and pressured to the point of decomposition—hence the dual reference of the title of the book.

As an extended family, the Ríos are brought up with such traditional values as uncalculated love and close emotional ties. The harsh urban realities and the ethics of survival of slum life, however, have rendered these values untenable. The members of the family find themselves suspended in a vacuum created by the sudden cancellation of old traditional values by emerging urban actualities. They live in a limbo of lovelessness, prostitution, delinquency, betrayal, and temporary consensual marriages which transform the house from a center of emotional stability into a lodging for successive men. Children seek in vain the figure of the absent father in each new "lodger." A sense of the severance of all ties develops: "I felt that I had no father or mother or brother or anybody and that I was on my own, come what may" (p. 485). Marcelo, like his friend Simplicio, floats in an emotional vacuum and hopes for an anchor, a place to develop roots and people to share his feelings with. The search leads most members of the Ríos family to alien lands where they hope to regenerate themselves. Instead, they find themselves doubly estranged:

suffering from both emotional alienation and cultural deracination.

Members of the Ríos family, like other urban refugees, are gradually initiated into a pattern of values which forms a sophisticated code of survival. They learn to ignore the unusable past and the uncontrollable future. Without yesterday and tomorrow, they find themselves enmeshed in the present moment, which must be enjoyed and lived with utmost possible intensity. The present, however freakish in its behavior, is at least tangible; their sensory organs testify to its concrete existence. From this attitude toward time emerges a carefree, hedonistic life-style which finds the future-oriented, plan-ridden, middle-class life gray, cold, and almost dead. Amid the crumbling of their traditional values under the onslaught of technological culture, the Ríos maintain a human cheerfulness and hope. The hope, however, seems less the outcome of a tough resiliency than a vague belief in a miraculous intervention of hidden powers to rescue them from their miseries. Cruz's daydream of a winning lottery number and Felicita's wish to "hit at numbers" symbolize this forlorn waiting for help. The Ríos all believe in superstition in one form or another and fear that a spell which only supernatural powers can lift hovers over their lives. Life in a crisis situation degenerates into such an aberrant series of events; the only match for its arbitrariness seems to be the occult, astrology, and other forms of para-rational explanations:

> "Why did you light the candle?" Rosa asked.
> "It's for Saint Expedito, the one who spends his time in corners. . . . On Mondays you blow smoke into every corner of the house. Then you put out a glass of water or a shot of rum. This saint comes and drinks it and that gives you good luck." [p. 281]

The living conditions of the Ríos, both in Puerto Rico and in New York, amount to a literalization of the "behavioral sink." Their houses are squalid, gloomy, and shabby. In the alleys are piles of uncollected garbage into which chamber pots are constantly emptied. The movie houses, steeped in the odor of urine, are referred to as "Pee Houses." The ceaseless noise of radios, televisions, and juke boxes seems to dull their senses and ease the pain and boredom of long vacant hours. The reduction of life to an almost animal subsistence is clear in Flora's sudden reaction in a New York supermarket: "As they pushed their shopping cart toward the front of the store, they passed a shelf that held cans of dog food. 'Mother of God!' exclaimed Flora. 'To think of buying special food for a dog. Who'd dream of doing that in Puerto Rico? Down there you can't afford to buy enough food for people, let alone a dog' " (p. 420). Their shelter too is shared by animals: "A cockroach ran across the floor and disappeared behind the refrigerator. *'Ay, Dios mío!'* Flora said. 'These tiny cockroaches are worse than the ones we have in Puerto Rico. I throw powder and the men come every month to clean them out, but they come back stronger than ever' " (p. 421). The "cockroaches" that keep coming back are symbols of the wretchedness and animality from which the Ríos family flees but cannot escape. Escape is the obsession of the wretched of La Esmeralda. Like Felicita, they dream about it: "I wish I were a tiny fish, a tiny swimming fish," and all their energies are devoted to freeing themselves, geographically as well as mentally, so they can realize their foremost desire and have, in Gabriel's words, "some peace!"

Though they try to establish a meaningful relationship with society by taking jobs, they usually become victims of exploitation (p. 213). They wind up selling bolita, "a forbidden game, an illegal lottery," picking tomatoes in some remote field in the States, and selling their bodies as whores to the U.S. sailors, middle-aged men, or homeless youths looking for some mother image—the ultimate mockery of their relentless search for roots and a sense of belonging. In an extreme situation, the most common mode of connecting to another person is not through abstract notions like "love," but by means of concrete, harsh touching. Soledad's cynical statement, "There is a whore in heaven whose name is Magdalen," can be taken as either a literal reference attempting to justify her life as a prostitute or as a mute, subtle intimation of the pervasiveness of the ethics of whoring.

Prostitution generates a pattern of action and a way of looking at reality: the mother and children must behave according to the code of toughness, which makes aggressive and callous people of essentially loving and love-seeking individuals. Fernanda, the hot-tempered mother of the Ríos family, has learned how to survive in such an environment:

> I often carry a razor because if someone tries to hit you, you have to defend yourself. When I was in the life, I kept a *Gem* blade in my mouth all the time. I could eat with it there, drink, talk and fight without anybody noticing it. I'd break off one corner of the blade to form a little handle and then I'd slip it between my lower gum and my cheek, with the cutting edge up. . . . When I know I'm going to get into a fight I have the *Gem* ready in my hand, hidden between my fingers. Then, when I get the chance, I quickly cut the cheek or lip. [pp. 26–27] [54]

Eventually the violence is internalized and the result is a drying up of all human emotions. Soledad is quite frank about this: "I don't care about affection any more nor about any kind of love. What I want is money."

The narrative stance of *La Vida* registers the curve of deeds and the texture of people's language. The descriptions of sexual experiences, for example, reach a transparency and vivid intensity that match the most erotic passages in fiction. Kal Wagenheim compares erotic scenes in *La Vida,* told in the words of simple, reputedly inarticulate people, to "Henry Miller's most wildly erotic outbursts." [55] Soledad's recounting of her sexual experience, in power of imagery and intensity of feeling, matches Molly Bloom's language. Molly's description of Boylan's penis as "that tremendous big red brute of a thing" lacks vigor in comparison with Soledad's felt expression of Benedicto's prick "as

54. Her life is so fictive that Philip Stevick has reprinted Fernanda's factual autobiographical account in his collection of contemporary experimental fiction—between stories by Roethke and William Gass. See Stevick, *Anti-Story* (New York: The Free Press, 1971), pp. 117–28.

55. Kal Wagenheim, "Voices of the Poor," *New Leader,* Dec. 5, 1966, p. 14.

big as a water pipe. If he didn't wear a jock it would hang down to the floor." The bizarre permutations of their fictionlike lives gradually make them into schizoids whose only authentic mode of self-communion becomes the nervous breakdown. All members of the Ríos family show nervous symptoms. The gap between the inner self and the social self reaches its pathological intensity in Soledad (p. 202). The trip within is frightening in its revelation of the well-hidden corners of consciousness, and, of course, is socially humiliating. Soledad is painfully aware of this: "But just because a person is nervous and falls in a fit, is that any reason to send her to crazy house?" Her concealment is similar to the silence of Mrs. Clutter and her family (in *In Cold Blood*) about the nervous trouble she goes through. Both women are suddenly exposed to interior spaces; both are running away from them in fright and social shame. Suspended in a valuational vacuum, the respectable middle-class housewife in Kansas and the Puerto Rican prostitute in self-exile in New York experience the same gradual psychic disintegration.

To read *La Vida* is to come into possession of horror. But the fantastic actuality can be comic as well as horrific. The slapstick effects result from the same permutations of events that generate dark horror:

> "So you're looking for a fight, you daughter of a great whore."
> "You're a bigger son of a bitch!"
> When I said that he came over and gave me a kick that knocked me into an open dresser drawer. Then he picked me up in the air by one arm and one leg and dumped me into a chamber pot full of piss. [pp. 312–13]

In his prefatory note to *La Vida*, Lewis says: "In order to maintain the anonymity of the subjects of this study, the names of all the family members, their friends and neighbors have been changed. I have also changed the name of the slum and the names of some of the streets, Stop numbers, bars, hotels and other public places. The names of historical figures and public officials have not been changed."

This change of actual names raises a question asked several years ago by Robert Tracy in his review of *In Cold Blood:* "Does nonfiction become fiction if the facts of a case are followed but the names of the actors are changed?" [56] As I have suggested before, such questions are based on a bipolar approach to prose narrative and a rather unsophisticated view of the relationship between empirical data and the imagined fictive situation. The generic identity of the nonfiction novel is not determined by the mere use of empirical data—the naturalistic novel and most realistic novels share this feature with the nonfiction novel. What makes a narrative fictional or nonfictional depends not on the quantity of facts used or on such relatively minor modifications as the change of personal or place names but on the manner in which facts are approached and the way they are put to use. The facts are used endorsively in fictive novels to support an integrated world view of the novelist, who totalizes the "human condition." Facts are part of the writer's technical battery. But the nonfiction novel does not employ facts to support a private reading of reality—it is written not *about* facts but *in* facts. The approach of the nonfiction novelist to facts is phenomenalistic, not compositional. Whether Lewis changes the names of people and places in *La Vida* is not important. The significant question is whether he uses the empirical data to support an interpretation of life. The disguised names can easily be decoded by the data provided in the book, which lead the reader to the available research files. The nonfiction novel is an open set. Its full range of experience is not limited to the materials contained within the two covers but goes beyond the book and establishes a dialectical relationship with actual life. Research files and all other supporting documents are an integral part of the book. The concept of "achieved content" does not apply to supramodern literature, which refuses to confine itself to the space between two cloth covers. The change of names in a nonfiction novel would change its generic identity only if that change was part of a strategy to manipulate facts, hap-

56. Robert Tracy, "In Cold Blood," *Southern Review,* 3, n.s. (1967), 245.

pened events, and living people to assert a reading of reality.

Oscar Lewis himself has published a book in which he provides the key for decoding the materials covered in *La Vida*.[57] Nevertheless, La Vida, like other nonfiction novels, has a built-in checking system through which the reader can determine whether the registered events are indeed actual or are dreamed up by the author for climactic and dramatic effects. If, as we read *La Vida*, we make a mental map of the streets, we will construct a topography for events which exactly corresponds with the actual geographical map of San Juan and New York. The disguised places are actual, undergoing fictive transformation by mere name changes motivated by practical considerations (concern for the safety of the people and the reputation of the places), rather than an overall fictional design for a private metaphysics.

The built-in checking system, however, is not limited to the topography of the cities. The book provides evidence to lead the reader outside to verify the materials. There are dates and flight numbers for the trips of family members to New York and San Juan (pp. 3, 127, 148, 204, 363) and discussions of public events (pp. 4, 361, 451). Misinformation in the text is corrected by the "author" in the footnotes (e.g. pp. 3, 87). Public figures and their actions are discussed, and their deeds directly affect the lives of the persons in *La Vida*. Muñoz Marin, the governor (pp. 83–84), President Kennedy (p. 236), Fidel Castro and his revolutionary ideas (pp. 358–59, 453) are all referred to. The discussion of ideas and opinions brings to *La Vida*, like any other nonfiction novel, a discursive mode. In these discursive passages, the narrative moves toward the world outside, the felt life and actual events, rather than toward the book itself. This creates the out-referential axis of *La Vida*. The racial problem, for example, sparks a debate which refers to the actualities of the world outside (pp. 450–51).

As a noninterpretive transcription of a fictual situation, *La Vida* has been vulnerable to criticism. A reviewer in the

57. Oscar Lewis, *A Study of Slum Culture: Backgrounds for "La Vida"* (New York: Random House, 1968).

Times Literary Supplement, for example, objected to the absence of interpretation: "So, one might say, in place of Dickens or Dostoevsky raging and protesting . . . we have anthropologists like Mr. Lewis; in place of the direct experience *squeezed to its essence and plumbed to its depth by the imagination,* we have the tape-recorder . . ." (emphasis added).[58] The reader's demand for "squeezing" the experience to its essence and "plumbing" it to its depth with the imagination, of course, presupposes a notion of the essence of experience not available to Lewis and his subjects, who all refuse to will such an understanding. The same kind of criticism is voiced by V. S. Pritchett, who believes "any intelligent novelist would have had the powers of selection and discrimination which Mr. Lewis uses very little." [59] But the principle according to which certain elements are selected and formulated into a "significant form" is lost to the contemporary consciousness, which has been forced to suspend totalization of life experiences to get as close as possible to the actualities.[60]

La Vida registers a fictual situation born out of an incredible contemporary reality. Its refusal to totalize or comment on the reported situations is a refusal to violate the authority of reality, for, as one critic concludes, in an extreme situation: "It is enough to write the facts in a clear hand: it is a mistake to attempt to embellish or improve upon the fantastic actuality." [61]

58. *Times Literary Supplement,* Sept. 21, 1967, p. 829.
59. *New Statesman,* Sept. 29, 1967, p. 404.
60. For similar criticism of lack of "guidance" and absence of "interpretation" in *La Vida* and other books by Lewis, see *Current Anthropology,* 8 (1967), 480–500. Also E. B. Leacock, ed., *The Culture of Poverty* (New York: Simon and Schuster, 1971), pp. 193–225.
61. Stephen Schneck, Review of Hunter Thompson, *The Hell's Angels,* in *Ramparts,* March 1967, p. 54.

Coda

The focal narrative genre of modernist American literature was the totalizing novel, which interpreted the experience of the self in its cultural environment and shaped that experience into fictional constructs which were by and large continuous with the structure of feelings and events in the empirical world. These fictions functioned as paradigms of the experience of the times, because the nature of the novelist's relationship with reality allowed him to totalize various manifestations of life around him into rationally significant and mimetically recognizable microcosms. Before World War 2, the imagination of the fictionist was ahead of the actualities, thus enabling him to formulate a private metaphysics of life in his culture and weave his vision—his view of man and his experience in relation to a larger order—into the fabric of his novels to provide his reader with a pattern of the underlying order of external reality. The advent of technetronic culture in the postwar years, however, has changed the nature of the relationship between the fictionist and the world around him: the actualities, in their freakish behavior, now move far ahead of the imagination of the writer. Contemporary reality is invested with fictive power and unfolds with a shape so fictional that not even Kafka, Joyce, or Beckett could have fully anticipated it. The forces unleashed by postwar scientific and technological innovations have created such historical disruption and discontinuity that the permutations of events have now reached a degree of bizarreness beyond the wildest imaginings. The contemporary fictive novelist can no longer find what Wallace Stevens has called the "sovereign images" with which to explore the emerging realities and organize the engulfing chaos in imaginative forms. The interpretive authority of the totalizing novel has been historically undermined.

The failure of the traditional novel to offer a total picture of recent culture and the situation of the individual within this radically altered milieu has caused many postwar critics to announce the "death of the novel," but even those humanist critics who, disliking metaphors of terminality, differ with such views have expressed their disappointment with the relationship between the contemporary fictive novelist and the culture. Philip Rahv, whose norm for fiction was the writings of the masters of modernism, voiced this dissatisfaction when he observed in his second collection of *Modern Occasions* that the present literary situation in America is marked by a confusion and fragmentation of creative minds. The present-day American novelist, Rahv maintains, has failed "to gain a coherent view of experience and to develop a creative strategy by means of which the raw material at his disposal can be so structured as to produce significant patterns that appeal at once to our imagination and our sense of truth." The question, however, is not so much the decline of fiction and the failure of individual novelists as it is the passing of an era in history in which such total statements about the nature of reality and humankind can be made. Reaching "a coherent view" of contemporary human experience requires a high degree of moral and metaphysical certitude. John Bayley, another liberal-humanist critic, demands such certitude when, in *Tolstoy and the Novel* (1966), he insists: "Anyone writing a novel . . . must have a clear and firm idea as to what is good and bad in life." There are not many left at present who can in good faith claim such an assurance; those who do so and attempt to totalize contemporary experience end up interpreting the present by reference to a preestablished code of values inherited from bygone days. Their fiction, consequently, turns out to be either the fiction of entertainment or, in the most dangerous sense of the word, escapist fiction. They ignore the newness of new realities and, by inventing a myth of continuity based on an assumption of a coherent external reality, lie to their readers as they give false assurances about a nonexistent order. The novels of Saul Bellow, Bernard Malamud, and Philip Roth, which Rahv found to be very close to his ideal fiction, are excellent examples of the fiction of entertainment and neo-escapist literature. The large readership and mass appeal of the fictions of these and other writers such as John Updike and Joyce Carol Oates stem from their escapist value. These fictions provide the readers with an escape from the incongruous realities of the times rather than exposing them to an imaginative exploration of such realities. The gap between the aesthetic order willfully imposed on contemporary experience in these fictions and the discontinuous facts of current actualities is so wide that the present totalizing novel has all but lost the most important function of the genre: the communalizing of values and cultural meanings.

The changes in the empirical and cultural realities in the postwar years (which have historically canceled the role of the totalizing novel) and the internal dynamics of the literary tradition (causing a gradual diminishing of the narrative energies of the fictive novel) have brought about a shift of the narrative "dominant" in contemporary American literature. The totalizing novel has been "backgrounded," and new forms of narrative have come to the fore. The shared epistemology of these new kinds of narrative is their noninterpretive stance toward external reality. Their narrative forms and strategies, however, differ radically from one another, as is evident in the most significant of these nontotalizing kinds of narratives, the nonfiction novel and transfiction. The nonfiction novel replaces "interpretation" with a "transcription" of naked facts. The various modes of transfiction employ a variety of strategies to avoid hiding the reality of chaos and the invading entropy in contemporary life under an imposed interpretive order. Metafiction, for example, uses a highly elaborate mock-interpretation and meta-commentary tinged with dark humor to reveal the absurdity of the contemporary totalizing novel's claim to a metaphysics of experience. And science fiction, another form of transfiction, operates with extrapolation rather than straight interpretation. The rejection of what Leslie Fiedler calls the "platitude of meaning" has become the matrix of the contemporary literature of silence. The traditional humanistic urge to find significance in all aspects of experience is considered by most writers of the postwar period (in Jack Gelber's words) "something perverse"; even adopting an "attitude" toward the mind-boggling realities of the contemporary stress situation is viewed as a disease—a "form of epilepsy," to use the expression of Heathcote Williams.

Epistemologically, the nonfiction novel is rooted in the idea that the experiencing mind, confronted with the impossibility of reaching a total view of contemporary life and the unavailability of any communal values which could endow experience with a shared significance, is left with a stripped reality: the facts of the phenomenal world of events, its surfaces and appearances. Thus, the nonfiction novel uses transcription, not interpretive analysis, as the most authentic way to deal with a reality which has no precedent and defies all established norms. This stance, however, should not be taken to imply that the nonfiction novelist believes in the existence of an "objective" reality "out there," independent of the consciousness of the human perceiver. As Niels Bohr observes in his *Atomic Theory and the Description of Nature:* ". . . we are both onlookers and actors in the great drama of experience." The "fact" in the nonfiction novel, in other words, is not a category of reality but an experiential *donnée.* The nonfiction novel concentrates on the perceived object without any claim to "objectivity" in either a conventional philosophical sense or in a literary naturalistic sense. To approach the genre in terms of an objective-subjective segmentation of experience is to ignore its complexity and reduce it to a conventional mono-referential narrative. The nonfiction novelist goes beyond the myth of mutually exclusive categories of "objective" and "subjective" and in the dual modes of his narrative acknowledges the inherently ambiguous nature of human knowledge of the external world. As a writer, he is also aware that his very medium—language—is the main carrier of attitudes and values and knows, as the narrator of Borges's "Alef" points out, language changes whatever it describes. Because of the nature of language, all attempts at objectivity are rendered subjective, but, nonetheless, there is an ontological difference between the nonfiction novel and the fictive novel. The reality which is mapped in a nonfiction novel is not a staged reality invented by the narratist and patterned in a way which endorses his interpretation of the order of the world. The events and actions in a nonfiction novel are actual phenomena in the world accessible to ordinary human senses and, unlike the contents of fictive novels, exist outside the covers of the book. The subjectivity involved in all acts of human perception of the external world does not deny the phenomenalistic status of the experiences transcribed by the nonfiction novelist.

The nonfiction novel is the narrative of the phenomenal world in its literalness. The literal, however, has been heavily invested with fictivity, both inwardly under the pressures of new forces created by various technologies and outwardly through such new communications media as television, which uncovers the dramatic texture and quality of the events constituting our perceptual environment. The new technological, economic, moral, and cultural forces operating in the postwar years and the information revolution which has accompanied them have created what might be called a dramatized society in which events have the substance of actuality and the shape of fiction. The transcription of the literal phenomena of this society in the nonfiction novel, without any intentional pattern-making and fictive structuring on the part of the narratist, assumes the shape of fiction and unravels with the paralogic of a "happening."

The result is what Frederick Wiseman calls "reality fiction." The tension between the centrifugal energies of reality and the centripetal forces of fiction produce double fields of reference in the nonfiction novel and distinguish the genre through its bi-referentiality from such mono-referential narratives as the fictive novel or factual history. Through its bi-referential narrative mode, the nonfiction novel registers the ontological ambiguity of events and in doing so moves beyond the polar perspectives which view experience as either factual or fictional. Contrary to the fictive novelist and the factual narratist, both of whom owe their allegiance either to the self-referential aesthetic artscript or the out-referential empirical factscript, the nonfiction novelist maps the unresolved tension between fact and fiction in contemporary society in his fictual narrative.

The fictual zone of experience emerges from the breakdown of the established boundaries between fact and fiction in recent times. In primarily addressing itself to the registration of this sphere of experience, the nonfiction novel is a distinctly postmodern genre. The blurring of such fact-fiction boundaries of reality in previous cultural periods has always been transitory; the violation of the underlying order has resulted from a stress situation or a passing crisis. Such proto-nonfiction novels as Defoe's *A Journal of the Plague Year* are not dominant forms of their times, because the extreme situation they register is more an accident than the given of everyday life. Since the end of World War 2, however, the matrix of daily life has become more and more like an extended stress situation, and the nonfiction novel has assumed a more central position in contemporary literature.

The newness of the nonfiction novel genre has understandably caused various misreadings of the works within it. The most common of such misreadings is the approach which, considering nonfiction novels as either factual narratives (reportage) or fictional projections (novels), ignores their bi-referentiality, and reduces them to narratives with a single field of reference. The fictuality of the nonfiction novel cannot be understood as long as such polar readings are maintained and as long as the capacity for constantly counterpointing the contradictory categories of fact and fiction—which is an acknowledging of the ontological doubleness of experience—is not developed.

The contemporary situation, as John Cage argues, is a "yes-and-no" situation. Giles, too, in his third descent into the belly of WESCAC, in Barth's transfiction, *Giles Goat-Boy*, discovers that reality is no longer totalizable into a "yes" or "no." The nonfiction novel is an enactment of the "yes-and-no" situation.

Selected Bibliography

1. THEORY OF FICTION

Collections of essays such as John Aldridge's *Critiques and Essays on Modern Fiction: 1920–1951* and Philip Stevick's *The Theory of the Novel* are not included. Nor are anthologies like Miriam Allott's *Novelists on the Novel,* George Perkins's *The Theory of the American Novel,* or Elke Platz-Waury's *English Theories of the Novel.* A few books on general literary theory with significant implications for the poetics of fiction are included.

Allott, Miriam. "The Temporal Mode: Four Kinds of Fiction." *Essays in Criticism,* 8 (1958), 214–16.

Alter, Robert. *Partial Magic: The Novel as a Self-Conscious Genre.* Berkeley: University of California Press, 1975.

Amis, Kingsley. "Real and Made-up People." *Times Literary Supplement,* July 27, 1973, pp. 847–48.

Angenat, Marc. "The Classic Structure of the Novel: Remarks on Georg Lukacs, Lucien Goldmann, and René Girard." *Genre,* 3 (1970), 205–13.

Auerbach, Erich. *Mimesis: The Representation of Reality in Western Literature.* Trans. W. R. Trask. Princeton: Princeton University Press, 1953.

Bachelard, Gaston. *The Poetics of Space.* New York: Orion Press, 1964.

Barthes, Roland. "Littérature littéral." *Critique,* Nos. 100–101, Sept.-Oct. 1955, pp. 820–26.

———. "Introduction à l'analyse structurale récite." *Communications,* 8 (1966), 1–27.

———. "Historical Discourse," in *Introduction to Structuralism.* Ed. Michael Lane. New York: Basic Books, 1970, pp. 145–55.

———. *Critical Essays.* Trans. Richard Howard. Evanston, Ill.: Northwestern University Press, 1972.

———. *S/Z.* Trans. Richard Miller. New York: Hill and Wang, 1974.

Bateson, F. W. "The Novel's Original Sin: A Lecture," in *Essays in Critical Dissent.* Totowa, N.J.: Rowman and Littlefield, 1972, pp. 242–53.

Bentley, Phyllis. *Some Observations on the Art of Narrative*. London: Howe and Van Thal, 1946.

Berthoff, Warner. "Fiction, History Myth: Notes Toward the Discrimination of Narrative Forms," in *The Interpretation of Narrative: Theory and Practice*. Ed. M. W. Bloomfield, Harvard English Studies I. Cambridge, Mass.: Harvard University Press, 1970, pp. 263–87.

Booth, Wayne C. *The Rhetoric of Fiction*. Chicago: University of Chicago Press, 1961.

Bradbury, Malcolm. *Possibilities: Essays on the State of the Novel*. London: Oxford University Press, 1973.

Brady, Frank, and John Palmer and Martin Price, eds. *Literary Theory and Structure*. New Haven: Yale University Press, 1973.

Brainerd, Barron. "An Exploratory Study of Pronouns and Articles as Indices of Genre in English." *Language and Style*, 5 (1972), 239–59.

———. "On the Distinction between a Novel and a Romance: A Discriminant Analysis." *Computer and Humanities*, 7 (1973), 259–70.

Bree, Germaine. "The Break-up of Traditional Genres: Bataille, Leiris, Michaux." *Bucknell Review*, 21, Nos. 2–3 (1973), 3–20.

Bremond, Claude. *Logique du récit*. Paris: Seuil, 1973.

Bronzwaer, W. J. M. *Tense in the Novel*. Groningen: Walters-Noordhoff, 1970.

Bruss, Elizabeth W. "Modes and Metaphors for Narrative Analysis." *Centrum*, 2 (1974), 14–41.

Burke, Kenneth. *A Rhetoric of Motives*. Englewood Cliffs, N.J.: Prentice-Hall, 1950.

Butor, Michel. *Inventory*. Ed. Richard Howard. New York: Simon and Schuster, 1968.

Chabrol, Claude, ed. *Semiotique narrative et textuelle*. Paris: Larousse, 1973.

Champigny, Robert. *Ontology of the Narrative*. The Hague: Mouton, 1972.

Chatman, Seymour. "New Ways of Analyzing Narrative Structure." *Language and Style*, 2, No. 1 (1969), 3–36.

———. "The Structure of Fiction." *University Review*, 37, No. 3 (1971), 199–214.

———. "On the Formalist-Structuralist Theory of Character." *Journal of Literary Semantics*, 1 (1972), 57–79.

———. "Towards a Theory of Narrative." *New Literary History*, 6 (1975), 295–318.

————, ed. *Approaches to Poetics.* New York: Columbia University Press, 1973.

Chomsky, Noam. *Aspects of the Theory of Syntax.* Cambridge, Mass.: M.I.T. Press, 1965.

————. *Topics in the Theory of Generative Grammar.* The Hague: Mouton, 1966.

————. *Language and Mind.* Enlarged ed. New York: Harcourt Brace, 1972.

————. *Studies on Semantics in Generative Grammar.* The Hague: Mouton, 1972.

Cioran, E. M. "Beyond the Novel," in *The Temptation to Exist.* Trans. Richard Howard. Chicago: Quadrangle, 1968, pp. 136–50.

Clareson, Thomas D. *SF: The Other Side of Realism.* Bowling Green, Ohio: Bowling Green University Popular Press, 1971.

Cohn, Dorrit. "Narrated Monologue: Definition of a Fictional Style." *Comparative Literature,* 18, No. 2 (1966), 97–112.

Collins, R. G., ed. *The Novel and Its Changing Form.* Winnipeg: University of Manitoba Press, 1972.

Crane, R. S. "The Concept of Plot and the Plot of *Tom Jones,*" in *Critics and Criticism: Ancient and Modern.* Chicago: University of Chicago Press, 1952, pp. 616–47.

Culler, Jonathan. *Structuralist Poetics.* London: Routledge and Kegan Paul, 1975.

van Dijk, T. A. *Some Aspects of Text-Grammar: A Study of Theoretical Linguistics and Poetics.* The Hague: Mouton, 1972.

Dolezel, Lubomir. "The Typology of the Narrator: Point of View in Fiction," in *To Honor Roman Jakobson: Essays on the Occasion of His Seventieth Birthday.* The Hague: Mouton, 1967, I, 541–52.

————. "Toward a Structural Theory of Content in Prose Fiction," in *Literary Style.* Ed. S. Chatman. New York: Oxford University Press, 1971, pp. 95–110.

————. "Narrative Semantics." *PTL: A Journal for Descriptive Poetics and Theory of Literature,* 1 (1976), 129–51.

Donato, Eugenio. "The Shape of Fiction: Notes Towards a Possible Classification of Narrative Discourse." *Modern Language Notes,* 86 (1971), 807–22.

————. "Structuralism: The Aftermath." *Sub-Stance,* No. 7 (1973), 9–26.

Dudley, Andrew J. "The Structuralist Study of Narrative: Its History, Use and Limits." *Bulletin of the Midwest Modern Language Association,* 6 (1973), 45–61.

Eaton, Trevor. *The Semantics of Literature*. The Hague: Mouton, 1966.

Ehrenpreis, Irvin. *The "Types" Approach to Literature*. New York: King's Crown Press, 1945.

Ferrara, Fernando. "Theory and Model for the Structural Analysis of Fiction." *New Literary History*, 5 (1974), 245–68.

Fiedler, Leslie. "Death of the Novel." *Ramparts*, 2 (1964), 2–14.

Forster, E. M. *Aspects of the Novel*. London: Arnold, 1927.

Fowler, Alastair. "The Life and Death of Literary Forms." *New Literary History*, 2 (1971), 199–216.

Fowler, Roger. "Style and the Concept of Deep Structure." *Journal of Literary Semantics*, 1 (1972), 5–24.

Freedman, Ralph. "The Possibility of a Theory of the Novel," in *The Discipline of Criticism*. Ed. Peter Demetz et al. New Haven: Yale University Press, 1968, pp. 57–77.

Friedman, Norman. "Forms of the Plot." *Journal of General Education*, 8 (1955), 241–53.

———. "Point of View: The Development of a Critical Concept." *PMLA*, 70 (1955), 1160–84.

Frye, Northrop. *Anatomy of Criticism: Four Essays*. Princeton, N.J.: Princeton University Press, 1957.

Garvin, Paul L., ed. and trans. *A Prague School Reader on Esthetics, Literary Structure and Style*. Washington, D.C.: Georgetown University Press, 1964.

Gass, William. *Fiction and the Figures of Life*. New York: Knopf, 1970.

Goldknopf, David. *The Life of the Novel*. Chicago: University of Chicago Press, 1972.

Goldman, Lucien. "Genetic Structuralism and the History of Literature," in *Velocities of Change*. Ed. Richard Macksey. Baltimore, Md.: Johns Hopkins University Press, 1974, pp. 89–102.

Goode, John. " 'Character' and Henry James." *New Left Review*, No. 40 (1966), 55–75.

Grant, Douglas. "The Novel and Its Critical Terms." *Essays in Criticism*, 1 (1951), 421–29.

Gras, Vernon W., ed. *European Literary Theory and Practice*. New York: Dell, 1973.

Greimas, A. J. "Narrative Grammar: Units and Levels." *Modern Language Notes*, 86 (1971), 793–806.

Grossvogel, David I. *Limits of the Novel: Evolution of the Form from Chaucer to Robbe-Grillet*. Ithaca, N.Y.: Cornell University Press, 1968.

Guillen, Claudio. *Literature as System*. Princeton, N.J.: Princeton University Press, 1971.

Guirard, Pierre. *Semiology*. London: Routledge and Kegan Paul, 1975.

Gullon, Ricardo. "On Space in the Novel." *Critical Inquiry*, 2 (1975), 11–28.

Halperin, John, ed. *The Theory of the Novel*. New York: Oxford University Press, 1974.

Hamburger, Kate. *The Logic of Literature*. Trans. M. J. Rose. Bloomington: Indiana University Press, 1973.

Hanneborg, Knut. *The Study of Literature: A Contribution to the Phenomenology of Humane Sciences*. Oslo: Universitetsforlaget, 1967.

Hardwick, Elizabeth. "Reflections on Fiction." *New York Review of Books*, Feb. 13, 1969, pp. 12–17.

Hardy, Barbara. *The Appropriate Form*. London: Athlone Press, 1964.

———. "Towards a Poetics of Fiction: 3) An Approach through Narrative." *Novel*, 2 (1968), 5–14.

Harvey, W. J. *Character and the Novel*. London: Chatto and Windus, 1965.

Hawkes, Terence. *Structuralism and Semiology*. London: Methuen, 1975.

Heller, L. G., and James Macris. *Toward a Structural Theory of Literary Analysis*. Worcester, Mass.: Clark University, 1970.

Henricks, William. *Essays on Semiolinguistics and Verbal Art*. The Hague: Mouton, 1973.

Hernadi, Paul. *Beyond Genre*. Ithaca, N.Y.: Cornell University Press, 1972.

Hirsch, E. D., Jr. *Validity in Interpretation*. New Haven, Conn.: Yale University Press, 1967.

Hutchens, E. N. "Towards a Poetics of Fiction: 5) The Novel as Chronomorph." *Novel*, 5 (1972), 215–24.

Ihwe, Jens. "On the Foundation of a General Theory of Narrative Structure." *Poetics*, 3 (1972), 5–14.

Irvine, Peter L. "The 'Witness' Point of View in Fiction." *South Atlantic Quarterly*, 69 (1970), 217–25.

James, Henry. *Theory of Fiction: Henry James*. Ed. James E. Miller. Lincoln: University of Nebraska Press, 1972.

Jameson, Fredric. *The Prison-House of Language: A Critical Account of Structuralism and Russian Formalism*. Princeton, N.J.: Princeton University Press, 1972.

Jennings, E. M. *Science and Literature.* Garden City, N.Y.: Doubleday, 1970.

Josipovici, Gabriel. *The World and the Book.* Stanford, Calif.: Stanford University Press, 1971.

Kahler, Erich. *The Inward Turn of Narrative.* Trans. Richard and Clara Winston. Princeton, N.J.: Princeton University Press, 1973.

Kahn, Edward. "Finite State Models of Plot Complexity." *Poetics,* 9 (1973), 5–20.

Kavanagh, Thomas M. "Time and Narrations: Indexical and Iconic Models." *Modern Language Notes,* 86 (1971), 823–34.

Kenner, Hugh. *Flaubert, Joyce and Beckett: The Stoic Comedians.* Boston: Beacon Press, 1962.

———. "Art in a Closed Field," in *Learners and Discerners: A Newer Criticism.* Ed. Robert Scholes. Charlottesville: University Press of Virginia, 1964, pp. 109–33.

Kermode, Frank. *The Sense of an Ending: Studies in the Theory of Fiction.* New York: Oxford University Press, 1967.

———. "Novel, History and Type." *Novel,* 1 (1968), 231–38.

———. "Novels: Recognition and Deception." *Critical Inquiry,* 1 (1974), 103–21.

Kern, Edith. "The Self and the Other: A Dilemma of Existential Fiction." *Comparative Literature Studies,* 5 (1968), 329–37.

Khrapchenko, Mikhail. "The Typological Study of Literature." *Social Sciences* (USSR Academy of Sciences), No. 4 (10), 1972, pp. 116–33.

Kristeva, Julia. *Semiotike: Recherches pour une semanalyse.* Paris: Seuil, 1969.

Kuspit, Donald B. "Fiction and Phenomenology." *Philosophical and Phenomenological Research,* 29 (1968), 16–33.

Lawall, Sarah. *Critics of Consciousness.* Cambridge, Mass.: Harvard University Press, 1968.

Lemon, Lee T., and M. J. Reis, eds. and trans. *Russian Formalist Criticism.* Lincoln: University of Nebraska Press, 1965.

Lévi-Strauss, Claude. "The Structural Study of Myth," in *Myth: A Symposium.* Ed. Thomas Sebeok. Bloomington: Indiana University Press, 1955, pp. 81–106.

———. *Structural Anthropology.* New York: Basic Books, 1963.

Liddell, Robert. *Treatise on the Novel.* London: Jonathan Cape, 1947.

———. *Some Principles of Fiction.* London: Jonathan Cape, 1953.

Lodge, David. *The Language of Fiction.* New York: Columbia University Press, 1966.

———. *The Novelist at the Crossroads.* Ithaca, N.Y.: Cornell University Press, 1971.

Lord, Albert B. *The Singer of Tales.* Cambridge, Mass.: Harvard University Press, 1960.

Lubbock, Percy. *The Craft of Fiction.* London: Cape, 1921.

Lukacs, Georg. *The Theory of the Novel.* Trans. Anna Bostock. Cambridge, Mass.: M.I.T. Press, 1971.

Macksey, Richard, ed. *Velocities of Change.* Baltimore: Johns Hopkins University Press, 1974.

Macksey, Richard, and E. Donato, eds. *The Structuralist Controversy.* Baltimore: Johns Hopkins University Press, 1972.

Martin, Harold C. *Style in Prose Fiction.* New York: Columbia University Press, 1959.

Matejka, Ladislav, and Krystyna Pomorska, eds. *Readings in Russian Poetics: Formalist and Structuralist Views.* Cambridge, Mass.: M.I.T. Press, 1971.

Mercier, Vivian. *The New Novel.* New York: Farrar, Straus and Giroux, 1971.

Morrissette, Bruce. "Narrative 'You' in Contemporary Literature." *Comparative Literature Studies* 2, No. 1 (1965), 1–24.

Mudrick, Marvin. "Character and Event in Fiction." *Yale Review,* 50 (1960), 202–18.

Muir, Edwin. *The Structure of the Novel.* London: Hogarth Press, 1928.

Murdoch, Iris. "The Sublime and the Beautiful Revisited." *Yale Review,* 49 (1959), 247–71.

"New Frontiers in the Theory of Fiction." *Times Literary Supplement,* Sept. 3, 1971, pp. 1055–56.

Nin, Anaïs. *The Future of the Novel.* New York: Macmillan, 1968.

Novak, Michael. "Philosophy and Fiction," in *Philosophy Today No. 2.* Ed. Jerry H. Gill. New York: Macmillan, 1969, pp. 209–24.

Ortega y Gasset, José. *Meditations on Quixote.* Trans. Evelyn Rugg and Diego Marin. New York: Norton, 1961.

———. *The Dehumanization of Art: And Other Essays on Art, Culture, and Literature.* Trans. Helene Weyl et al. 1925; rpt. Princeton, N.J.: Princeton University Press, 1968.

Pavel, Thomas G. "Some Remarks on Narrative Grammars." *Poetics,* 8 (1973), 5–30.

Pavlova, Nina. "New Research on the Novel." *Soviet Literature,* No. 10 (1974), 163–66.

Piaget, Jean. *Structuralism.* New York: Harper and Row, 1971.

Pizer, Donald. "A Primer of Fictional Aesthetics." *College English*, 30 (1969), 572–80.

Price, Martin. "The Other Self: Thoughts about Character in the Novel," in *Imagined Worlds*. Ed. Maynard Mack and Ian Gregor. London: Methuen, 1968, pp. 279–98.

Prince, Gerald. "Notes toward a Categorization of Fictional 'Narratees.'" *Genre*, 4, No. 1 (1971), 100–106.

———. *A Grammar of Stories*. The Hague: Mouton, 1973.

———. "On Presuppositions and Narrative Strategy." *Centrum*, 1 (1973), 23–31.

Rabkin, Eric S. *Narrative Suspense*. Ann Arbor: University of Michigan Press, 1973.

Ransom, John Crowe. "The Understanding of Fiction." *Kenyon Review*, 12 (1950), 189–218.

Rayfield, J. R. "What Is a Story?" *American Anthropologist*, 74 (1972), 1085–1106.

Reichert, John. "'Organizing Principle' and Genre Theory." *Genre*, 1 (1968), 1–12.

Rimmon, Shlomith. "A Comprehensive Theory of Narrative: Genette's *Figures III* and the Structuralist Study of Fiction." *PTL: A Journal for Descriptive Poetics and Theory of Literature*, 1 (1976), 33–62.

Robbe-Grillet, Alain. *For a New Novel: Essays on Fiction*. Trans. Richard Howard. New York: Grove Press, 1965.

Roberts, Thomas J. *When Is Something Fiction?* Carbondale and Edwardsville: Southern Illinois University Press, 1972.

Rodway, Allan, and Brian Lee. "Coming to Terms." *Essays in Criticism*, 14 (1964), 109–25.

van Rossum-Guyon, Françoise. "Point de vue ou perspective narrative; theories et concepts critiques." *Poetique*, 4 (1970), 478–97.

Russ, Joanna. "Towards an Aesthetic of Science Fiction." *Science-Fiction Studies*, 2 (1975), 112–19.

Salm, Peter. "The Borderlines of Literature: Toward a Generic Distinction." *Bucknell Review*, 21, Nos. 2–3 (1973), 21–25.

Scholes, Robert. "Towards a Poetics of Fiction: 4) An Approach through Genre." *Novel*, 2 (1969), 101–11.

———. *Structuralism in Literature*. New Haven, Conn.: Yale University Press, 1974.

———. *Structural Fabulation*. Notre Dame, Ind.: University of Notre Dame Press, 1975.

Scholes, Robert, and Robert Kellogg. *The Nature of Narrative*. New York: Oxford University Press, 1966.

Schroder, Maurice Z. "The Novel as Genre." *Massachusetts Review,* 4 (1963), 291–308.

Schwartz, Elias. "The Problems of Literary Genres." *Criticism,* 13 (1971), 113–30.

Searle, John R. "The Logical Status of Fictional Discourse." *New Literary History,* 6 (1975), 319–32.

Segre, Cesare. *Semiotics and Literary Criticism.* The Hague: Mouton, 1973.

Seltzer, Alvin J. *Chaos in the Novel, the Novel in Chaos.* New York: Schocken, 1974.

Shapiro, Michael. "Ideas toward a Coherent Conceptualization of Literary Theory." *Journal of Literary Semantics,* 1 (1972), 89–94.

Souvage, Jacques. *An Introduction to the Study of the Novel.* Ghent: E. Story-Scientia, 1965.

Spencer, Sharon. *Space, Time and Structure in the Modern Novel.* New York: New York University Press, 1971.

Stanzel, Franz. *Narrative Situations in the Novel.* Trans. James P. Pusack. Bloomington: Indiana University Press, 1971.

Stern, J. P. *On Realism.* London: Routledge and Kegan Paul, 1973.

Stern, Laurent. "Fictional Characters, Places, and Events." *Philosophy and Phenomenological Research,* 26 (1965–66), 202–15.

Stevick, Philip. "Novel and Anatomy: Notes toward an Amplification of Frye." *Criticism,* 10 (1968), 153–65.

———. "Metaphors for the Novel." *TriQuarterly,* No. 30 (1974), pp. 127–38.

Stone, Ronald J. "The Novel in the Age of the Movies." *Modern Occasions,* 1 (1971), 547–72.

Style (special issue on French Stylistics), 8 (Winter 1974).

Sukenick, Ronald. "Twelve Digressions toward a Study of Composition." *New Literary History,* 6 (1975), 429–37.

Suvin, Darko. "On the Poetics of the Science Fiction Genre." *College English,* 34 (1972), 372–82.

Swinden, Patrick. *Unofficial Selves.* London: Macmillan, 1973.

Szanto, George H. "The Phenomenological Novel: A Third Way in Modern Fiction." *Texas Quarterly,* 11 (1968), 119–26.

Tate, Allen. "Techniques of Fiction." *Sewanee Review,* 52 (1944), 210–25.

Tillotson, Kathleen. "The Tale and the Teller," in *Mid-Victorian Studies.* Ed. Geoffrey and Kathleen Tillotson. London: Athlone Press, 1965, pp. 1–23.

Tillyard, E. M. "The Novel as a Literary Kind." *Essays and Studies,* 9 (1966), 73–86.

Times Literary Supplement (special issues on semiotics), Oct. 5 and Oct. 12, 1973.

Todorov, Tzvetan. "Les categories du récit littéraire." *Communication*, 8 (1966), 135–51.

———. *Grammaire du Decameron*. The Hague: Mouton, 1969.

———. *Poetique de la prose*. Paris: Seuil, 1971.

———. "The 2 Principles of Narrative." *diacritics*, 1 (1971), 37–44.

———. *The Fantastic*. Trans. Richard Howard. Ithaca, N.Y.: Cornell University Press, 1975.

Toliver, Harold. *Animate Illusions: Explorations of Narrative Structure*. Lincoln: University of Nebraska Press, 1974.

Townsend, Dabney W. "Phenomenology and the Form of the Novel." *Philosophical and Phenomenological Research*, 34 (1974), 331–38.

20th Century Studies (special issue on Russian Formalism), Nos. 7/8 (Dec. 1972).

Uspensky, Boris. *A Poetics of Composition: The Structure of the Artistic Text and Typology of a Compositional Form*. Trans. Valentina Zavarin and Susan Wittig. Berkeley: University of California Press, 1973.

Vickery, John B., ed. *Myth and Literature*. Lincoln: University of Nebraska Press, 1966.

Vivas, Eliseo. "Literary Classes: Some Problems." *Genre*, 1 (1968), 97–105.

Watt, Ian. *The Rise of the Novel*. London: Chatto and Windus, 1957.

Weimann, Robert. "Point of View in Fiction," in *Preserve and Create: Essays in Marxist Literary Criticism*. Ed. Gaylord C. LeRoy and Ursula Beitz. New York: Humanities Press, 1973, pp. 54–75.

Wellek, René. *Concepts of Criticism*. New Haven, Conn.: Yale University Press, 1963.

———. *Discriminations*. New Haven, Conn.: Yale University Press, 1970.

Wellek, René, and Austin Warren. *Theory of Literature*. 3d ed. New York: Harcourt, 1962.

Wicker, Brian. *The Story-Shaped World: Fiction and Metaphysics, Some Variations on a Theme*. London: Athlone Press, 1975.

Wiendold, Gotz. "On Deriving Models of Narrative Analysis from Models of Discourse Analysis." *Poetics*, 3 (1972), 15–28.

Winner, Thomas G. "The Aesthetics and Poetics of the Prague Linguistic Circle." *Poetics*, 8 (1973), 77–96.

Winters, Yvor. *In Defense of Reason.* Denver, Colo.: University of Denver Press, 1947.

2. AMERICAN FICTION SINCE WORLD WAR II

This section lists selected studies of general trends in American fiction since World War II.

Aldridge, John W. *After the Lost Generation.* New York: Macmillan, 1951.
———. *Time to Murder and Create: The Contemporary Novel in Crisis.* New York: McKay, 1966.
Alter, Robert. "The New American Novel." *Commentary,* Nov. 1975, pp. 44–51.
Barth, John. "The Literature of Exhaustion." *Atlantic,* Aug. 1967, pp. 29–34.
Bell, Pearl K. "American Fiction: Forgetting the Ordinary Truth." *Dissent,* 20 (1973), 26–34.
Bellamy, Joe David, ed. *The New Fiction: Interviews with Innovative American Writers.* Urbana: University of Illinois Press, 1974.
Bellow, Saul. "Distractions of a Fiction Writer," in *The Living Novel.* Ed. G. Hicks. New York: Macmillan, 1957, pp. 1–20.
———. "Some Notes on Recent American Fiction." *Encounter,* Nov. 1963, pp. 22–29.
Bergonzi, Bernard. *The Situation of the Novel.* London: Macmillan, 1970.
Berthoff, Warner. "The Novel in a Time of Troubles," in *Fictions and Events.* New York: Dutton, 1971, pp. 102–17.
Book Week (special issue on postwar fiction), Sept. 26, 1965.
Brodin, Pierre. *Présences contemporaines: écrivains américains d'aujourd'hui.* Paris: Nouvelles Editions Debresse, 1964.
———. *Vingt-cinq américains: littérature & littérateurs américains des années 60.* Paris: Nouvelles Editions Debresse, 1969.
Brustein, Robert. "Who's Killing the Novel?" *New Republic,* Oct. 23, 1965, pp. 22–24.
Bryant, Jerry H. *The Open Decision: The Contemporary American Novel and Its Intellectual Background.* New York: Free Press, 1970.
Butscher, Edward. "The American Novel Is Alive and Well . . . Now." *Georgia Review,* 27 (1973), 393–97.
Coleman, Francis X. J. "Is the Novel Dead?," in *Modern Occasions,*

No. 2. Ed. Philip Rahv. Port Washington, N.Y.: Kennikat Press, 1974, pp. 73–87.

Dickstein, Morris. "Fiction and Kool: Dilemmas of the Experimental Writer." *TriQuarterly*, No. 33 (1975), 257–72.

Ditsky, John. "The Man on the Quaker Oats Box: Characteristics of Recent Experimental Fiction." *Georgia Review*, 26 (1972), 297–313.

Dolmetsch, Carl Richard. "Camp and Black Humor in Recent American Fiction," in *Amerikanische Literatur im 20. Jahrhundert*. Ed. Alfred Weber and D. Haack. Göttingen: Vandenhoeck & Ruprecht, 1971, pp. 147–74.

Federman, Raymond. *Surfiction: Fiction Now . . . and Tomorrow.* Chicago: Swallow Press, 1975.

Fiedler, Leslie. "The Novel in the Post-Political World." *Partisan Review*, 23 (1956), 358–65.

———. *Love and Death in the American Novel.* Rev. ed. New York: Stein and Day, 1966.

Fogel, Stanley. " 'And All the Little Typopies': Notes on Language Theory in the Contemporary Experimental Novel." *Modern Fiction Studies*, 20 (1974), 328–36.

French, Michael. "The American Novel in the Sixties." *Midwest Quarterly*, 9 (1968), 365–79.

Galloway, David. *The Absurd Hero in American Fiction.* Rev. ed. Austin: University of Texas Press, 1970.

Gardner, John. "The Way We Write Now." *New York Times Book Review*, July 9, 1972, pp. 2, 32–33.

Glicksberg, Charles I. "Experimental Fiction: Innovation versus Form." *Centennial Review*, 18 (1974), 127–50.

Gold, Herbert. "Fiction of the Sixties." *Atlantic,* Sept. 1960, pp. 53–57.

Graff, Gerald. "Babbitt at the Abyss: The Social Context of Postmodern American Fiction." *TriQuarterly*, No. 33 (1975), 305–37.

Guerard, Albert J. "Notes on the Rhetoric of Anti-Realist Fiction." *TriQuarterly*, No. 30 (1974), 3–50.

Hansen, Arlen J. "The Celebration of Solipsism: A New Trend in American Fiction." *Modern Fiction Studies*, 19 (1973), 5–15.

Harper, Howard M., Jr. "Trends in Recent American Fiction." *Contemporary Literature*, 12 (1971), 204–29.

Harris, Charles B. *Contemporary American Novelists of the Absurd.* New Haven, Conn.: College and University Press, 1971.

Hassan, Ihab. *Radical Innocence: The Contemporary American Novel.* Princeton, N.J.: Princeton University Press, 1961.

————. *Contemporary American Literature 1945–1972: An Introduction.* New York: Frederick Ungar, 1973.

Heidenry, John. "Yes, Virginia, the Novel Is Not Dead." *Commonweal,* May 12, 1972, pp. 233–37.

Henkle, Roger, ed. "Wrestling (American Style) with Proteus." *Novel,* 3 (1970), 197–207.

Hicks, Jack. "Down More Muddy Roads." *Carolina Quarterly,* 24 (1972), 82–98.

Kazin, Alfred. "Form and Anti-Form in Contemporary Literature." *Barat Review,* 4 (1969), 92–98.

Kennard, Jean E. *Number and Nightmare: Forms of Fantasy in Contemporary Fiction.* Hamden, Conn.: Archon Books, 1975.

Klein, Marcus Neil. *After Alienation: American Novels in Mid-Century.* Cleveland: World, 1964.

————, ed. *The American Novel since World War II.* New York: Fawcett World Library, 1969.

Klinkowitz, Jerome. "How Fiction Survives the Seventies." *North American Review,* 258 (1973), 69–73.

————. *Literary Disruptions: The Making of a Post-Contemporary American Fiction.* Urbana: University of Illinois Press, 1975.

Kostelanetz, Richard. "The Point Is That Life Doesn't Have Any Point." *New York Times Book Review,* June 6, 1965, p. 3.

Krim, Seymour. "An Enemy of the Novel." *Iowa Review,* 3 (1972), 59–62.

Lee, L. L. "What's new in fiction, if it's possible." *Style,* 9 (1975), 335–52.

Leonard, John. "The Last Word: The Novel Redux." *New York Times Book Review,* Nov. 14, 1971, p. 71.

Levine, Paul. "The Intemperate Zone: The Climate of Contemporary American Fiction." *Massachusetts Review,* 8 (1967), 505–23.

McConnell, Frank. "The Corpse of the Dragoon: Notes on Postmodern Fiction." *TriQuarterly,* No. 33 (1975), 273–303.

McNamara, Eugene. "The Post-Modern American Novel." *Queen's Quarterly,* 69 (1962), 265–75.

Mailer, Norman. "Modes and Mutations." *Commentary,* March 1966, pp. 37–40.

Major, Clarence. "On New Fiction and Criticism." *Fiction International,* Nos. 2–3 (1974), 151–54.

Mathews, Richard B. "Intermedia Fictions and Critical Consciousness." *Style,* 9 (1975), 353–69.

Mayberry, George, and Sharon Mayberry. "Recent American Fiction." *The Nation,* Feb. 5, 1973, pp. 180–83.

Miller, James E., Jr. "The New American Novel," in *Quests Surd and Absurd*. Chicago: University of Chicago Press, 1967, pp. 3–30.

Newman, Charles. "Beyond Omniscience: Notes toward a Future for the Novel." *TriQuarterly*, 10 (1967), 37–52.

Olderman, Raymond M. *Beyond the Wasteland: A Study of the American Novel in the Nineteen-Sixties*. New Haven: Yale University Press, 1972.

Podhoretz, Norman. "Bringing the News." *Book Week*, Sept. 26, 1965, pp. 8, 14.

Roth, Philip. "Writing American Fiction." *Commentary*, 31 (March 1961), 223–33.

Rovit, Earl. "Some Shapes in Recent American Fiction." *Contemporary Literature*, 15 (1974), 539–61.

Rubin, Louis. *The Curious Death of the Novel*. Baton Rouge: Louisiana State University Press, 1967.

Russell, Charles. "The Vault of Language: Self-Reflective Artifice in Contemporary American Fiction." *Modern Fiction Studies*, 20 (1974), 349–59.

Ryf, Robert S. "Character and Imagination in the Experimental Novel." *Modern Fiction Studies*, 20 (1974), 317–27.

Said, Edward W. "Contemporary Fiction and Criticism." *TriQuarterly*, No. 33 (1975), 231–56.

Saporta, Marc. *Histoire du roman américain*. Paris: Seghers, 1970.

Scholes, Robert. *The Fabulators*. New York: Oxford University Press, 1967.

———. "Metafiction." *Iowa Review*, 1 (1970), 100–115.

Schultz, Max F. *Black Humor Fiction of the Sixties*. Athens: Ohio University Press, 1973.

Stevick, Philip. "Scheherezade Runs Out of Plots, Goes on Talking; the King Puzzled, Listens: An Essay on New Fiction." *TriQuarterly*, No. 26 (1973), 332–62.

Sukenick, Ronald. "Reinventing the Novel." *Fiction International*, Nos. 2/3 (1974), 133–34.

Tanner, Tony. *City of Words*. London: Jonathan Cape, 1971.

Trema, No. 1 (1976), special issue on "Déconstruction & fragmentation dans la fiction américaine contemporaine."

Vanderbilt, Kermit. "Writers of the Troubled Sixties." *The Nation*, Dec. 17, 1973, pp. 661–65.

Waldmeir, Joseph J. "Only an Occasional Rutabaga: American Fiction since 1945." *Modern Fiction Studies*, 15 (1969–70), 467–81.

————, ed. *Recent American Fiction: Some Critical Views*. Boston: Houghton Mifflin, 1963.

Zollman, Sol. "Propaganda for Theory of Human Nature in Current American Novels." *Literature & Ideology*, No. 12 (1972), pp. 59–66.

3. THE CONTEMPORARY CONSCIOUSNESS

This section lists studies of the postmodern literary imagination and works which provide an overview of the cultural matrix of contemporary narrative literature.

Aldridge, John W. *The Devil in the Fire: Retrospective Essays on American Literature and Culture, 1951–1971*. New York: Harper's Magazine Press, 1972.

Alvarez, Alfred. "The Literature of the Holocaust." *Commentary*, Nov. 1964, pp. 65–69.

"America Now: A Failure of Nerve? A Symposium." *Commentary*, July 1975, pp. 16–87.

American Imagination. New York: Atheneum, 1960.

Angrist, Stanley, and Loren G. Hepler. *Order and Chaos: Laws of Energy and Entropy*. New York: Basic Books, 1967.

Arnheim, Rudolf. *Entropy and Art*. Berkeley: University of California Press, 1971.

"Art and Technology: A Dialog Between Harold Rosenberg and Benjamin Nelson." *Salmagundi*, No. 27 (1974), pp. 40–56.

Battcock, Gregory, ed. *Minimal Art: A Critical Anthology*. New York: E. P. Dutton, 1968.

Behar, Jack. "Notes on Literature and Culture." *Centennial Review*, 18 (1974), 197–220.

Bell, Daniel. *Toward the Year 2000*. Boston: Houghton Mifflin, 1968.

————. "The Cultural Contradictions of Capitalism," in *Capitalism Today*. Ed. D. Bell and I. Kristol. New York: Basic Books, 1971, pp. 16–43.

————. *The Coming of Post-Industrial Society: A Venture in Social Forecasting*. New York: Basic Books, 1973.

Bellow, Saul. "Culture Now: Some Animadversions, Some Laughs." *Modern Occasions*, 1 (1971), 162–78.

————. "A World Too Much with Us." *Critical Inquiry*, 2 (1975), 1–9.

Benthall, Jonathan. *Science and Technology in Art Today.* New York: Praeger, 1972.

Bergonzi, Bernard, ed. *Innovations: Essays on Art and Ideas.* London: Macmillan, 1968.

Berman, Ronald. *America in the Sixties: An Intellectual History.* New York: Free Press, 1968.

Birnbaum, Norman, and Christopher Lasch. "America Today: An Exchange." *Partisan Review,* 42 (1975), 361–73.

Bohr, N. *Atomic Theory and the Description of Nature.* Cambridge: Cambridge University Press, 1934.

Bork, Alfred M. "Randomness and the Twentieth Century." *Antioch Review,* 27 (1967), 40–61.

Bornstein, George. "Beyond Modernism," *Michigan Quarterly Review,* 12 (1973), 278–84.

Boulding, Kenneth E. *The Meaning of the Twentieth Century: The Great Tradition.* New York: Harper and Row, 1966.

Brackman, Jack. *The Put-On.* New York: Bantam, 1972.

Brand, Stewart, ed. *The Last Whole Earth Catalog.* Menlo Park, Calif.: Portola Institute/New York: Random House, 1971.

———. *The Whole Earth Epilog.* Baltimore: Penguin, 1974.

Brockman, John. *Afterwords: Explorations of the Mystical Limits of Contemporary Reality.* Garden City, N.Y.: Doubleday, 1973.

Brockman, John, and E. Rosenfeld, eds. *Real Time 1.* Garden City, N.Y.: Doubleday, 1973.

———. *Real Time 2.* Garden City, N.Y.: Doubleday, 1973.

Brooks, Harvey. "Scientific Concepts and Cultural Change." *Daedalus,* 94, No. 1 (1965), 66–83.

Brown, Norman O. *Love's Body.* New York: Random House, 1966.

———. *Closing Time.* New York: Random House, 1973.

Brzezinski, Zbigniew. *Between Two Ages: America's Role in the Technetronic Era.* New York: Viking Press, 1971.

Cage, John. *Silence.* Middletown, Conn.: Wesleyan University Press, 1961.

———. *A Year from Monday.* Middletown, Conn.: Wesleyan University Press, 1969.

Capek, Milic. *The Philosophical Impact of Contemporary Physics.* Princeton, N.J.: D. Van Nostrand, 1961.

Cox, C. B., and A. E. Dyson, eds. *The Twentieth-Century Mind 3: 1945–65.* London: Oxford University Press, 1972.

"Culture and the Present Moment: A Round-Table Discussion." *Commentary,* Dec. 1974, pp. 31–50.

Dallaporta, Nicola. "The Crises of Contemporary Physics." *Diogenes,* No. 89 (Spring 1975), 66–86.

Davis, Douglas M., ed. *The World of Black Humor.* New York: E. P. Dutton, 1967.

DeMott, Benjamin. *Supergrow: Essays and Reports on Imagination in America.* New York: Dutton, 1969.

———. "Looking Back on the Seventies: Notes toward a Cultural History." *Atlantic,* March 1971, 59–64.

Derrida, Jacques. "The Ends of Man." *Philosophical and Phenomenological Research,* 30 (1969), 31–57.

———. "Differance," in *Speech and Phenomena.* Trans. David B. Allison. Evanston, Ill.: Northwestern University Press, 1973, pp. 129–60.

Dhiegh, K. A. *The Eleventh Wing: An Exposition of the Dynamics of I Ching Now.* New York: Nash, 1973.

Dneprov, Vladimir. "What Is Meant by 'Modernism.'" *Soviet Literature,* 325 (1975), 157–63.

Ehrlich, Paul R. *The End of Affluence.* New York: Ballantine, 1974.

Ellul, Jacques. *The Technological Society.* New York: Knopf, 1964.

Enzensberger, Hans Magnus. *The Consciousness Industry: On Literature, Politics and the Media.* New York: Seabury Press, 1974.

Feldman, Morton. "After Modernism." *Art in America,* 59 (1971), 68–77.

Ferkiss, Victor C. *Technological Man: The Myth and the Reality.* New York: Braziller, 1969.

Fiedler, Leslie. *Collected Essays.* 2 vols. New York: Stein and Day, 1971.

———. "The Birth of God & the Death of Man." *Salmagundi,* No. 21 (1973), pp. 3–26.

Florman, Samuel C. *Existential Pleasures of Engineering.* New York: St. Martin's Press, 1976.

Friedman, Bruce J., ed. *Black Humor.* New York: Bantam, 1965.

Foucault, Michel. *The Archeology of Knowledge.* New York: Pantheon, 1972.

———. *The Order of Things: An Archaeology of the Human Sciences.* New York: Pantheon, 1970.

Fuller, R. Buckminster. *Utopia or Oblivion.* New York: Bantam, 1969.

Gilman, Richard. *The Confusion of Realms.* New York: Random House, 1969.

———. "The Idea of the Avant-Garde." *Partisan Review,* 39 (1972), 382–96.

Goodheart, Eugene. "The Avant-Garde: Status and Prospects." *Book Forum*, 1 (1974), 47–58.

Goodman, Paul. *Growing Up Absurd*. New York: Random House, 1960.

Graff, Gerald. "The Myth of the Postmodernist Breakthrough." *TriQuarterly*, No. 26 (1973), pp. 383–417.

Hassan, Ihab. "The Dismemberment of Orpheus: Reflections on Modern Culture, Language and Literature." *American Scholar*, 32 (1963), 463–84.

———. *The Literature of Silence*. New York: Knopf, 1967.

———. *Paracriticisms: Seven Speculations of the Times*. Urbana: University of Illinois Press, 1975.

———, ed. *Liberations: New Essays on the Humanities in Revolution*. Middletown, Conn.: Wesleyan University Press, 1971.

Heilbroner, Robert L. *An Inquiry into the Human Prospect*. New York: Norton, 1974.

Heilbrun, Carolyn G. *Toward a Recognition of Androgyny*. New York: Knopf, 1973.

Heisenberg, Werner. *Physics and Philosophy*. New York: Harper and Brothers, 1958.

———. "The Representation of Nature in Contemporary Physics." *Daedalus*, 87 (1958), 95–108.

Hermand, Jost. "The 'Good New' and the 'Bad New': Metamorphoses of the Modernism Debate in the GDR since 1956." *New German Critique*, 1 (1974), 73–92.

Howe, Irving. *Decline of the New*. New York: Harcourt Brace Jovanovich, 1970.

Huszar, Istvan. "The Scientific and Technological Revolution: A Socialist Assessment." *New Hungarian Quarterly*, No. 55 (1974), 6–20.

Jameson, Fredric. "Ideology of the Text." *Salmagundi*, Nos. 31–32 (1975–76), 204–46.

Kermode, Frank. *Continuities*. New York: Random House, 1968.

King, Larry. "You Must Be Kidding." *New Republic*, May 31, 1969, pp. 24–25.

Kostelanetz, Richard. *The End of Intelligent Writing*. New York: Sheed and Ward, 1974.

———, ed. *The New American Arts*. New York: Horizon Press, 1965.

Krim, Seymour. *Shake It for the World, Smartass*. New York: Dial Press, 1970.

Laing, R. D. *The Politics of Experience*. New York: Pantheon, 1967.

Leary, Timothy. *Politics of Ecstasy.* New York: Putnam, 1968.

Levin, Harry. "What Was Modernism?," in *Refractions: Essays in Comparative Literature.* New York: Oxford University Press, 1966, pp. 271–95.

Lifton, Robert Jay. *Boundaries: Psychological Man in Revolution.* New York: Vintage, 1970.

Lukacs, John. *The Passing of the Modern Age.* New York: Harper and Row, 1970.

McDonald, Daniel. "Science, Literature and Absurdity." *South Atlantic Quarterly,* 66 (1967), 42–49.

McElroy, Joseph. "Neural Neighborhoods and Other Concrete Abstracts." *TriQuarterly,* No. 34 (1975), pp. 201–17.

McLuhan, Marshall. *Understanding Media: The Extensions of Man.* New York: New American Library, 1964.

———. *The Gutenberg Galaxy: The Making of Typographic Man.* New York: New American Library, 1969.

Mailer, Norman. *Cannibals and Christians.* New York: Dial Press, 1966.

———. *Existential Errands.* Boston: Little, Brown, 1972.

Marcuse, Herbert. *One Dimensional Man.* Boston: Beacon Press, 1964.

Marx, Leo. "Technology and the Study of Man." *The Key Reporter,* 39 (1974), 2–4, 8.

Matson, Floyd W. *The Broken Image: Man, Science and Society.* 1964; rpt. Garden City, N.Y.: Doubleday, 1966.

Mercer, Peter. "The Culture of Fictions; or the Fiction of Culture?" *Critical Quarterly,* 12 (1970), 291–300.

Mesthene, Emmanuel G. *Technological Change: Its Impact on Man and Society.* Cambridge, Mass.: Harvard University Press, 1970.

Meyer, Leonard B. *Music, the Arts and Ideas: Patterns and Predictions in Twentieth-Century Culture.* Chicago: University of Chicago Press, 1967.

Meyer, Ursula. *Conceptual Art.* New York: Dutton, 1972.

Millett, Kate. *Sexual Politics.* Garden City, N.Y.: Doubleday, 1970.

Moravia, Alberto. "Notes on the Word," in *Man as an End: A Defense of Humanism.* Trans. Bernard Wall. New York: Farrar, Straus and Giroux, 1966, pp. 167–77.

Newman, Charles. "Death as a Metaphor Is Dead." *New York Times Book Review,* July 1, 1973, p. 27.

———. "The Uses and Abuses of Death: A Little Rumble through the Remnants of Literary Culture." *TriQuarterly,* No. 26 (1973), pp. 3–41.

Nuttall, Jeff. *Bomb Culture.* New York: Dell, 1968.

Oglesby, Carl, ed. *The New Left Reader.* New York: Grove Press, 1969.

"On the New Cultural Conservatism: A Symposium." *Partisan Review,* 39 (1972), 397–453.

Ong, Walter J. *Rhetoric, Romance and Technology: Studies in Interaction of Expression and Culture.* Belmont, Calif.: Wadsworth, 1971.

Onopa, Robert. "The End of Art as a Spiritual Project." *TriQuarterly,* No. 26 (1973), 363–82.

Peckham, Morse. *Man's Rage for Chaos: Biology, Behavior and the Arts.* Philadelphia: Chilton, 1965.

The Pentagon Papers. New York: Bantam Books, 1971.

Pirsig, Robert M. *Zen and the Art of Motorcycle Maintenance.* New York: William Morrow, 1974.

Planck, Max. *The New Science.* Trans. James Murphy and W. H. Johnston. New York: Meridian, 1959.

Poggioli, Renato. *The Theory of the Avant-Garde.* Trans. G. Fitzgerald. Cambridge, Mass.: Belknap Press of Harvard University Press, 1968.

Poirier, Richard. *The Performing Self.* New York: Oxford University Press, 1971.

———. "The Aesthetics of Radicalism." *Partisan Review,* 41 (1974), 176–96.

Reich, Charles A. *The Greening of America.* New York: Random House, 1970.

Revel, Jean-François. *Without Marx or Jesus: The New American Revolution Has Begun.* New York: Dell, 1972.

Rochberg, George. "The Avant-Garde and the Aesthetics of Survival." *New Literary History,* 3 (1971), 71–92.

Rosenberg, Bernard, and David M. White, eds. *Mass Culture Revisited.* New York: Van Nostrand, 1971.

Rosenberg, Harold. *The Tradition of the New.* New York: McGraw-Hill, 1965.

———. *Discovering the Present: Three Decades in Art, Culture, and Politics.* Chicago: University of Chicago Press, 1973.

Roszak, Theodore. *The Making of a Counter Culture: Reflections on the Technocratic Society and Its Youthful Opposition.* Garden City, N.Y.: Doubleday, 1969.

———. *Where the Wasteland Ends: Politics and Transcendence in Post-industrial Society.* Garden City, N.Y.: Doubleday, 1972.

Rubin, Louis D. "Susan Fagan and the Camp Followers." *Sewanee Review*, 82 (1974), 503–10.

Said, Edward W. "What Is beyond Formalism?" *Modern Language Notes*, 86 (1971), 933–45.

Sarraute, Nathalie. *The Age of Suspicion*. Trans. M. Jolas. New York: George Braziller, 1963.

Scholes, Robert. "The Illiberal Imagination." *New Literary History*, 4 (1973), 521–40.

Sears, Sallie, and Georgianna W. Lord, eds. *The Discontinuous Universe: Selected Writings in Contemporary Consciousness*. New York: Basic Books, 1972.

Shattuck, Roger. "After the Avant-Garde." *New York Review of Books*, March 12, 1970, pp. 41–47.

Skinner, B. F. *Beyond Freedom and Dignity*. New York: Knopf, 1971.

Slater, Philip. *The Pursuit of Loneliness: American Culture at the Breaking Point*. Boston: Beacon Press, 1970.

Snow, C. P. *The Two Cultures: And a Second Look*. New York: New American Library, 1963.

Solotaroff, Theodore. *The Red Hot Vacuum; and Other Pieces on the Writing of the Sixties*. New York: Atheneum, 1970.

Sontag, Susan. *Against Interpretation and Other Essays*. New York: Farrar, Straus and Giroux, 1966.

———. *Styles of Radical Will*. 1968; rpt. New York: Farrar, Straus and Giroux, 1969.

Spanos, William V. "The Detective and the Boundary: Some Notes on the Postmodern Literary Imagination." *Boundary 2* 1 (1972), 147–68.

Steiner, George. *Language and Silence*. New York: Atheneum, 1970.

———. *Extraterritorial: Papers on Literature and the Language Revolution*. New York: Atheneum, 1971.

———. "A Future Literacy." *Atlantic*, Aug. 1971, pp. 41–44.

———. *In Bluebeard's Castle: Some Notes towards the Redefinition of Culture*. New Haven: Yale University Press, 1971.

Stern, Richard G. "Events, Happenings, Credibility, Fictions." *Yale Review*, 57 (1968), 577–85.

Stover, Carl F., ed. *The Technological Order*. Detroit: Wayne State University Press, 1963.

Sukenick, Ronald. "The New Tradition." *Partisan Review*, 39 (1972), 580–88.

————. "Author as Editor and Publisher." *New York Times Book Review*, Sept. 15, 1974, p. 55.

Sypher, Wylie. *Loss of Self in Modern Literature and Art.* New York: Random House, 1962.

————. *Literature and Technology: The Alien Vision.* New York: Random House, 1968.

Szabolcsi, Mikos. "Avant-garde, Neo-avant-garde, Modernism: Questions and Suggestions." *New Literary History*, 3 (1971), 49–70.

Tatham, Campbell. "Critical Investigations: Language Games: (Post)Modern(Isms)." *Sub-Stance*, No. 10 (1974), pp. 67–80.

————. "Correspondence/Notes/Etceteras." *Chicago Review*, 26 (1975), 112–32.

Thompson, W. I. *At the Edge of History: Speculations on Transformation of Culture.* New York: Harper, 1971.

————. *Passages about Earth: An Exploration of the New Planetary Culture.* New York: Harper and Row, 1974.

Toffler, Alvin. *Future Shock.* New York: Random House, 1970.

Trilling, Lionel. *The Liberal Imagination.* New York: Viking Press, 1950.

————. *Gathering of Fugitives.* Boston: Beacon Press, 1956.

————. *Sincerity and Authenticity.* Cambridge, Mass.: Harvard University Press, 1972.

Wasson, Richard. "Notes on a New Sensibility." *Partisan Review*, 36 (1969), 460–77.

————. "From Priest to Prometheus: Culture and Criticism in the Post-Modern Period." *Journal of Modern Literature*, 3 (1974), 1188–1202.

The Watergate Hearings: Break-in and Cover Up. New York: Bantam Books, 1973.

Webster, Richard. "Frank Kermode's *The Sense of an Ending.*" *Critical Quarterly*, 16 (1974), 311–24.

The White House Transcripts. New York: Bantam Books, 1974.

Widmer, Kingsley. "American Apocalypse: Notes on the Bomb and the Failure of Imagination," in *The Forties: Fiction, Poetry, Drama.* Ed. Warren French. Deland, Fla.: Everett/Edwards, 1969, pp. 141–51.

Wiener, Norbert. *The Human Use of Human Beings: Cybernetics and Society.* Boston: Houghton Mifflin, 1950.

Williams, Duncan. *Trousered Apes: Sick Literature in a Sick Society.* New Rochelle, N.Y.: Arlington House, 1972.

"The Writer's Situation: A Symposium I." *New American Review*, No. 9 (1970), pp. 61–99.

"The Writer's Situation: A Symposium II." *New American Review*, No. 10 (1970), pp. 203–37.

"The Writer's Situation: A Symposium III." *New American Review*, No. 11 (1971), pp. 202–31.

4. THE NONFICTION NOVEL

Novels Cited

The following list includes nonfiction novels analyzed in this book and the nonfiction novels and proto-nonfiction novels mentioned in passing.

Agee, James. *Let Us Now Praise Famous Men.* 1941; rpt. New York: Ballantine Books, 1972.

Capote, Truman. *In Cold Blood.* New York: Random House, 1966.

Castaneda, Carlos. *The Teachings of Don Juan.* Berkeley: University of California Press, 1968.

———. *A Separate Reality.* New York: Simon and Schuster, 1971.

———. *Journey to Ixtlan.* New York: Simon and Schuster, 1972.

———. *Tales of Power.* New York: Simon and Schuster, 1974.

Clemens, Samuel Langhorne. *Life on the Mississippi.* Introduction by Edward Wagenknecht. Ed. Willis Wager. New York: Limited Editions Club, 1944.

Cummings, E. E. *The Enormous Room.* New York: Boni and Liveright, 1922.

Defoe, Daniel. *A Journal of the Plague Year.* Ed. Louis Landa. London: Oxford University Press, 1969.

Hemingway, Ernest. *Green Hills of Africa.* New York: Scribner's Sons, 1935.

Hersey, John. *Hiroshima.* New York: Knopf, 1946.

———. *The Algiers Motel Incident.* New York: Knopf, 1968.

Kaplan, Bruce. "Convention Coverage." *Chicago Review,* 20–21 (1969), 124–73.

Lewis, Oscar. *Five Families.* New York: Basic Books, 1959.

———. *The Children of Sanchez.* New York: Random House, 1961.

———. *La Vida.* New York: Random House, 1966.

Mailer, Norman. *The Armies of the Night.* New York: New American Library, 1968.

Miller, Henry. *Tropic of Cancer.* 1934; rpt. New York: Grove Press, 1961.

Orwell, George. *Homage to Catalonia.* 1938; rpt. New York: Harcourt, Brace, 1952.

Rosengarten, Theodore. *All God's Dangers: The Life of Nate Shaw.* New York: Knopf, 1975.

Sack, John. *M.* New York: New American Library, 1967.

Styron, William. *The Confessions of Nat Turner.* New York: Random House, 1967.

Terkel, Studs. *Division Street: America.* New York: Pantheon, 1967.

———. *Hard Times.* New York: Pantheon, 1970.

———. *Working.* New York: Pantheon, 1974.

Thompson, Hunter S. *Fear and Loathing in Las Vegas.* New York: Random House, 1971.

Wambaugh, Joseph. *The Onion Field.* New York: Delacorte Press, 1973.

Warhol, Andy. *a.* New York: Grove Press, 1968.

Wolfe, Tom. *The Electric Kool-Aid Acid Test.* New York: Farrar, Straus and Giroux, 1968.

Criticism

I do not know of any full-length study of the nonfiction novel. Critical reactions to books discussed in this study can be examined in reviews occasioned by their publication, easily located through standard reference books. Here I have listed a few reviews whose writers show some interest in the overall generic issues involved in reading individual works. I have also included a few works on the authors I have dealt with and on the relationship between fact and fiction.

Adams, George, et al., eds. *Studies in the Nature of Facts.* University of California Publications in Philosophy, Vol. 14. Berkeley: University of California Press, 1932.

Alvarez, Alfred. "Reflections in a Bloodshot Eye." *New Statesman,* Sept. 20, 1968, pp. 351–52.

Barsam, Richard M. *Nonfiction Film: A Critical History.* New York: Dutton, 1973.

Barzun, Jacques. "Proust's Way." *The Griffin,* 5 (1956), 4–13.

Bastian, F. *"Journal of the Plague Year* Reconsidered." *Review of English Studies,* n.s., 16 (1965), 151–73.

Behar, Jack. "Fiction and History." *Novel,* 3 (1970), 260–65.

Bendiner, Elmer. "Outside the Kingdom of the Middle Class." *The Nation*, Jan 2, 1967, pp. 22–23.

Berthoff, Warner. "Witness and Testament: Two Contemporary Classics." *New Literary History*, 2 (1971), 311–27.

Block, Haskell M. *Naturalistic Triptypch: The Fictive and the Real in Zola, Mann, and Dreiser*. New York: Random House, 1970.

Brady, Frank. "Fact and Factuality in Literature," in *Directions in Literary Criticism*. Ed. Stanley Weintraub and Philip Young. University Park: Pennsylvania State University Press, 1973, pp. 93–111.

Braudy, Leo. *Narrative Form in History and Fiction*. Princeton, N.J.: Princeton University Press, 1970.

Brower, Brock. "Of Nothing but Facts." *American Scholar*, 33 (1964), 613–18.

Calenhead, I. E., ed. *Literature and History*. University of Tulsa Monographs Series, No. 9. Tulsa, Okla.: University Tulsa, 1970.

Capote, Truman. "Interview." *Playboy*, March 1968, pp. 51–53, 56–62, 160–170.

Carroll, Paul. "What's a Warhol?" *Playboy*, Sept. 1969, pp. 133–34, 140, 278–82.

Clarke, J. H., ed. *William Styron's Nat Turner: Ten Black Writers Respond*. Boston: Beacon Press, 1967.

Clifford, James L., ed. *Boswell's Life of Johnson*. Englewood Cliffs, N.J.: Prentice-Hall, 1970.

Cousins, Norman. "John Hersey." *Saturday Review of Literature*, March 4, 1950, p. 15.

Crone, Rainer. *Andy Warhol*. Trans. John W. Gabriel. New York: Praeger, 1970.

DeMott, Benjamin. "In and Out of Universal City: Reflections on New Journalism and the Old Fiction." *Antioch Review*, 29 (1969), 7–13.

Dennis, Everette E., ed. *The Magic Writing Machine*. Eugene: University of Oregon School of Journalism, 1971.

Dennis, Everette E., and William Rivers. *Other Voices: The New Journalism in America*. San Francisco: Canfield Press, 1974.

Eaton, Marcia. "The Truth Value of Literary Statements." *British Journal of Aesthetics*, 12 (1972), 163–74.

Edel, Leon. *Literary Biography*. London: Rupert Hart-Davis, 1957.

Fischer, John. "The Rise of Non-Fiction," in *Mass Media and the Popular Arts*. Ed. F. Rissover. New York: McGraw-Hill, 1971, pp. 247–49.

Fishwick, Marshal, ed. "New Journalism." *Journal of Popular Culture,* 9 (1975), 95–151.

Fleishman, Avrom. *The English Historical Novel: Walter Scott to Virginia Woolf.* Baltimore, Md.: Johns Hopkins University Press, 1971.

Follett, Wilson. "The Novelist's Use of History." *The Bookman,* 68 (1928), 156–62.

Friedman, Melvin J. *"The Confessions of Nat Turner:* The Convergence of 'Nonfiction Novel' and 'Meditation on History.' " *Journal of Popular Culture,* 1 (1967), 166–75.

Garrett, George. "Crime and Punishment in Kansas: Truman Capote's *In Cold Blood." Hollins Critic,* 3 (Feb. 1966), 1–12.

Gay, Peter. "History and the Facts." *Columbia Forum,* n.s., 3, No. 2 (1974), 7–14.

Gidal, Peter. *Andy Warhol.* New York: Dutton, 1971.

Gold, Herbert. "Truth and Falsity in the Novel." *Hudson Review,* 8 (1955), 410–22.

Haack, Dietmar. "Faction: Tendenzen zu einer Kritischen Faktographie in den USA," in *Amerikanische Literatur im 20. Jahrhundert.* Ed. Alfred Weber and Dietmar Haack. Göttingen: Vandenhoeck and Ruprecht, 1971, pp. 127–46.

van den Haag, Ernest. "History as Factualized Fiction," in *Philosophy and History: A Symposium.* Ed. Sidney Hook. New York: New York University Press, 1963, pp. 212–26.

Harris, Robert T. "Plausibility in Fiction." *Journal of Philosophy,* 49 (1952), 5–10.

Hogarth, Paul. *The Artist as Reporter.* New York: Reinhold, 1967.

Honan, Park, ed. "Realism, Reality and the Novel." *Novel,* 2 (1969), 197–211.

"Is That a Fact?" *Times Literary Supplement,* Nov. 25, 1965, pp. 1061–62.

Isaac, Dan. "Theatre of Fact." *TDR/The Drama Review,* 15 (1971), 109–35.

Jameson, Storm. "Autobiography and the Novel." *The Bookman,* 72 (1931), 557–65.

Johnson, Michael. *The New Journalism.* Lawrence: University Press of Kansas, 1971.

Kazin, Alfred. "Autobiography as Narrative." *Michigan Quarterly Review,* 3 (1964), 210–16.

———. "The Imagination of Fact: Capote to Mailer," in *Bright Book of Life.* Boston: Little, Brown, 1973, pp. 207–41.

Kendall, Paul Murray. *The Art of Biography*. New York: Norton, 1965.

Krieger, Murray. "Fiction, History, and Empirical Reality." *Critical Inquiry*, 1 (1974), 335–60.

Lahr, John, and Jonathan Price. *Life Show: How to See Theater in Life and Life in Theater*. New York: Viking Press, 1963.

Lang, Victor. "Fact and Fiction." *Comparative Literature Studies*, 6 (1969), 253–61.

Langbaum, Robert. "Capote's Nonfiction Novel." *American Scholar*, 35 (1966), 570–80.

Leeds, Barry H. *The Structured Vision of Norman Mailer*. New York: New York University Press, 1969.

Leonard, John. "The Return of Andy Warhol." *New York Times Magazine*, Nov. 10, 1968, pp. 32, 142–50.

Levi, Albert William. "Literary Truth." *Journal of Aesthetics and Art Criticism*, 54 (1966), 373–82.

Levin, Harry. "From Gusle to Tape Recorder." *Comparative Literature Studies*, 6 (1969), 253–61.

Levine, George. *The Boundaries of Fiction: Carlyle, Macaulay, Newman*. Princeton, N.J.: Princeton University Press, 1968.

Levine, Paul. "Reality and Fiction." *Hudson Review*, 19 (1966), 135–38.

Lewis, Oscar. *A Study of Slum Culture: Backgrounds for "La Vida."* New York: Random House, 1968.

Lukacs, John. *Historical Consciousness or the Remembered Past*. New York: Harper and Row, 1968.

McCarthy, Mary. "The Fact in Fiction," in *On the Contrary*. New York: Farrar, Straus and Cudahy, 1961, pp. 249–70.

Macdonald, Dwight. "The Triumph of the Fact," in *Against the American Grain*. New York: Random House, 1962, pp. 393–427.

"A Machine and Sympathy." *Times Literary Supplement*, March 17, 1966, p. 223.

Madden, David. "Approaching Autobiography as Art," in *The Poetic Image in Six Genres*. Carbondale: Southern Illinois University Press, 1969, pp. 218–36.

Mahoney, John, and John Schmittroth, eds. *New Fiction, Non-Fiction*. Cambridge, Mass.: Winthrop, 1971.

Mailer, Norman. "Interview." *Playboy*, Jan. 1968, pp. 69–84.

Mazzocco, Robert. "aaaaaa." *New York Review of Books*, April 24, 1969, pp. 34–37.

Mew, Peter. "Facts in Fiction." *Journal of Aesthetics and Art Criticism*, 31 (1973), 329–37.

Miller, Ross. "Autobiography as Fact and Fiction: Franklin, Adams, Malcolm X." *Centennial Review,* 16 (1972), 221–32.

Mink, Louis O. "History and Fiction as Modes of Comprehension." *New Literary History,* 1 (1969–70), 541–58.

Mouton, Jean. *Litterature et sang-froid.* Paris: Desclée de Brouwer, 1967.

Nance, William. *The Worlds of Truman Capote.* New York: Stein and Day, 1960.

Pascal, Roy. "The Autobiographical Novel and the Autobiography." *Essays in Criticism,* 9, No. 2 (1959), 134–50.

Pinni, Richard. "Fiction et réalité chez Truman Capote." *Les Langues Moderns,* 63 (1969), 76–85.

Pizer, Donald. "Documentary Narrative as Art: William Manchester and Truman Capote." *Journal of Modern Literature,* 2 (1971), 105–18.

Plimpton, George. "The Story behind a Nonfiction Novel." *New York Times Book Review,* Jan. 16, 1966, pp. 2–3, 38–43.

————. "A Shared Ordeal: Interview with William Styron." *New York Times Book Review,* Oct. 8, 1973, pp. 2–3, 30–32, 34.

Podhoretz, Norman. "The Article as Art," in *Doings and Undoings.* New York: Farrar, Straus and Co., 1964, pp. 126–42.

Poirier, Richard. *Norman Mailer.* New York: Viking Press, 1972.

Pritchett, V. S. Review of Alfred Kazin, *Bright Book of Life. New York Times Book Review,* May 20, 1973, pp. 3, 30.

"Prying into Poverty." *Times Literary Supplement,* Sept. 21, 1967, pp. 829–30.

Puzo, Mario. "Generalissimo Mailer: Hero of His Own Dispatches." *Book World,* April 28, 1968, pp. 1, 3.

Raban, Jonathan. "The New Mongrel." *London Magazine,* n.s. 13 (1973), 96–105.

Rader, Ralph W. "Literary Form in Factual Narrative: The Example of Boswell's Johnson," in *Essays in Eighteenth-Century Biography.* Ed. Philip B. Daghlian. Bloomington: Indiana University Press, 1968, pp. 3–121.

Renault, Mary. "History in Fiction." *Times Literary Supplement,* March 23, 1973, pp. 315–16.

Review of *The Children of Sanchez, Pedro Martinez,* and *La Vida. Current Anthropology,* 8 (1967), 480–500.

Rockwell, Joan. *Fact in Fiction: The Uses of Literature in the Systematic Study of Society.* London: Routledge and Kegan Paul, 1974.

Rodway, A. E. "The Truth of Fiction: A Critical Dialogue." *Essays in Criticism,* 8 (1958), 405–17.

Salter, R. D. "The Place of Reality and Fantasy in Fiction." *Critical Survey*, 5 (1972), 285–91.

Sanders, David. *John Hersey.* New Haven, Conn.: College and University Press, 1967.

Schneck, Stephen. Review of Hunter Thompson, *The Hell's Angels. Ramparts*, March 1967, pp. 52–56.

Scholes, Robert. "Double Perspective on Hysteria." *Saturday Review*, Aug. 24, 1968, p. 37.

———. "The Tape-Recorded Unreality." *Saturday Review*, Dec. 21, 1968, p. 41.

Sconhorn, Manuel. "Defoe's *Journal of the Plague Year:* Topography and Intention." *Review of English Studies*, n.s. 19 (1968), 387–402.

Seib, K. A. "Mailer's March: The Epic Structure of *The Armies of the Night." Essays in Literature*, 1, No. 1 (1974), 89–95.

Solotaroff, Robert. *Down Mailer's Way.* Urbana: University of Illinois Press, 1974.

Sparshott, F. E. "Truth in Fiction." *Journal of Aesthetics and Art Criticism*, 26 (1967), 3–7.

Stern, Laurent. "Fictional Characters, Places, and Events," in *Philosophy and Phenomenological Research*, 26 (1965–66), 202–15.

Stevick, Philip. "Lies, Fictions and Mock-Facts." *Western Humanities Review*, 30 (1976), 1–12.

Stoehr, Taylor. "Realism and Verisimilitude." *Texas Studies in Literature and Language*, 11 (1969), 1269–88.

Sullivan, Nancy. Review of Oscar Lewis's *La Vida. Novel*, 1 (1967), 92–93.

Tanner, Tony. "Death in Kansas." *The Spectator*, March 18, 1966, pp. 331–32.

Taylor, A. J. P. "Fiction in History." *Times Literary Supplement*, March 23, 1973, pp. 327–28.

Taylor, H. O. *Fact: The Romance of Mind.* New York: Macmillan, 1932.

Tomlinson, T. B. "Literature and History—The Novel." *Melbourne Critical Review*, No. 4 (1961), pp. 93–101.

Tompkins, Philip K. "In Cold Fact." *Esquire*, June 1966, pp. 125, 127, 166–71.

Trachtenberg, Alan. "Mailer on the Steps of the Pentagon." *The Nation*, May 27, 1968, pp. 701–2.

Tracy, Robert. "In Cold Blood." *Southern Review*, n.s., 3 (1967), 251–54.

Vivas, Eliseo. "Reality in Literature." *Iowa Review*, 1 (1970), 117–27.

Wagner, Geoffrey. "Sociology and Fiction." *Twentieth Century*, 167 (1960), 108–14.

Warhol, Andy. "Interview with G. R. Swenson," in *Pop Art Redefined*. Ed. John Russell and Suzi Gablick. New York: Praeger, 1969, pp. 116–19.

———. *The Philosophy of Andy Warhol*. New York: Harcourt Brace Jovanovich, 1975.

Weber, Ronald, ed. *Reporter as Artist*. New York: Hastings House, 1974.

Wells, H. G. "Digression about Novels," in *An Experiment in Autobiography*. New York: Macmillan, 1934, pp. 410–24.

Wiegand, William. "The 'Non-Fiction Novel.' " *New Mexico Quarterly*, 37 (1967), 243–57.

Williams, John. "Fact in Fiction: Problems of the Historical Novelist." *Denver Quarterly*, 7 (1973), 1–12.

Wolfe, Tom. "The Author's Story." *New York Times Book Review*, Aug. 18, 1968, pp. 2, 40–41.

Wolfe, Tom, and E. W. Johnson, eds. *The New Journalism*. New York: Harper and Row, 1973.

Woodward, C. Vann, ed. "The Uses of History in Fiction." *Southern Literary Journal*, 1 (1969), 57–90.

Index